Holding and Psychoanalysis

A Relational Perspective

Relational Perspectives Book Series

Stephen A. Mitchell and Lewis Aron
Series Editors

Holding and Psychoanalysis
A Relational Perspective

Joyce Anne Slochower

Published by The Analytic Press, Inc.
Editorial Offices: 101 West Street, Hillsdale, NJ 07642

Typeset in Palatino by Laserset, Inc., New York City

Library of Congress Cataloging-in-Publication Data

Slochower, Joyce Anne, 1950-
  Holding and psychoanalysis : a relational perspective / Joyce Anne Slochower
    p.   cm.
  Includes bibliographical references and index.
  ISBN 0-88163-200-7
  1. Holding (Psychoanalysis) 2. Psychotherapist and patient.
I. Title.
RC489.H64S56   1996
616.89'17--dc20   96-16197
                                                          CIP

Printed in the United States of America
10 9 8 7 6 5 4 3 2 1

Contents

Acknowledgments

As is usually the case, this book has multiple roots and requires acknowledgments on a variety of levels. My interest in the holding process and its many functions has been deepened enormously by my patients. They have worked with me (and at times alone) in ways that have enriched my understanding of the value of both holding and explicit intersubjective work. Their contributions appear throughout the text, although always in disguised or composite form.

Steve Mitchell is the best of editors. Consistently enthusiastic and excited by my ideas, he responded generously to the manuscript and engaged actively with the issues I raised. I am enormously grateful to Steve for doing all this while always communicating a clear respect for my process and giving me plenty of room to go my own way.

Susan Kraemer indefatigably read and responded to numerous chapter drafts, making a multiplicity of contributions to the final version. In addition, Neil Altman, Andrew Druck, Stephanie Glennon, and Jim Stoeri read portions of the manuscript, raising important questions that clarified areas of ambiguity. I am also grateful to my husband, Bruce, for creating the space within our busy family life that allowed me to work and rework the book and for his stellar editorial help.

The contributions of colleagues, supervisees, and students, especially members of my Winnicott class at the N.Y.U. Postdoctoral Program in Psychotherapy and Psychoanalysis, have enriched and challenged my thinking about many clinical issues.

On several levels, I am enormously grateful to Larry Epstein and Ruth Gruenthal, who were extraordinarily generous in facilitating the development of ideas that were not their own. Although my work has evolved very much along its own lines, I am not sure that this book would have been written without them.

My children, Jesse, Alison, and Avi, have contributed richly (though mostly unknowingly) to my understanding of holding processes. It is with them that I experience the parental sides of holding and mutuality and of living through easier and more difficult moments.

Although my father, Harry Slochower, died before I began writing this book, it is dedicated to his memory.

Holding and Psychoanalysis
A Relational Perspective

Chapter 1

A Relational Holding Model

It has always been easy for analysts to think about the practice of psychoanalysis and psychotherapy in terms of how best to communicate our understanding of dynamic process to our patients. After all, much of psychoanalysis is focused on clarifying *meaning*: the meaning of unconscious process, of early experience, of transference material. When we are engaged in this endeavor, we may feel more or less "on the ball," that is, more or less clear about the implicit message embedded in our patients' communications. In any event, we know why we are there with the patient, and our task is apparently clear—to help our patients make therapeutic use of a deeper level of self-understanding. To that end, we study our patients and ourselves with the aim of enhancing and broadening our capacity to gather and effectively communicate meaning to our patients. And for good reason. Most of us have experienced firsthand the powerful impact that a good interpretation can have on self-experience and ultimately on our capacity for change.

The purpose of this book, however, is to examine a dimension of psychoanalytic practice that is *not* devoted explicitly to the study and elaboration of meaning. That dimension is described not by the analyst's activity but by its relative absence. It addresses the analyst's affective presence and its impact, especially the analyst's provision of an emotionally protective space in difficult periods of work while she[1] struggles with, and yet also brackets, aspects of her own complex emotional experience. The analyst's willingness to contain her understanding of the patient's process as well as of her own is, in my view, an essential and frequently overlooked aspect of psychoanalytic work.

It is my belief that the analyst's capacity for restraint, that is, her willingness to suspend temporarily an active investigation of meaning, is a core element in effective psychoanalytic process. It is essential because of the important limitations to the therapeutic efficacy of intersubjective work. There are times when interpretations about split-off affective states or work around intersubjective experience may be

---

[1] Throughout this book, for simplicity's sake, unless I am describing a particular patient–analyst pair, I have chosen the female pronoun to refer both to analyst and to patient. These pronouns should be read to refer equally to individuals of both genders.

anything but helpful to the patient. At those moments, clinical movement is effected not as a result of an active analysis (or interpretation) of dynamic process or of mutual enactments, but because of the analyst's capacity to create an emotional space that more or less *protects* the patient from the impact of the analyst's "otherness." Here, a focus on the nature and therapeutic action of a core affective dimension of the patient's treatment experience actually more or less *excludes* the analyst's separate subjecthood. Winnicott (1960a) called this process "holding," and I will be using that term here, although with a very expanded meaning.

My focus brings together two apparently disparate analytic perspectives on the nature of the treatment process. The first derives from a relational clinical tradition. Contemporary relational theories have a variety of psychoanalytic roots, including interpersonal (see, for example, Levenson, 1972; Gill, 1983) and traditional, especially object relations, theories (see, for example, Fairbairn, 1952; Bowlby, 1969; Winnicott, 1958, 1965, 1971, 1989; Klein, 1975). Relational models share with these theories a focus on the analyst's active exploration of the derivative meanings embedded in the patient's unconscious and conscious processes. Relational perspectives, however, especially emphasize the intersubjective origins of the patient's experiences. It is understood to be necessary that the analyst actively address both the patient's own process and the impact of the analyst on that process. Within that context, interpretations represent an important aspect of the work. However, interpretations are not viewed to derive from anything like "objective truth," because the analyst's understanding characteristically is seen to include her ever-present subjectivity, which inevitably informs her understanding, and frequently colors it in ways that are unique. For this reason, the analyst's subjective responses to the patient are viewed as a legitimate arena for study. It is assumed that the analyst's subjectivity in part is reflective of her personal process, yet is also *reactive* to the patient's in a mixture so complex as to render impossible any clear allocation of emotional "responsibility" to one party or the other. As a consequence, enactments between analyst and patient are inevitable, and frequently represent an essential element that ultimately will deepen the patient's self-experience. The relational position, therefore, is an intersubjective one; it assumes that both patient and analyst always impact on the therapeutic interchange, and, furthermore, that the treatment process ideally involves a relatively mutual, though asymmetrical, interchange between the two.[2]

---

[2]Increasingly, other psychoanalytic schools of thought also embrace at least aspects of a perspective within which enactments are to be studied rather than simply avoided (see, for example, Druck, 1989).

It is my intention to integrate a view of holding processes within a contemporary relational perspective. In that context, I address the intersubjective implications of the suspension of active investigatory or interpretive analytic work. This perspective develops a contemporary understanding of the holding theme and clarifies the therapeutic role that holding processes play in those treatment situations in which neither straightforward interpretation nor intersubjective interchange moves the treatment. I emphasize the impact of holding on both patient and analyst, and especially the implicit meaning embedded in the analyst's holding stance. Although I believe the analyst to be partially "outside" the intersubjective interchange during moments of holding, I nevertheless believe that she is engaged actively in a struggle around her own process as a holding object. That struggle is complex. In Chapter 2, I trace in detail the evolution of the holding metaphor in psychoanalytic thinking and then the theoretical basis for my own perspective. Here, however, I would like to outline briefly the core of my understanding and use of the holding metaphor.

The Therapeutic Holding Function

I view the holding process in psychoanalytic treatment to be both a real affective experience and a metaphor that may be useful in describing a core dimension of the work between patient and analyst. That dimension will become pivotal primarily during moments of especially difficult psychoanalytic interchange. The holding process describes the analyst's struggle to provide an emotionally protective, contained space for the patient in order to facilitate the evolution of the patient's self-experience. Within that holding space, the patient is largely protected from those aspects of the analyst's subjectivity (i.e., separate perspective) that would feel disruptive. For this reason, holding excludes both interpretive work that implicitly expresses the analyst's cognitive or emotional separateness and intersubjective interchange within which the analyst communicates her distinct affective experience.

The holding space is created by the analyst with the patient's implicit cooperation as a result of the specifics of the patient's needs as well as the analyst's responses to those needs. In contrast to the traditional view of holding, I propose that the shape and central affective tone of a holding process frequently does not involve issues of dependence at all but, instead, a variety of other emotional states.

What is the purpose of the holding process? The holding metaphor describes the creation of an experience in which the patient is permitted to remain unaware of elements of her emotional effect on the analytic object. During moments of holding, patient and analyst *coconstruct* an *illusion of analytic attunement* that creates a feeling of emotional safety and resonance within the treatment space in a way that allows a variety of affective states to be articulated. It does not necessarily describe a feeling of caring or closeness between analyst and patient. Instead, the illusion of attunement refers to the ways in which the analyst neither questions nor challenges but instead accepts the patient's experience of the analyst's affective impact, whatever its particular color. The analyst allows this illusion to remain temporarily unchallenged, so that she remains, in Winnicott's (1969) terms, subjectively perceived. The analyst contains, and does her best not to express (either directly via interpretation or indirectly), those aspects of her reaction that feel dystonic to the patient. By not communicating these affective responses directly or covertly, the analyst protects the patient from experiencing their impact. For certain patients, it is only within this highly contained and bounded space that a full elaboration of split-off or dissociated aspects of self-experience can take place. The ultimate goal of a holding process includes both the patient's deepened capacity for self-elaboration, and, ultimately, for self-holding within a collaborative analytic relationship.

I believe that a close study of the nature of holding processes within psychoanalytic and psychotherapeutic work indicates that a theme associated with the concept of a holding experience is ubiquitous. At times, holding processes represent a core element of psychoanalytic work, while at other times they are more in the background. The frequency with which the holding element occurs within therapeutic experience suggests that there are probably moments in every treatment when the patient is changed in some way as a function of the analyst's holding capacity rather than by deepened meaning. In many treatments this impact can sooner or later be articulated, that is, integrated with meaning; in some it cannot. Paradoxically, the latter is most likely to be true in those very treatment contexts wherein the holding dimension plays a critical role.

In underlining the centrality of the holding theme in psychoanalytic work, I am attempting to spotlight a treatment dimension that often remains a backdrop to ordinary therapeutic interchange, especially within a relational framework. Certainly, holding processes are not pivotal in all treatment situations. In more everyday therapeutic work, patient and analyst engage in an ever-shifting pattern of interchange around the patient's experience. Exploration, interpretation, and affective elaboration characterize that process. To the extent that the patient can make use of the analyst's separate understanding (expressed via both interpretation and other emotional communications), the analytic process to some degree is characterized by mutuality (Aron, 1991). By mutuality I do not mean to imply shared or alternating need or responsiveness, but instead an implicit negotiation around the experience that each member of the therapeutic pair has of the other. This negotiation remains unarticulated much of the time. It is nevertheless present, and it involves the patient's potential awareness of her impact on the analytic object.

However, what of those for whom collaboration is elusive? Some of our patients are a long way from being truly capable of assimilating the analyst's separate subjective presence. To tolerate collaborative interchange, the patient must be able to sustain a reasonably solid sense of internal intactness in the face of the analyst's inevitably unsettling interpretations or observations, or, at least, to work with interpretations about experienced disruptions. In the absence of a capacity to sustain difference, the analyst's interventions may be intensely disturbing to the patient—no matter how gently and carefully they are worded. To the extent that the patient hears the analyst to be saying something *different* from what the patient expected to hear, the analyst's separate subjectivity becomes undeniable. There are patients for whom mutuality and intersubjective dialogue present a genuine and powerful threat rather than an enrichment.

The holding element therefore becomes absolutely central in work with patients who, for a variety of reasons, cannot assimilate or even tolerate the ordinary exchange that we take for granted in much of psychoanalysis. For individuals who struggle with split-off or dissociated affective issues (for example, dependence, self-involvement, self-hate, or rage) it may be only within the highly protective space that is created when the analyst brackets aspects of her active input that the patient can contact and integrate these experiences. For this reason, holding processes tend to be especially pivotal in work with extremely dependent, narcissistic, and borderline patients.

However, the holding theme also may appear as a subtext of the work even when the patient does not ever require an ongoing holding experience. In this sense, a close study of almost any psychoanalytic treatment may reveal some moments during which a holding function has played an important role.

A crucial difference exists between the containment that is characteristic of the holding situation and that which is an ongoing aspect of the analytic position during any treatment situation. Certainly, the analyst always contains much of her subjectivity; to do otherwise would represent acting out based on countertransference issues. However, in everyday therapeutic interchange, the analyst *makes use* of both the patient's material and her response to it via her questions and reflective and interpretive statements. These both move the process forward and help the analyst. They do the latter because by creating and communicating meaning about subjective process, the analyst has the opportunity to work in the way that she has been trained, and at the same time, to clarify confusing or disturbing aspects of her own response to the patient.

Interpretations provide a vehicle through which the analyst can *think* about her affective reactions. By linking subjective process with the patient's material and then organizing these links into communicable ideas, the analyst can organize, diffuse, and integrate aspects of her own experience. The act of "linking" (Bion, 1962) that is involved in the work of interpretation provides organization and structure to potentially disturbing emotional responses for the analyst as well as for the patient. It also may help the analyst to diffuse the stronger aspects of her countertransference response, and to integrate these in ways that will be helpful to her as well as to the patient (Jacobs, 1994). In contrast, during moments of holding, the analyst is deprived of the possibility of making use of herself via interpretation or other interventions that would explicitly or implicitly embody her separate subjectivity. As a result, she may find it more difficult to continue privately to make links between the patient's associations and between her process and the patient's. Even if she continues to interpret silently, her limited opportunity to express her experience and thereby create shared meaning around it will increase her sense of strain.

Why is it sometimes necessary that the analyst so fully contain her subjectivity? It is precisely the analyst's willingness to protect the patient from her (the analyst's) reactions, and particularly from her emotionally separate responses, that permits the holding process to operate in a therapeutic way. During moments of holding, it is essential that the analyst be experienced by the patient as absolutely attuned—that is, simultaneously affectively present and contained. For some patients, the emotional risks inherent in exposing split-off or hidden aspects of the self (including dissociated or denied anxieties, rage, dependency, and so on) are enormous. During a holding experience, the patient has the opportunity to explore fully and express aspects of affective life that have heretofore been dissociated or denied and to do so in a setting where the danger of external intrusion is minimal. This is possible precisely because the highly protective role taken by the analyst makes this process sufficiently safe (Winnicott, 1963b). It is the analyst's willingness to receive material *without* changing its meaning, and to remain emotionally present at the same time, that creates a feeling of safety. That feeling of safety is essential at moments for all patients; it is most often pivotal in work with those patients who cannot tolerate the impact of the analyst's separateness.

My perspective on holding processes emphasizes the systematic study of the analyst's emotional response to a therapeutic holding process of any sort. Inevitably, that response will vary enormously. The analyst's experience always will involve a complex mixture of her own subjectivity and that of her patient. The nature of the patient's particular needs and the analyst's personal way of assimilating them impact powerfully on the overall emotional effect of the holding experience. My central concern is to study the patient's and analyst's separate and joint contributions to various holding processes.

Holding and Interpretation

Can a holding process occur simultaneously with an interpretive one, or are the two functions mutually exclusive? To the extent that interpretations derive from the analyst's separate understanding of the patient's processes, they may be quite disruptive of the holding process. This will be true when the analyst's interpretations are felt primarily to be so impinging, controlling, or destructive that the patient is unable to examine her reactions to such interventions, and instead only can live them. However, at other times a holding process may occur alongside an interpretive one. This is especially so when the analyst's interpretation itself functions as a container for the patient's experience. Of course, the analytic holding function may carry its own symbolic communication to the patient, and thus may represent an implicit interpretation. That interpretation is embedded in the analyst's *action* or stance, which may contain important meaning to the patient. It is therefore not my intention to discount, override, or ignore the therapeutic function of interpretive work, but, rather, to focus on the way in which interpretations can be used to support a holding process. At times, interpretations and holding may occur side by side because of the patient's capacity to find a holding process within an interpretation (Winnicott, 1972; Pine, 1984); at other times, however, the patient's need for a holding experience is so intense that any interpretive input is excessively disruptive.

The Ubiquity of the Holding Function

The holding metaphor developed out of Winnicott's association between psychoanalysis and the mother–infant relationship and, for that reason, has been viewed to depict a highly idealized, nurturing and protective analytic stance. The Winnicottian analyst held the very vulnerable patient in order to protect her from noxious environmental impingements while she contacted previously hidden aspects of "true self" experience (Winnicott, 1960b). To the degree that the analytic holding function recapitulated the parents' even, affectively responsive stance, the patient who needed a holding experience was viewed to be struggling with the dependency needs characteristic of infancy.

Although the containing element classically has been associated with the mother–infant metaphor, I hope that a closer examination of that metaphor will reveal the far broader implications of the holding theme. I do not make a tight link between holding and infancy, and thus do not limit the holding function to the analyst's containing response to dependency needs. In contrast, I understand the holding stance to include times when the analyst functions in anything but an idealized way because what is held often is not dependence but a variety of other difficult and painful affective states. I believe that in fact there is a theme related to holding that pervades the life span. That theme is not unique to a periodic need for a holding process during moments of dependence. It also surrounds other core emotional experiences, including self-involvement, ruthlessness, and rage.

Holding therefore includes a far more complex set of analytic functions than those associated with an idealized view of infancy and the maternal role. The analyst holds in multiple emotional situations by providing the patient with a containing and relatively even emotional space within which to safely experience and express a range of difficult affective states. At the same time, the analyst holds by tolerating, more or less unexpressed, her sometimes intense emotional reactions to the patient's emotional communications. I thus use the word "holding" to describe a therapeutic position in which the analyst, like the parent of either sex, functions more as a container than as an actor within the psychoanalytic dyad.

It frequently is assumed that, when the need for a holding experience emerges within the treatment context, it does so because of a profound developmental failure, usually reflected in the absence of such holding experiences during infancy. The analyst who "holds" is thus typically understood to be offering the patient a reparative experience that, with time, will allow the patient to move beyond such needs.

I do not believe, however, that these developmental assumptions are necessarily implicit in the notion of holding or that the need for holding experiences follows a linear developmental progression. Instead, I view the analyst's movement toward a holding process to reflect her experience of the patient as highly reactive to any manifestation of the analyst's subjectivity. The persistence of such reactivity suggests a history of trauma at a variety of points in the patient's life. Such trauma is often organized around repetitive experiences in which the parent's separate subjectivity was felt to be disturbing, if not traumatic. In adulthood, the patient carries an ongoing sensitivity to the analyst's input. This sensitivity is especially evident in the treatment situation because of a breakdown of the usual defensive barriers with which the adult patient defends against experiencing the object's simultaneous emotional power and its separateness. The patient's sensitivity to analytic interventions is reflective of the presence of early trauma but does not in fact replicate such trauma. In work with a very reactive patient, the analyst tends to move, through trial and error, toward a holding stance because it is less likely to activate a level of defensiveness that causes a therapeutic impasse.

The Holding Moment or Period

To what degree does the holding process represent a momentary or transient experience? Does the patient move from *moments* of holding to *moments* of intersubjective work, or does the analytic process evolve in such a way that the patient experiences a prolonged period of holding that subsequently shifts toward more fully intersubjective exchange?

I believe that a close study of many treatments will reveal that in nearly every session there are moments that are characterized by a holding process, even when a more prolonged holding experience is absent. It is probably most common for the holding theme to represent a momentary, rather than an ongoing, treatment element. I am, of course, familiar with treatment situations in which the patient needed a prolonged holding experience. As I discuss the holding dimension in more detail in subsequent chapters, I focus on especially difficult treatment situations in which the holding theme dominated the work, sometimes for fairly long periods of time. These clinical situations were chosen because of the centrality of the holding process within them. Lest the reader be left with the impression that I view holding processes always to be extended rather than more transient aspects of the treatment experience, it is important to underscore that the holding moment, while more difficult to "catch" at times, is also a core treatment dimension with patients who never become involved in prolonged periods of holding work.

I believe that a pivotal analytic goal involves the development of a capacity for collaborative interchange between patient and analyst. For this reason, I understand holding moments or periods increasingly to give way to moments of mutual interchange as the treatment process evolves. To some degree, I view the holding process as a temporary rather than a permanent dimension of analytic process. However, on a deeper level, the need for holding processes is ubiquitous within the analytic context. In this sense, the analyst probably always holds aspects of the process. Further, the periodic need for more acute holding experiences around core affective issues continues to be felt throughout our lives, and thus also throughout the analytic process. Although individual patients may present with a predominant need for a particular kind of holding, all of these varied themes probably appear at moments in any analytic treatment. If there are times in almost every treatment context when multiple versions of the holding metaphor may apply, any system of categorization represents a somewhat arbitrary and artificial delineation of processes that may actually crosscut developmental periods and patient groups. Although it will be necessary separately to describe these processes as they relate to different affective states, I hope to make clear that the holding theme frequently may reemerge in different forms with the same patient over the course of treatment.

Holding experiences alone cannot effect a satisfactory treatment outcome. Virtually any successful analytic process includes a mixture of holding processes, interpretive and explorative work, and enactments of many kinds that ultimately yield to understanding. It is my view that a central goal of psychoanalytic work involves the patient's deepened and better integrated self-experience in an intersubjective context. This includes the patient's capacity for collaboration, that is, her ability to work with the analyst's separate understanding and to make use of that separateness without a loss of self-experience. For those patients who cannot tolerate collaborative work, the holding experience may facilitate a move toward collaboration. The holding thread, whether momentary or prolonged, thus describes a crucial contributor to the change process. It is my hope that in pulling out this single treatment dimension for study, I may more fully elucidate its complexities and meaning within psychoanalytic practice.

Structure of the Book

As you read this book, I hope that you will join me in an attempt to delineate the role of the holding process and of the analyst's subjectivity as both impact on a multiplicity of therapeutic situations. Whereas some of these treatment contexts seem quite clear, in that the patient's need is explicit and her response to a holding experience markedly therapeutic, in other situations there is far more ambiguity. It is my intention not to offer a perspective that fully resolves that ambiguity but, instead, to raise what I view to be the relevant issues that come up with patients who seem to need the partial illusion of a holding experience. It is my assumption that ambiguity is implicit and inevitable, especially during holding processes, and that far more danger resides in attempting to resolve it than in accepting and living with it.

The concept of holding is not a new one, and has been used in somewhat varied ways to describe aspects of psychoanalytic work. In Chapter 2, I review the evolution of the holding metaphor and related concepts in psychoanalytic thinking. I then elaborate more fully on my own understanding of the holding process.

To highlight the variety of core issues that present themselves in therapeutic contexts that may involve the patient's need for a holding experience, I address separately what I view to be the three primary emotional issues that tend to need a holding response. The first of these is, of course, holding with issues of dependence. In addition to this better known model, when certain narcissistic issues predominate, and also when issues surrounding the patient's hate and self-hate are at the forefront, holding becomes an important treatment element. The clinical difficulties of working with patients in need of a regression and holding around issues of self-involvement, ruthlessness, and rage are addressed separately in Chapters 3, 4, and 5.

A particularly difficult treatment problem is raised by patients who appear to be very much in need of a holding experience and yet simultaneously are emotionally allergic to anything resembling the holding experience. In Chapter 6, I consider the treatment difficulties raised by patients who are "on the edge" in this sense, and who need to work toward a holding process. Because these patients seem to want and need precisely what they cannot tolerate, particularly complex issues arise in this work.

There are, of course, treatments that stall or even fail. In Chapter 7, I consider how we may understand holding processes that appear to break down. In that context, I address the separate and joint contributions of the analyst's and the patient's inability to work within the holding metaphor.

I view the therapeutic holding function to pervade the life cycle, and to be potentially present in some interpersonal, nontherapeutic situations in crucial ways. In Chapter 8, I examine Jewish mourning ritual, and the multiple holding functions that it can serve, in a way that illustrates the manner in which a variety of holding processes may be necessary in times of life crisis.

Although I believe that my perspective on holding processes is within a relational psychoanalytic tradition, there has been considerable controversy among relational theorists concerning the plausibility of the holding notion. In Chapter 9, I take on the relational critique of holding. I attempt to demonstrate that the holding theme is compatible with a relational perspective because the analyst's subjectivity remains very much alive during periods dominated by holding processes.

Because my position emphasizes the necessity for the analyst to function in a nonintrusive way during periods of holding, there are areas of overlap between these ideas and those of some Freudian and self psychologists. In the second part of Chapter 9, I sort out some of the similarities and differences between our perspectives.

Although the thrust of this book addresses the therapeutic function of holding, it is quite evident that both psychotherapy and psycho-analysis consist of much more than holding processes. Because the holding experience is one during which the patient is largely protected from the analyst's subjectivity, holding does not allow for truly mutual interchange, and to some extent keeps the patient highly dependent on the analyst's holding capacity. In Chapter 10, I examine the limitations of the holding dimension and the necessity for an evolution toward mutual interchange between patient and analyst. I believe that it is the transition from the holding experience toward collaboration (object usage in Winnicott's [1969] sense) that facilitates the movement toward more mutual dialogue between analyst and patient.

Chapter 2

Holding as Metaphor

Before elaborating further on the nature of holding processes in psychoanalysis, I would like to examine the theoretical evolution of the holding metaphor. Until recently, holding was linked inextricably to an idealized maternal metaphor in which the analyst/mother was viewed as all-knowing and all-giving. That metaphor generated a powerful but mixed response. Much of its appeal was associated with the hope that appeared to lie in the maternal analyst's potential reparative powers. If the analyst can symbolically become the mother, the possibility of reworking early trauma is enormously increased; what cannot be remembered can be reexperienced and then repaired; the patient can, in fact, be a baby again, but with a better, more responsive mother (see also Slochower, 1996a).

The Winnicottian Model

The maternal metaphor is perhaps most widely associated with Winnicott (1960a, 1963a, b), who explicitly tied analytic process to the mother–infant relationship. Winnicott noted that the mother's profound, if temporary, identification (primary maternal preoccupation) with her infant's needs allows her to experience these needs *as if they were her own*. It is this maternal identification that allows her to provide what is needed by the infant in a highly sensitive way and to set aside her own subjective responses when these are not reciprocal with those of her infant. Winnicott emphasized the centrality of holding as a reliable ego support for the infant during the period of absolute dependence.

Winnicott (1960b) tied the maternal metaphor to a particular aspect of analytic work with patients who could not make good use of "ordinary" technique. He especially studied the analytic holding function in his work with schizoid patients whose ongoing self experience was characterized by an *as if* quality. Winnicott described this as false self functioning. Here, the true self (i.e., the patient's authentic experience of both self and object worlds) responds to persistent environmental failures by abandoning attempts to make itself and its needs known. Instead, the true self progressively retreats and allows the false self to take over.

People who consistently make use of the false self in this way may function quite well, yet suffer from a pervasive sense of disconnection that makes it difficult for them fully to integrate and own their experiences. Winnicott found that interpretive process tended to be assimilated in line with false self functioning by these patients, resulting in superficially based insight but no internal change. Winnicott (1964b) believed that if real change were to take place, the schizoid patient needed a regressive experience in which false self functioning was turned over to the analyst. Here, the analyst temporarily "takes over" the adaptive functions of the false self, creating a protected setting in which the true self can be exposed safely.

During the regression to dependence, the therapeutic holding environment involves the analyst's emotionally responsive, highly attuned presence. It mimics the maternal holding process because the analyst continually adapts to the patient's needs. The analyst protects the patient from external impingements through her consistent and sensitive emotional "handling." Affective and sometimes literal support might be required as the regression intensifies, and interpretations are used primarily to support the holding function rather than to convey new information or stimulate insight. During a regression to dependence, the patient, like the infant, becomes extremely sensitive to environmental impingements because of the vulnerability of the true self. The holding analyst attempts to protect the patient from unnecessary impingements by especially careful attention to all aspects of the analytic setting that relate to its constancy (for example, during a regression, the analyst would be particularly reluctant to cancel or reschedule sessions, move the office furniture around, and so on).

Winnicott believed that the holding experience ultimately would allow the patient to recontact and integrate aspects of true self experience that had previously been split off or repressed. In this sense, he viewed the regression to dependence as serving a reparative function that would facilitate the patient's movement toward a fuller and deeper level of self-experience. The analyst–patient pair, like the mother and baby, were viewed to be engaged in an ongoing attempt first to understand and then to meet the patient's needs, and to repair disruptions when they occurred. It was assumed that this holding process would be a temporary one, and would gradually give way to more "ordinary" interpretive work as the patient internalized the protective holding function.

Winnicott's (1947) view of the holding process suggested that at times such holding absolutely lost its metaphoric quality. He wrote:

> For the neurotic the couch and warmth and comfort can be *symbolical* of the mother's love; for the psychotic it would be more true to say that these things *are*

the analyst's physical expression of love. The couch *is* the analyst's lap or womb, and the warmth *is* the live warmth of the analyst's body. And so on [p. 199].

It is not clear to what extent Winnicott believed that the analyst temporarily joined the patient in this belief, thus at least momentarily losing contact with the symbolic nature of the maternal metaphor. Winnicott sometimes appears to view the holding process to be quite literal, with respect to both the analyst's actions, and more importantly, her experience. At other moments, however, it retains its metaphoric element.

Other Versions of the Maternal Metaphor

Although Winnicott's concept of the holding environment is especially evocative of the relationship between psychoanalysis and aspects of maternal care, many others have described the analytic process in similar ways. What is central to these characterizations is the use of (preoedipal) mothering as a tool with which to understand psychoanalysis (Phillips, 1993). Within the maternal metaphor not only is the patient a baby in crucial ways, but the analyst becomes, at least in part, the maternal object. As a maternal object, the analyst's behavior and affective responses mirror those of her patient. Even more importantly, the analyst's symbolic function overrides her interpretive one, and in some cases is essential to cure.

The use of the maternal metaphor is sometimes implicit, but often quite explicit. Bion's (1959, 1962) concept of the analyst's containing function described a process that permits the infant/patient to detoxify experiences by projecting them into the mother, who transforms these projected affects via a reverie.[1]

Little (1959) described the need of certain vulnerable patients to establish a "basic unit," or feeling of total undifferentiatedness from the analyst in ways reminiscent of earliest infancy. Loewald (1960) explicitly linked the parent–child relationship to the analytic one, and emphasized the parent's capacity to be simultaneously empathically attuned, and somewhat more knowing than the child. Sandler (1960) described the background of safety as having developed "from an integral part of the primary narcissistic experience. . . . These safety-signals are related to such things as the awareness of being protected; for example by the reassuring presence of the mother" (p. 354).

Khan (1963), borrowing from Freud (1920), discussed the mother's function as a protective shield. "The analyst's task is not to *be* or *become*

---

[1] The concept of containment has been further elaborated by Ogden (1979, 1994) and Hamilton (1990). Here, the patient ultimately introjects the containing aspect of the analyst.

the mother. . . . What we do provide are some of the functions of the mother as a protective shield and auxiliary ego" (p. 67). Balint (1968) elaborated on the analyst's maternal role in meeting the needs of the patient suffering from a basic fault. "Here too, the only thing that the analyst can do is to accept the role of a true primary substance . . . which *eo ipso* is there to carry the patient" (p. 167). He underlined the importance of permitting a regression to the level of the basic fault.

Bollas (1978) described the transformational object to be "an object that is experientially identified by the infant with the process of the alteration of self experience" (p. 97). He (1987) notes that although the analyst does not become the patient's parent, the analyst's function as a transformational object includes her capacity to offer "through holding and interpretation . . . a more skilled and appropriate intervention than prevailed when the analysand was a child" (p. 115). Kohut's (1971) discussion of the narcissistic patient's need for idealizing and mirroring selfobject experiences is similarly based on the maternal metaphor. Grunes (1984) delineated the concept of the therapeutic object relationship to describe the more permeable and intimate relationship needed by regressed patients who suffer from object hunger. Bromberg (1991) describes therapeutic regression as a process during which "one aspect of the analytic situation is the creation of a relational environment that . . . allows the individual partially to surrender the role of protecting his own ego stability because he feels safe enough to share the responsibility with the analyst" (p. 416). Sandbank (1993) makes an explicit link between the dual tasks of holding and encouraging autonomy in mothering and in psychoanalysis.

In his discussion of differences among Freudian analysts, Druck (1989) describes what he calls the right and left wings of classical technique. He notes that left wing analysts (including Loewald, Grunes, Freedman, Bach, Modell, and others) view work on developmental issues as an integral part of analysis rather than merely preparation for analysis. These developmental issues are seen to be based implicitly, if not explicitly, on the maternal metaphor.

There is, then, a convergence of opinion concerning the applicability of the maternal model to at least some analytic functions. These writers generally emphasize the analyst's capacity to facilitate a therapeutic process through the symbolic yet paradoxically real provision (cf. Pizer, 1992) of necessary ego supports. Notably omitted from most of these descriptions is a consideration of any difficulties that the analyst or patient might experience during periods of holding. What is overridingly emphasized is the nurturing nature of the analyst's subjective and explicit response to the patient. Intrinsic to the maternal metaphor is the assumption that the analyst/mother can, and should, be sufficiently identified with the patient/baby's needs to provide the appropriate, emotionally responsive atmosphere in order to facilitate growth, and that the patient/baby will easily take in and make use of the holding process. The holding process around dependence typifies what Stern (1994) calls Paradigm II, in which the therapeutic relationship is based on the patient's need for a reparative experience. This stands in contrast to Paradigm I, in which the treatment is viewed as evoking the repetition of the original pathogenic situation.

Yet despite Winnicott's rather poetic perspective on the maternal function, he (Winnicott, 1947) was careful to note that there are good and sufficient reasons for the mother to hate her baby (and thus implicitly for the holding analyst to hate her patient). In this sense, he opened the way for a consideration of the impact of maternal subjectivity (First, 1994) on the parenting process. However, Winnicott believed that the nature of primary maternal preoccupation was such that the mother and the holding analyst could largely override such feelings of strain. To a significant extent, the mother is so identified with her baby's needs that her own recede—if they do not disappear altogether. Her sense of self is largely defined by her capacity to mother or to hold, and in this sense she derives adequate sustenance from her nurturing capacity.

The Contemporary Mother

Although there is something enormously soothing about this portrait of the mother–infant relationship (and implicitly about the analytic one), on closer examination it is quite problematic. Winnicott's "mother" is deeply embedded in a romantic, idealized portrait of the nurturing object that no longer fits our contemporary understanding of motherhood. It is quite evident to those of us who have parented, directly or indirectly (with our patients), that this idealized portrait is, in fact, far removed from the reality of daily infant care (or of psychoanalytic work). It is rare that the mother can so fully set aside her own internal state to provide what is needed for the baby, or that the baby so passively receives the mother's holding.

Contemporary writers from feminist (Chodorow, 1978; Bassin, Honey, and Kaplan, 1994) as well as psychoanalytic perspectives (Benjamin, 1988, 1994; Kraemer, 1995) have cogently argued for a more complex view of mothering. Central to this position is an attempt to explicitly include the mother's nonmirroring responses to the role of parent, and especially the mother's ongoing state of conflict concerning her responses to the infant's needs. Rather than spontaneously offering a holding experience from a position of pure identification with her baby's needs, maternal care is often offered with a bit of and sometimes much reluctance. The mother of an infant struggles intensely because she *cannot* be fully identified with her baby. Instead, her own needs maintain a latent and sometimes manifest press that is incompatible with the baby's necessities. It is not possible for the mother to set these aside as she quite simply provides for her baby, because the mother rarely loses complete contact with her subjectivity. Instead, she is engaged in an continuous struggle surrounding the dysjunctive nature of her emotional responses to her baby—her frustration, rage, or sense of helplessness at the baby's dependency and her desperate need for space of her own, time, sleep, nurturing from her own mother, and adult contact. To the extent that the mother provides her baby with the necessary holding, she does so through ongoing internal work. That work allows her not to delete her subjective experience, but instead to own and embrace it sufficiently so that she does not unconsciously or reflexively enact her needs vis-à-vis her baby.

The contemporary mother, then, is permitted quite a bit more emotional breathing room than was the idealized mother of a more romantic period. As the maternal metaphor has been systematically deconstructed, we have a new opportunity to define both motherhood and psychoanalysis. What constitutes good-enough mothering, though, becomes more problematic. To the extent that a mother's and infant's needs are intrinsically and diametrically opposed, there inevitably will be a loser in the situation. It may be tempting to redefine the mother's emotional relationship to her baby by minimizing the delicacy and centrality of the mother's role or by emphasizing the infant's capacity to tolerate and respond to the mother's subjectivity. However, I believe that this shift in perspective risks negating the reality of the baby's profound dependence on the mother as a unique object. When we acknowledge the absoluteness of the baby's greater need, we are left with an essentially unresolvable tension created by the impossibility of deleting the subjectivity of either baby or mother.

The Contemporary Analyst and the Parental Holding Function

It is within the framework of holding-as-metaphor that the centrality of the holding function must be considered, while simultaneously rendering both analyst and patient more complex. In order for the analyst to provide a holding function for the patient, it is not merely possible, but, rather, absolutely *inevitable* that the analyst experience a variety of emotionally dystonic states. It seems to me that the recent criticisms leveled at the maternal metaphor in psychoanalysis (Mitchell, 1988; Aron, 1991; Stern, 1992; Tansey, 1992; Shabad, 1993; Mayes and

Spence, 1994) have highlighted the problems inherent in a model that takes the idea of an idealized, holding analyst too literally. That analyst, like the placid, contained, holding mother of infancy, remains in a remarkably unflappable position vis-à-vis the patient/baby. The maternal analyst would seem to know what the patient needs and also how to meet those needs. She would not experience conflict, either about meeting the patient's needs or about the tension between those needs and her own. The analyst working within a holding framework would thereby be forced into a rather limited emotional space, required to attend to the patient's deficits and to delete her own subjectivity from the analytic interchange. At this juncture, such a view of either motherhood or psychoanalytic practice is both implausible and unacceptable. (I will discuss these issues in depth in Chapter 9.)

In a similar way, it is unlikely that the patient in need of a holding experience could enter it in a simple, unconflicted way. Such an unambivalent, smooth transition to a holding relationship would exclude the patient's tendency to reexperience old, repetitive object relationships even as she moves toward a new, reparative experience. Further, that struggle would have its own impact on the analyst, resulting in a complex rather than simple level of interchange between the two.

The Analytic Functions: Being and Doing

The holding moment within psychoanalytic work is a highly complex emotional process that places special demands on analyst and patient. The very presence of dysjunctive subjective elements within the analyst and the patient renders the holding experience a transient one. Nevertheless, any good treatment will include at least moments of holding and, ultimately, a movement toward more fully intersubjective clinical interchange.

I propose that two relatively separate analytic functions may usefully be described within the treatment process. One of these relates to the analyst's capacity to provide an opportunity for affective growth largely *without* the active introduction of the analyst's externality. Here, it is the analyst's affectively responsive *presence* that plays a key therapeutic role and the holding process that predominates.

The second core aspect of the analytic task is for the most part absent during moments of holding. It concerns the analyst's ability to respond to the patient in a manner that allows for the introduction of *new* ways of understanding, experiencing, and deepening the patient's process. That work explicitly includes the analyst's more separate way of understanding the patient, that is, the introduction of external factors into the patient's internal world. In part it is reflected in the analyst's directly interpretive stance. However, on a more subtle level, the analyst also functions as an "actor" by virtue of her willingness to actively present herself as a separate object to the patient. The "active" analytic function may involve interventions that are less explicit than interpretations. "Action" may be reflected in virtually any signal given by the analyst that overtly or implicitly demonstrates that the analyst's own separate subjectivity remains present despite the patient's experience (see also Seinfeld, 1993).

It seems to me that each of these analytic functions is separately related to an essential dimension of human experience. Winnicott (1966) called these the female and male elements of "being" and "doing." Winnicott believed that these two elements exist, as shifting figure and ground, in all of us. He related them to gender because the mother's function was defined by her capacity to contain rather than to introduce her subjectivity into infant care, to "be there" for her child. In large part, it has been the mother's even, available presence ("being") that defined her maternal function.[2] That role contrasted with what was classically the father's position—of "doing" rather than of "being." The father "does" with the child, and his role as a bridge to activity involved his more external place in the child's emotional world.

Our contemporary understanding of the maternal and paternal roles makes clear, however, that in fact neither position is inextricably gender linked (Butler, 1990; Dimen, 1991; Harris, 1991; Aron, 1995). Instead, there are moments when both mother and father struggle with the dual tasks of "being" and "doing" because they both represent essential aspects of human experience that are not gender specific.

Winnicott did not associate "being" and "doing" with variations in the analytic function. I would like to extend and modify his position by suggesting that key dimensions of the analytic function are associated with these separate elements, while explicitly distinguishing those elements from their association with gender. In this context, I connect the analyst's capacity to tolerate the holding dimension of psychoanalytic work to her capacity to "be." The analyst's role as a more relational, interpretive, or active, boundary-setting rather than

---

[2]Winnicott (1963e) differentiated between what he called the environment mother and the object mother. He linked the former to the maternal holding position, that is, the mother who provides the infant with reliable, even management, whereas the latter, the object mother, was the mother of the infant's excited attacks. Interestingly, however, Winnicott viewed both the environment and the object mother as functioning largely within a frame that excludes their subjectivity. That is, both of the maternal functions involve the mother's capacity to receive, respond to, and contain the infant's desires. The mother is not herself seen as a major source of (subjective) stimulation for the infant.

containing object is associated with the "doing" element of self-experi-ence, and is relatively absent from the holding process.

Classically, different schools of psychoanalytic thought have con-nected these ideas to gender. For example, Bion, Kohut, Sandler, and others use maternal imagery to describe the analyst's holding function. These writers contrast with the more penetrating, interpretive "male" stance characteristically ascribed, for example, to Freud and Kernberg. Rather than viewing either one *or* the other of these functions as piv-otal, some examinations of analytic process have emphasized the interweaving of the two dimensions; for example, the ways in which interpretations themselves can serve a holding function (Winnicott, 1954; Pine, 1984; Stolorow, 1993).

In fact, the analytic process probably can never successfully be ascribed to a single affective stance or gender dimension. Rather, I would suggest that these two quite distinct analytic functions must both be used at different moments within any treatment context. To varying degrees, all analytic work inevitably involves both elements in an idiosyncratic mix that varies from treatment to treatment as a func-tion of both individual and relational factors.

It seems necessary and inevitable that as analysts we retain aspects of an identification as both *container* and *actor*. These two dimensions relate to the separate functions of the analyst in response to the patient's need for a holding process or for more active uncovering, especially of conflict. The analyst functions in widely varying ways; at times she soothes, reflects affective states, and contains the patient. At other times, she provides a stimulating function—probing, elaborat-ing, interpreting, or questioning the patient's experience and actively setting boundaries that structure the analytic interaction.

It is clear that the relative weight of these two dimensions will vary from analyst to analyst—as a function of both theoretical bias and per-sonal style and in response to the affective demands of different patients. Some analysts reject the therapeutic efficacy of a holding pro-cess, and argue instead that correctly timed interpretive work that includes their separate perspective will more quickly move the ana-lytic process forward. Others, who are not theoretically opposed to the notion of holding, simply feel that they "can't stand" keeping them-selves out in the manner necessary to work within a holding frame. Instead, they prefer to persevere in an attempt to make themselves known to the patient, hoping that eventually they will find a way of being that the patient can tolerate. For some analysts, the commitment to intersubjectivity and mutual *knowing* dominates, and "holding" is rejected both on theoretical and personal grounds. At the other extreme, there are analysts who absolutely reject the therapeutic use-fulness of challenging interpretations or confrontation, and instead remain within a model that more totally excludes their own subjectivity. Such a choice may reflect theoretical preferences and/or personal style.

The capacity to work within a holding frame also is based to some degree on the analyst's tolerance for strain, especially for self-doubt. Strain and self-doubt are occupational hazards within our field; however, this is nowhere more evident than when the analyst attempts to work in a way that deprives her of the opportunity to do her job (i.e., to deepen the patient's self-understanding) and thereby clarify her ideas about the patient and, indirectly, validate her self-experience as a good-enough analyst. My own view is that only a capacity to tolerate that strain and a willingness to work with a mixture of analytic functions, including both holding and nonholding interpretations, will address the needs of patients who vary in their capacity to tolerate and work with the analyst's distinct "otherness."

Holding in Context

What is unique about a perspective that simultaneously places the analyst's subjectivity (potential for "action") and her capacity to bracket that subjectivity (to "be") at the center of a holding process? Certainly, the notion of holding is not a new one; neither is the idea that the analyst must work within an empathic frame. In general, however, theorists who have used the maternal metaphor (Little, 1959; Loewald, 1960; Sandler, 1960; Balint, 1968) have done so while implicitly *deleting* certain aspects of the analyst, especially her struggle around maintaining a holding position. In contrast, I have tried to make explicit my commitment to a relational perspective within which the analyst's subjectivity remains alive. I simultaneously underscore the analyst's pivotal ability to contain both the patient's intense affective experience and her own dysjunctive subjectivity.

In that context, the therapeutic impact of the analyst's affective position vis-à-vis the patient becomes central. Clearly, interpretive work also has a powerful therapeutic impact on the change process. The holding theme, however, spotlights the mutative effect of the relational matrix in the context of the analyst's capacity to *contain* her subjectivity while surviving intact, in a way that the patient experiences to be *related* rather than disengaged. By remaining affectively "in" the treatment without raising questions about the patient's experience of me, I do not "challenge" the patient's transference by interpreting its meanings or sources. Thus, my holding stance does not confront the patient with evidence of my externality or with the possibility that her own process needs to be questioned.

Within this framework, holding does not represent an empathically responsive, nurturing analytic position whereby the analyst meets the patient's dependency needs. Instead, holding describes the analyst's containing response to a wide variety of emotional states, which include the complex process that presents itself with self-involved and hateful patients. The holding concept provides the analyst with a framework that may allow her more easily to maintain an actively engaged, yet containing, stance. It addresses the particularly difficult transference–countertransference matrices that often evolve in work with difficult patients. Holding simultaneously may facilitate an elaboration of the patient's emotional process while helping the analyst to live with the rather intense and difficult feelings that can be aroused in work with some patients.

The Nature of Holding Processes

How can we understand the holding process? What *is* held during such moments—the patient or the process? To the degree that the analyst's holding presence facilitates the emergence of heretofore split-off or dissociated affective states, on one level it is clear that the holding analyst actually holds the *process* even more than she does the patient. That is, the holding function frequently is represented by the analyst's ability to create a sense of emotional space with firm edges—a room large enough to allow for wide and intense affective expression, yet simultaneously bounded enough always to feel containing to the patient.

To the degree that we view the analyst to be holding the process rather than the patient, we may more fully open up the possibility of understanding holding outside the constraints of the parental metaphor. The analyst who holds the process certainly is not compelled to view the patient as a baby or herself as parent. Instead, the holding function becomes an ongoing aspect of the nature of psychoanalytic work at all times.

Yet it seems to me that we may miss out on an important dimension of the holding experience unless we address the ways in which the holding analyst actually holds the patient as well as the process. Within this perspective, it is the nature of the actual and fantasied object relationship assimilated by the patient that creates an explicit sense of being held by the analyst. The patient is held to the degree that the analyst's protective position provides the patient with an experience of safety within which self-exposure becomes possible. The affective tone of holding moments may be characterized by dependence; on the other hand, they may not. For some patients, the holding analyst facilitates the expression of rage, feelings of internal chaos, self-involvement, or other extremely painful self-states. It is important, then, to understand that the analyst who holds the patient is not necessarily engaged in an experience of emotional closeness in the usual sense of the word; instead, the analyst's protective presence may be viewed as opening up the possibility for a deeper level of self-exposure.

I suggest that the holding process must be viewed from both perspectives; the holding analyst holds the process, but sometimes also holds the patient. The relative weight of these two experiences may be related to the patient's sense of reliance on the analyst as a unique object or on the analysis as a unique process.

Self-Holding and the Analyst's Bracketed Subjectivity

It is a truism that psychoanalytic work inevitably evokes some brief and even more prolonged countertransference responses in the analyst. It is my assumption that countertransference always includes the analyst's experience of the patient in an idiosyncratic mixture of her more reactive and more subjective responses to that patient. That is, the analyst's countertransference is in large part intersubjectively derived. The analyst's countertransference reactions at times fit with the patient's experience and at other times do not. Thus, for example, the needy patient may expect and receive a nurturing response; the angry patient a somewhat tough one. At other moments, however, the analyst's countertransference may be less overtly reciprocal with the patient's transference. This may occur because the analyst in fact is reactive to split-off aspects of the patient's affective state, because the analyst may have her own subjective response to the patient's needs, or both. For example, the analyst may feel suffocated by a needy patient's demands even when the patient is absolutely unaware of that aspect of her impact.

To varying degrees, the analyst always works by internally studying and moving among different aspects of her experience of the patient. In "ordinary" therapeutic moments, the analyst explicitly makes use of both her affectively resonant responses and her more separate way of understanding the patient's process. She makes use of her responses via a complex of interventions, including but not limited to interpretations.

The analyst's separate understanding of the patient's experience presents a special dilemma during moments of work that are characterized by a holding process. During those moments, the patient is in such an emotionally reactive state that she cannot tolerate the analyst's separate input because it is felt to be too emotionally dysjunctive, that is, too "out of sync" with the patient's affective experience. This dysjunctive element introduces the reality of the analyst's separate subjectivity, and at these times disrupts the patient's attempt to elaborate on her own process. To the extent that aspects of the patient's self-experience have been dissociated (Bromberg, 1995), the work of contacting and integrating such states is potentially disorganizing to the patient.

Owing to the patient's rather delicate affective position during moments dominated by holding processes, the analyst will tend to feel somewhat constricted in her ability to make use of the complexity of her inner world, that is, of the full range of her reactions to her patient. She especially will struggle with those thoughts or responses that she believes may jar the patient, that do not fit with the patient's affective experience. I shall call that element of the analyst's experience her *dysjunctive subjectivity*.[3]

An analyst working with a patient within a holding process frequently experiences enormous pressure to *actually feel* what the patient needs her to feel. In addition, it may at moments be quite difficult for the analyst to be absolutely certain that her subjective response to her patient *is* in fact her own; the possibility exists of a shared subjectivity, that is, of an area of confusion between the patient's and analyst's responses to the holding process. This is particularly likely with patients who make extensive use of projective identification (Klein, 1955; Bion, 1959; Ogden, 1994). To the degree that the patient has split off or disowned aspects of her own experience, for example, in an unconscious sadistic attack on her dependent self, the analyst may tend to experience these attacking feelings as internally generated. In such a situation, the analyst may be uncertain as to whether her ambivalence about bracketing her subjectivity reflects her questions about the process or an identification with the patient's self-attack.

Although work with these sorts of issues is always problematic, when the holding process remains unarticulated between patient and analyst it will be especially difficult for the analyst to sort out those elements of her experience that include the patient's projections. However, as I understand the nature of the holding function, it requires that

---

[3]My use of the term dysjunctive subjectivity is similar to Stolorow's (1994) use of "intersubjective" disjunction. Stolorow's concept, however, refers to the interpersonal experience during which the analyst absorbs the patient's material in ways that markedly shift its subjective meaning *for the patient*. My focus is instead on how the analyst copes with those aspects of her own experience that do not fit with her expectations of how she "should" feel.

the analyst retain contact with her own subjective center. In order to do this within a holding frame, the analyst must *bracket* her experience, that is, *neither delete nor introduce* her dysjunctive subjectivity during the therapeutic interaction. The analyst's willingness to bracket aspects of her experience implies that she remains at least potentially in contact with them, that she neither uses her dysjunctive responses in interpreting to the patient nor splits off, represses, or denies their existence. The analyst's capacity to *hold herself* therefore is pivotal to the therapeutic effectiveness of the holding metaphor. Self-holding does not refer simply to issues of timing, wherein the analyst avoids offering premature interpretation; instead, it describes the analyst's *ongoing struggle* with those aspects of her affective responses that may break into the patient's process. If the analyst altogether loses contact with her experience, holding will cease to be a metaphor. The analyst will be stripped of her ability to be a subject and will become an idealized container for the patient. That idealized view of the analytic function carries with it considerable dangers of its own.

Thus, there are moments in many treatments, and longer periods in some, during which the analyst's holding capacity is crucial. Yet, because I view the analyst to be very much present *as a subject* even during moments of holding, the fate of her subjectivity as well as her capacity to know what the patient needs must be addressed directly.

The Limits of Enactment

There are moments in every treatment when the analyst does not interpret dynamic process to the patient because, instead, analyst and patient play out a complex, painful, or gratifying emotional scenario based on each person's unconscious experience of the other. Such enactments previously were thought to be problematic because they represented a countertransference "acting out" on the part of the analyst that interfered with the work. However, there is increasing consensus among theorists from various psychoanalytic persuasions that the analyst is susceptible to subjective process in a way that periodically results in a series of necessary and inevitable enactments within the psychoanalytic interaction (Mitchell, 1991a, b; Burke 1992; Tansey, 1992; Bromberg, 1993). At least in part, these moments often carry important historical meaning to the patient and are thus pivotal analytic grist that contains a potential for change. To the degree that an analytic enactment can be worked with by the patient–analyst pair, these events may in fact represent crucial treatment moments that ultimately become a catalyst for forward movement. The analysis of such enactments is therefore sometimes a powerful analytic tool. This perspective on enactment underlines the ways in which patient and analyst engage collaboratively to clarify its meaning. That process enhances the patient's self-understanding and simultaneously tends to create a new, more mutual experience of the analytic relationship.

Simultaneously, however, enactments reflect the analyst's partial *failure*—to understand rather than to act—and there are therefore limits to their therapeutic usefulness. For some patients, at least at moments, the analyst's error so powerfully recapitulates early parental failures in form and/or content that the patient experiences the enactment as a near literal reenactment (of early trauma) and responds to the failure in a traumatic way. If the analyst's failure cannot be worked with and ultimately integrated by the patient, it instead may serve to reinforce the patient's defensive style or to precipitate a traumatic regression of one kind or another.

It is in more difficult treatment contexts, which provide very limited space to work with the analyst's misunderstandings, interpretive errors, or failures, that the holding metaphor becomes a dominant theme. When the patient's response to the analyst's input is consistently a toxic one, the analyst's capacity to make use of her subjectivity is limited in crucial ways. Some would argue that it is always the analyst's job to try to find a way to make her understanding known, to introduce her separate perspective into the psychoanalytic dialogue. I disagree, however.

There are times in work with more difficult patients when the analyst's separate existence, often defined by her separate understanding, presents a considerable threat to the patient that cannot easily be worked through. At critical junctures in many treatments, and for prolonged periods with more difficult patients, the analyst's subjective understanding of the patient's experience is experienced as toxic rather than as an intervention with therapeutic potential. It is precisely when the patient cannot work with such enactments that a holding stance presents a therapeutic alternative.

Does the holding process itself represent an enactment? To the degree that the analyst's participation in a holding process emerges out of the complex, mutual pulls of the patient–analyst dyad, the holding experience itself may be an enactment within which patient and analyst coconstruct the holding illusion. The analyst becomes the idealized, attuned parental object, often without a clear sense of how or why she ended up in that position. Additionally, the analyst may view herself as choosing to hold as a rationalization for a more unconsciously based enactment of the maternal metaphor. Such an enactment may be based on patient's and analyst's partially unconscious fantasies of cure. To some degree, the holding process—by definition—represents an enactment in the form of a powerful emotional experience, albeit one that is potentially mutative.

However, frequently there is also a powerful pull within the patient in the direction of recapitulating early parental failures. That pull may impact on the analyst in a way that results in a variety of therapeutic failures, all producing disruptions of the holding process. The simultaneous or alternating pulls toward contradictory scenarios (analyst-as-containing-object and analyst-who-fails-to-contain) make a simple playing out of the idealized maternal metaphor somewhat unlikely. Instead, the holding process usually involves an *element* of enactment for both patient and analyst that is mitigated by the analyst's capacity to retain contact with her subjective experience.

Patients' Responses to the Analyst's Subjectivity

I have found that when patients are involved in a more ordinary or mutual level of psychoanalytic interchange, my emotional variability will, unless extreme, either go nearly unnoticed or be responded to with a directness that allows it to be addressed explicitly. As Aron (1992) and others have so clearly elaborated, when the analyst's subjectivity is addressed, the resulting interchange often deepens both the patient's experience of herself and our relationship to one another. Although patients may have quite a variety of reactions to evidence of my subjectivity (including anger, pleasure, frustration, and so on), their struggle with it and with me is most often strengthening and ultimately results in a freer and deeper level of interchange between us.

Does the analyst's containment of her subjectivity imply its absence for the patient? This is usually not quite the case. During moments of holding, patients themselves often have a peripheral awareness that I have more complex feelings about our relationship (and am a more complex person) than they are fully prepared to assimilate. In this sense, I am suggesting that disruptions inevitably will occur even during a holding process. However, the patient's need for therapeutic holding implies—even requires—that she exclude the dysjunctive elements from her experience in the interest of preserving the holding frame. When the analytic holding function predominates, both analyst and patient temporarily suspend their engagement around the analyst's subjective experience. Although this suspension may lead both members of the dyad to an authoritarian, grandiose, and/or idealized view of the analyst's function, it is also quite likely that both know better.

The analytic dyad does not often enter a holding experience easily or seamlessly. Paradoxically, the apparent seamlessness of the experience both exists and is simultaneously illusory. That is, a negotiation between analyst and patient does take place around a holding moment. However, this negotiation is almost always tacit, never explicit. For a holding process to take place, the patient cannot challenge the boundaries of the analytic holding moment; instead, patient and analyst implicitly agree not to question the analyst's intactness, attunement, or capacity to hold. Yet the patient makes clear, through both conscious and unconscious communications, what is essential for her during the holding process, and the analyst also (sometimes unwittingly) asserts the limits of her capacity to sustain this stance. In my experience, these negotiations around both participants' needs and limits remain largely unarticulated (in a direct way) with the patient during moments of holding. This tacit negotiation stands in marked contrast to the very explicit bargaining that often takes place with patients who are engaged in more mutual analytic interchange.

The Nature of Illusion in Psychoanalysis

Contemporary relational theories view the whole of analytic process as involving a willingness to tolerate paradox and illusion, as the treatment space is transformed into the particular affective arena needed by the patient (Adler, 1989; Ghent, 1992; Pizer, 1992).[4] Mitchell (1988) notes that illusions may reflect narcissistic disturbances and/or may serve to preserve destructive object ties when taken too literally. Illusions, however, also may be used to enhance a capacity for play and creativity within and outside of the psychoanalytic situation. Winnicott (1951) called this arena of illusion transitional space. He linked it to the mother's willingness to adapt to the infant in a way that allowed for illusion. "The mother's adaptation . . . gives the infant the *illusion* that there is an external reality that corresponds to the infant's own capacity to create" (p. 239). For Winnicott, analytic process, like the mother–infant relationship, is the creation of a transitional space within which the nature of certain contradictory realities is not questioned but instead simply allowed to exist. In his discussion of analytic process, Ogden (1994) describes this space as the analytic "third," that is, the result of the meeting of the separate subjectivities of patient and analyst.

It seems to me that within the holding situation, the transitional space that is always characteristic of psychoanalytic experience takes

---

[4]The belief that a tolerance for illusion is an intrinsic aspect of the treatment process differs from traditional Freudian and interpersonal perspectives on illusion as a defense that will be resolved over the course of the treatment. (See Mitchell, 1988, for an in-depth discussion of this issue.)

on a particular quality. Whatever its affective ambience, the holding situation involves the mutual establishment by patient and analyst of a temporary *illusion of analytic attunement*. This illusion concerns the analyst's apparent capacity to remain evenly and consistently present, intact, and available to the patient. Although the analyst may remain consistently present as a nurturing object, at times her nonretaliatory aliveness, her firmness, or her consistent recognition of the patient's rage also may be central to the illusion of attunement. This attunement is illusory because its maintenance requires that both parties temporarily suspend their awareness of the more complex aspects of the analytic interchange, whatever their affective color.

During moments of holding, the separate subjectivities of patient and analyst are transformed in the direction of increased synchrony. To the extent that this synchrony develops in the absence of a sense of struggle on the analyst's part, there is likely to be a significant narrowing of the analytic play space. The holding situation offers patient and analyst a somewhat limited "third" space in Ogden's (1994) sense, because the patient is absolutely intolerant of the analyst's separate and potentially dysjunctive subjectivity. Holding may be play, but it is play rather narrowly defined because the high degree of overlap between analyst's and patient's experience limits the possibility for mutual interchange.

The holding situation requires that the analyst retain, largely unexpressed, her capacity to imagine the enlarged area created by their shared yet separate experience. However, it is absolutely essential that the analyst maintains at least her idea of the possibility for an expanded analytic third, that is, an arena within which patient and analyst potentially can negotiate around two separate sets of subjectivities. If that idea is lost altogether, then holding ceases to be a metaphor and analyst and patient lose all contact with the illusory quality of the holding experience. It is when holding ceases to be a metaphor in the analyst's mind that it is most likely to fail. Mitchell's (1988) discussion of the delicate balance that must be maintained in working with a patient's illusions underlines the ongoing nature of the analyst's struggle with this issue.

To the degree that we view the analyst's role as embedded within a relational frame, the notion of the holding analyst is a paradoxical one. On one hand, the analyst's capacity to hold the patient is real and powerful. The analyst's emotional and literal reliability, resilience, understanding, and sensitivity are a compelling reality at all times, and especially to the patient in a holding process.

On the other hand, how can the inevitably symbolic provision contained within the holding experience be reconciled with the reality of the patient's adult, potentially *knowing* status? The patient is not, after all, a baby, and neither patient nor analyst enters a holding situation with the complex biological/psychological ties that facilitate the holding process in motherhood. Further, there is ample evidence that even during earliest infancy, the baby is highly reactive to the inevitable variations in the mother's affective presence (Beebe and Lachmann, 1988). The holding metaphor requires that these be contained if not excluded from the process if the patient is to have a protected experience.

The analyst who is continually vulnerable to her own subjective process as well as to the patient's cannot hold with anything like the calm, contained, nonreactive evenness with which this concept is associated. The analyst is far too limited by the treatment setup itself, as well as by her own idiosyncratic reactions to her patient, to possibly respond in a smooth, reciprocal way to her patient's needs. In addition, her ability to know just what her patient needs may be quite limited; what the analyst perceives to be an affectively conjunctive response may not always feel conjunctive to the patient. Similarly, what feels dysjunctive to the analyst may at times actually fit within the patient's process far more closely than the analyst imagines. Thus, even the most empathic, attuned analyst is vulnerable to a multiplicity of responses to her patient that may limit her ability to work within the holding metaphor. (I elaborate further on the fate of the analyst's subjectivity and its theoretical implications in Chapter 9.)

The notion of analytic holding is an especially paradoxical one when viewed from a relational perspective. The analyst is *there* as a holding presence, and also is *not there*. Her holding capacity, even if good enough, inevitably will fail periodically because the analyst must and yet cannot possibly hold the patient in a sufficiently even way to protect the patient from her impact on the analytic object. The nature and boundaries of the analytic relationship are such that, even during moments characterized by holding, the patient ultimately may come up against the limits of the analyst's availability, attunement, and sensitive holding capacity. Further, by virtue of her willingness to bracket her subjectivity, the analyst inevitably reveals something of herself to her patient—if only her emotional resilience and willingness to struggle with her experience.

Yet there are times when the patient's need for a holding process is so pressing that the analyst's subjective presence or her failures to hold represent a serious threat to the patient's need. At those times, rather than reacting to analytic breaches, the patient may temporarily delete them from her experience.[5]

---

[5] When failures are registered, they often have a derailing effect on analytic process and are more disruptive than facilitative of therapeutic movement. This stands in marked contrast to the considerable therapeutic effect that the analysis of such disruptions can

In a sense, the holding process requires that the patient suspend disbelief, that is, her awareness of these limits, if she is to render such synchronous moments real and powerful. In order to make effective use of the holding moment, both parties may partially suspend their awareness of the illusory nature of analytic attunement for a time. Although it is certainly true that the analyst is incapable of complete emotional attunement, and, further, is rarely in a position to know fully what to do, both parties bracket this piece of awareness for a time, behaving "as if" it were not the case. The illusion of attunement—an illusion that patient and analyst share—reflects their confidence in the analyst's reparative powers. Yet it is only the deluded analyst who enters any kind of holding situation with absolute confidence about its therapeutic efficacy. To the extent that the analytic holding environment is functioning in a therapeutic way, and does not represent a *folie à deux* between analyst and patient, the analyst (and, at moments, the patient as well) retains the capacity to acknowledge the paradoxical nature of the holding metaphor even while it is experienced as simply real.

It is therefore only if we keep in mind the idea of holding-as-paradox that we can make use of the concept while avoiding the reductionism implicit in a more literal reading of this treatment dimension. In order for the patient to experience the analyst as absolutely attuned, the patient (and sometimes the analyst as well) must to some extent suspend, reframe, or temporarily set aside awareness of those elements that would put this attunement into question. These may include the analyst's absences, her inevitable emotional variability, and her affective "misses" or misunderstandings. That awareness, however, hovers at the edges of the analytic experience, occasionally breaking into the process. Yet it is simultaneously clear that explicit evidence of the analyst's misattunement (i.e., separateness), whether through unconsciously motivated interventions or through the inevitable unreliability of the setting itself (e.g., vacations and other interruptions), may in fact be profoundly disruptive during certain periods. These disruptions (which often themselves represent a reenactment of parental failure) once again underscore the temporary *reality* of the patient's need for a high degree of adaptation on the analyst's part. With most patients, this highly reactive state will be a transitory one that will alternate with and ultimately give way to a more complex and mutual level of relatedness.

---

have during other periods of treatment. For this reason, an analysis of the patient's reactions to object failures will often take place *before or after* rather than during acute periods of holding.

Illusion and Collusion in the Holding Metaphor

If we recognize but keep silent about our awareness that the holding experience is in part illusory, are we colluding with our patients? Certainly, we are participating in a shared experience that only in part is symbolically represented in reality. In this sense, we fail to disabuse our patients of this somewhat distorted view of us; we might even be accused of a limited degree of inauthenticity. Yet is it not possible that the illusion of analyst-as-ideal-parent may sometimes be critical for our patients and for ourselves? Are such partial illusions not, in fact, intrinsic to all intimate relationships? When my 5-year-old son said to me, "You are the best mommy in the whole world," was it necessary that I present a more complex view of myself and disabuse him of his feeling (or even modify it)? Perhaps I should have told him that I wasn't always so great, that he didn't always feel that way about me, or that I hoped he would one day feel similarly about another woman. Or was it instead essential that I did not question his feeling but rather appreciated and even shared it for that moment? Do we not permit such illusions to pervade our romantic love relationships (Mitchell, personal communication)? These illusions frequently are used by both participants to deepen their experience of the other and of themselves, and this is no less true within a psychoanalytic context. Within the context of such illusions, the patient may, for example, contact feelings of hope, safety, or even love for the first time. If analysts feel wedded to absolute authenticity, it becomes necessary to continually remind patients of the limits of our capacity to meet their needs, and thereby render the relationship devoid of an element of idealization that is sometimes crucial.

It is certainly true within the psychoanalytic relationship that there are unusually clear-cut limits within which the analyst may become the holding object. Yet if we simultaneously can accept that reality without feeling obligated to remind our patients or ourselves of it, we may find ourselves capable of participating in an illusion of a crucial kind. I view the holding metaphor as an illusion that contains within it powerful possibilities for enhanced self-experience. Further, it is inherent in the nature of such illusions that the analyst at times will share the patient's experience, so that it becomes temporarily quite real to both parties.

Chapter 3

Holding and Regression to Dependence
The Winnicottian Model

The holding model classically has been associated with that element of psychoanalytic treatment linked to the earliest period of the infant–mother relationship. A rosy vision of mother and child in tender embrace is deeply embedded in those images of motherhood rendered palpable by such painters as Renoir and Cassatt. There is something enormously compelling about the idea of an idyllic early period between mother and infant. This maternal figure lives for her baby; she delights in her infant's dependency and is sustained and enriched by her baby's greedy use of her. She easily gives up those aspects of her own life that are incompatible with motherhood because of her powerful positive response to her new baby. She never appears to be so fatigued or conflicted that she is unwilling or unable to meet her infant's needs. Within this romantic metaphor, the infant is similarly viewed—every feed is satisfying, every holding moment soothing. Colic, fatigue, frustration, or otherwise mismatched responses do not cause more than a momentary wrinkle in the smooth, satisfying interplay that characterizes the mother–infant bond. Clearly, the enormous appeal of this image speaks to our persistent longing for an utterly nonconflictual, intimate maternal connection.

It has, however, become necessary to render the maternal position more complex, even at the price of divesting the mother of her romanticism. The modern mother may adore her baby and delight in her maternal status; she nevertheless struggles with a variety of emotionally dystonic responses to her infant's relatively incessant demands. As much as she may feel gratified by her capacity to nurture, she is aware that she has set aside much of her life to do so. At least at moments and probably sometimes for far longer periods, she meets her baby's needs with a bit or much reluctance, and sometimes not at all (Chodorow, 1978; Kraemer, 1995).

In a similar way, the baby in the best of all possible worlds is unlikely to have quite the level of even, satisfying experience that the maternal metaphor implies. Instead, there will be moments and even longer periods when the baby reacts with frustration to its own internal discomfort or to the mother's inevitable misattunement. There also may be times when distress simply is caused by the baby's growing awareness of its absolute dependence on the mother. Further, recent infant research (Mayes and Spence, 1994) makes clear that the baby is far from a passive recipient of the mother's care. In fact, the infant provides the mother with an ongoing stream of responses (many of which are internally generated, not simply reactive to the mother's input) that represent a source of stimulation for the mother.

Yet despite the complex interchange between infant and mother, a pervasive expectation persists of near perfect maternal adaptability during her child's infancy. What makes maternal subjectivity especially problematic during this early period is the difficulty that the mother may have in tolerating the complexity of her own experience and her baby's without massive self-reproach. To the degree that she expects of herself (and implicitly of her infant) a smooth, affectively resonant response, an acknowledgment of either of their dystonic reactions may produce powerful feelings of shame at her failures to measure up to this idealized image. These failures are particularly disturbing since there is some consensus that the infant is, in fact, in need of responsive, relatively even handling. Kraemer (1995) has underlined the ongoing tension that exists between the mother's subjectivity and that of her baby, and points to the crucial importance of acknowledging the nature and reality of the mother's needs and of her endless, often unsuccessful struggle to contain them.

Holding in the Treatment Setting

Our increasingly complex perspective on infancy and mothering, along with the current emphasis among relational theorists on the importance of mutuality within the psychoanalytic setting, has raised questions about the viability of the maternal metaphor within the treatment process. Can the analyst and the patient replicate in any way the mother–infant experience? Given the mother's struggles with the infant's neediness, can the analyst be expected to offer the dependent patient even a partially "maternal" response? Can the analyst "hold" the dependent patient within the treatment setting? Is regression necessary? Is it possible? Can the patient ever "be" a baby, even momentarily? As we reexamine the idea of regression to dependence within a relational frame, we confront the unresolvable paradox presented by these needs. I address the relational critique of the "developmental tilt" (Mitchell, 1988) models in Chapter 9. Here, I underscore my conviction that, despite its inevitable complexities, it is essential that we include a perspective on regression that accepts the legitimacy and immediacy of the patient's needs.

The patient in need of a holding experience may be seen simultaneously as an adult and as a baby or child. In part, the patient's reactivity reflects the adult's struggle to ward off those disturbing emotional experiences that are easily evoked within the analytic situation. Yet, these experiences also have historical (and often traumatic) antecedents. The holding process addresses both the adult patient's struggle with the present-day residue of early trauma and her self-experience as child. As Ghent (1992) suggests, the paradox of patient as baby and adult is perhaps better tolerated than resolved. Bromberg (1991) states this idea beautifully:

> Therapeutic regression refers to the "raw" states of cognitive disequilibrium allowed by an analytic patient as part of the progressive, self-perpetuating restructuring of self and object representations . . . the deeper the regression that can be safely allowed by the patient, the richer the experience and the greater its reverberation on the total organization of the self. . . . The "child" in the patient is a complex creature; he is never simply the original child come to life again, but always an aspect of an aware and knowing adult. In this respect it is fair to portray the relationship between analyst and "child" as simultaneously real and metaphorical. Regression in one respect is a metaphor, but not *only* a metaphor. It is also a real state of mind. . . . [pp. 416–417].

To the degree that the analyst accepts the therapeutic potency of regressive process within the treatment, and to the extent that the patient can tolerate it, the two sometimes may work toward moments of powerful affective charge within a highly protective holding environment. Despite the paradoxical nature of regression, the analyst working with a dependent patient often experiences the patient's needs to be potent and utterly legitimate. The analyst actually may feel momentarily as if the patient were a baby and the analyst the parent; in the very next (or even in the same) moment, the analyst may feel the patient to be an adult.

How does the analyst "hold" the patient during these moments of regression to dependence? Balint (1968) emphasized the analyst's capacity to carry the patient "like water carries the swimmer or the earth carries the walker . . ." (p. 167).

The analyst working with a patient in the midst of a regression may respond to the dependent patient by attempting to provide her with an experience of near perfect emotional attunement, of what Little (1959) termed "basic unity." From this position, the analyst tries not to intrude on the patient with interpretations or emotional communications that relate to the analyst's own (subjective) understanding of the patient. Instead, the analyst attempts to maintain a position that largely protects the patient from the impact of the analytic object's external existence.

In part, the analyst may respond to the patient's dependency with a resonant nurturing stance. That stance is likely to be motivated both by a conscious choice to hold and by a less conscious pull to enact the metaphor of the idealized mother and baby. The holding position may leave the analyst feeling sustained by her positive therapeutic effect and gratified by her nurturing capacity. She may want to make herself available, to provide what is needed, and temporarily to become the maternal object. She even may have the fantasy that the patient is her baby, that she has the opportunity to meet *this* baby's needs in a near perfect way. That fantasy is particularly seductive because a draw toward the psychoanalytic profession has, for most of us, roots in our less-than-perfect experiences as infants (and also, for some of us, in our experiences as less-than-perfect parents).

Strain in Holding Dependence

Nevertheless, to work in this way with an extremely dependent patient places special pressures on the analyst. The analyst who tries to provide a holding experience for her patient inevitably confronts an enormous level of strain in response to the patient's need for such a high level of affective attentiveness. The analyst must tolerate the sense that the patient is profoundly vulnerable to minute therapeutic failures, and that her responsibility for keeping the patient emotionally or literally alive is great. Although the patient's needy or loving feelings can be gratifying, the analyst may develop a disturbing feeling that the patient is taking over her practice or is draining her emotionally. When holding a dependent patient, the analyst is likely to find remarkably little breathing room for herself—room for error, for misunderstanding, and certainly for her own needs. This is especially so since an uncamouflaged expression of the analyst's subjectivity tends to have a derailing effect on the patient during these periods. The analyst at times will struggle with her own emotionally dystonic responses to the patient, and especially with guilt or resentment about the level of attunement that seems to be required. Because such feelings do not fit with the maternal metaphor, they are especially difficult to assimilate. In this sense, the dependent patient's need for a holding experience will leave the analyst in a state characterized by paradox; she is likely to be simultaneously emotionally gratified and strained by her patient's need.

Similarly, little attention has been paid to the patient's difficulties in tolerating a holding experience during moments of intense dependency. To acknowledge need is always painful; during moments of dependence the patient is acutely reactive to the analyst's capacity to meet that need. Even when the patient responds to the holding experience with feelings of relief or gratitude at the analyst's sensitivity, to some degree, shame is likely to come up around the level of exposure associated with need, and may result in a resistance to the entire process. In addition, to the degree that the patient struggles with issues of envy, greed, or rage, the analyst's very giving potential may evoke in the patient an unconscious wish (and effort) to spoil the moment, to render the analyst inadequate in one way or another (Joseph, 1989). Finally, because it is unlikely that the analyst *is* in fact capable of fully holding the patient, the patient sometimes must contend with anger or resentment at whatever actual failures occur. Again, these feelings are particularly difficult because they do not fit the parental model, and in this sense represent a potential disruption of the holding experience. For that reason, there is often a strong unconscious pressure on both patient and analyst to exclude altogether such reactions during the holding process.

Countertransferential Resistances to Holding

Because of the multiple tensions inherent in a regressive process, it can be particularly tempting for the analyst to resolve those tensions by denying the emotional power and necessity of a regression. A common analytic response to the patient's regression is partially to minimize the nature of the patient's dependence on the analyst as a *specific* object of need. The analyst may attempt to do this by underlining the metaphoric nature of the treatment situation (i.e., by symbolically reminding herself and/or the patient that the patient is not, in fact, a baby; that the treatment involves a contract between adults).

A male analyst was working with Mr. S., a very vulnerable and emotionally labile middle-aged man who, with great difficulty, had reached a point in the treatment where he expressed the powerful conviction that he could not get through his day without the analyst. The analyst had, he felt, given him a sense of hope for the first time in his life. The analyst felt both gratified by his importance to Mr. S. and frightened by the potential implications of Mr. S.'s feelings, which included a fear that he would suffer a breakdown if the analyst were to fail him, especially by leaving even for brief periods. The analyst found it difficult to maintain a holding position; typically he would respond empathically to Mr. S.'s statements, and then would underline his very real strengths in the world and in the analysis in a way that implied that the patient did not need the analyst after all. In addition, when it seemed appropriate, the analyst interpreted Mr. S.'s unconscious conviction that he could be cared about only if he were as helpless as a baby. Mr. S. responded to these statements with apparent relief, and rarely disputed them. Yet, over months, the themes of vulnerability and need did not shift, and Mr. S. periodically became intensely depressed about his inability to "get over" his feelings. The analyst increasingly was left with a sense that something had not been fully addressed in the treatment.

Midway through this period, the analyst began to recognize the persistence and reality of Mr. S.'s experience of need, which in fact did not include any solid feeling of strength. The analyst failed, however, to register Mr. S.'s need for *him* as a unique object. The analyst responded to Mr. S.'s intensified distress prior to a vacation break by raising the possibility of his making use of substitute objects during the break (specifically, he suggested medication and a referral to a covering analyst). To the analyst's surprise, Mr. S. responded to these suggestions with massive distress and a pervasive feeling of despair, and it was at this point that the analyst sought a consultation.

Several implicit messages seemed to be embedded in the analyst's initial response to Mr. S.'s neediness, in which he emphasized Mr. S.'s potential strengths. Mr. S. apparently heard that the analyst supported his capacity for autonomous functioning. This can feel quite reassuring to a patient in the midst of a regression. Furthermore, in a sense it was true; Mr. S. *could* function in the world; he was not simply a dependent baby. However, also embedded in the analyst's communication was an implied (though largely unconscious) prohibition against need. That prohibition reflected the analyst's anxiety about how far the regression would go, and his ambivalence and doubts about his desire and capacity to meet it. To the degree that the analyst implicitly required that Mr. S. function at a higher emotional level than he was able to *without* sacrificing emotional authenticity, the analyst inadvertently truncated a process through which Mr. S. could fully contact, live with, and ultimately work through early vulnerabilities.

When the analyst came to recognize Mr. S.'s vulnerabilities, he attempted to meet them symbolically, by making substitute objects available. Interventions like these may at times be necessary and probably were necessary with this patient. However, they are potentially disastrous to the degree that the analyst makes use of them *in order to sidestep* his unique importance in the holding process. Here, the analyst failed the patient not so much by offering substitute objects, but by not explicitly communicating that he was simultaneously aware of how inadequate such substitutes were. It was only when the analyst was able to accept the reality and power of Mr. S.'s need for him—*without evading its implications*—that Mr. S. was able to expose his internal life and ultimately move forward in the treatment process. Paradoxically, the analyst's willingness to recognize Mr. S.'s feeling that nothing but the analyst would do did actually help Mr. S. to tolerate the separations more easily and did not result in an intensification of his need.

The analyst's confusion about the legitimacy of the patient's need may further be perpetuated by the paradoxical nature of the patient's communications. Ghent's (1992) important discussion of the distinction between neediness and need is relevant here:

> The likelihood is high that in the clinical process, particularly with some patients, both real need is expressed, and along with it, a curious species of camouflage, the blackwashing of need—neediness. The neediness, by being easily confounded with genuine need, is well designed to keep the real need from being known by the analyst let alone the patient. It is often expressive of true self, whereas neediness, garbed in protective coloration, is the impersonator. It is the expression of protector self, that aspect of false self that serves simultaneously as usurper of selfhood and protector of the integrity of true self. It is also hinting to us that behind the noisy fiction and the drama of neediness lives a true self whose genuine need is awaiting discovery and response. . . . My reason for using the word "paradoxical" here is that two equally valid but contradictory statements apply; There is no need; what looks like need is a manipulative, at times vengeful demandingness. . . . On the hand, there is need-genuine longings for human warmth, empathic responsiveness. . . . What so often complicates matters further is that one can often sense both thrusts in operation, oscillating unpredictably in ambiguous and overlapping ways [pp. 141–142].

In this sense, the patient's anxieties around dependence may be expressed in a pseudodependence that evokes in the analyst either iritation or a feeling of being manipulated. To the degree that the analyst remains unconscious of the defensive nature of the patient's neediness and need, the two may collude to avoid entering the arena of more deeply felt dependence.

It is, of course, not uncommon for an analyst to respond to a regressive process with considerable anxiety, reluctance, or ambivalence about meeting need (which then is viewed as neediness, gratifying the patient). When the patient is in, or moving toward, a regression, however, any such response will subvert the holding process. By emphasizing the patient's strengths, the analyst inadvertently supports a return to false self-functioning. The patient may, in effect, comply with the analyst's request that the patient act "grown up" by doing just that. On one level, this move actually can be an enormous relief to both parties; the patient may feel "bucked up" and the analyst will be able once again to do his work in the usual way.

Alternatively, the analyst's inability or unwillingness to recognize the reality of the patient's need may precipitate a traumatic regression. The patient who is told, in effect, not to need the analyst in quite the way that he does, may become disorganized and more needy than ever. Here, the patient responds to what feels like a rejection of his need by unconsciously raising the volume on the expression of dependence. This often is not, however, a simple manipulation on the patient's part; instead, the intensified regression may represent an unconscious protest against the analyst's denial of his need.

The analyst's difficulty in sustaining a regressive process may also be partially a response to the patient's unconscious communication that he cannot tolerate the prospect of regression or is afraid that the analyst cannot. In large measure, such failures frequently represent enactments based on the parental object's inability to adequately hold the child's dependence.

It has been my experience that a considerable number of those people who wish to return to treatment following a reasonably satisfactory therapy or analysis share a sense that the possibility for holding experiences (of widely varied kinds) was missed in their treatment. It is only after quite a bit of investigation that it becomes clear that they have carried, unexpressed, an impression that the analyst needed them to be a certain way, and that, as a result, they held a part of themselves together and "outside" the treatment. It is often this unarticulated feeling that crucial aspects of the transference (for some, the patient's dependence on the analyst; for others, the patient's greediness, rage, and so on) could not be fully experienced that leads to the need for more treatment.

Holding Dependence and the Analyst's Attunement

The dilemma posed by holding dependence requires that the analyst be willing to live with a variety of affective experiences that carry an unusually high level of strain. These concern the patient's potential for breakdown and the analyst's desire and unwillingness to symbolically become the parental object. In addition, the analyst may have particular difficulty tolerating her emotional states when they do not fit the holding experience from the patient's or analyst's point of view. Although these countertransference responses are always problematic to some degree, the level of affective synchrony that the patient needs during periods of regression makes such feelings especially difficult for the analyst. Much as contemporary views of mothering underline the mother's effort to set aside yet maintain contact with her own affective needs when these do not fit with the baby's, it is, I believe, implicit to the holding process that the analyst bracket rather than delete the dysjunctive aspects of her subjectivity. Although the holding process always necessitates that the analyst to a large extent set aside her own needs, this is never more explicit than when the patient struggles with powerful feelings of dependence.

In subsequent chapters I consider holding processes with affective states other than dependence. During work around issues of self-involvement and hate, it will become clear that there is some room for the analyst to make use of her dystonic affective reactions to the patient. Because dependent patients need such a high level of responsiveness from the analyst, however, the analyst has far less space within which either to process or to make use of her dysjunctive subjectivity.

In a parallel way, the patient who allows herself to experience a regression will temporarily exclude or bracket those aspects of her responses to the analyst and to the treatment situation that do not fit the holding metaphor. However, the need for a feeling of safety during a holding process requires that the analyst be experienced as near absolute in her capacity to hold. The patient either deliberately sets aside or unconsciously deletes those aspects of her response to the analyst that are incongruous with the holding metaphor.

Holding, Negotiation, and the Analyst's Subjectivity

Alan, a rather schizoid patient who entered a phase of intense regression following a very long and somewhat intellectualized period of self-analysis, told me, "I imagine that it must be hard for you to stand this—to have to be so absolutely available to me. I even think that you might be mad at me sometimes because I react to every little shift in you. I don't want to know, though. I need you to just *be* this way, to keep *you* out at least for now."

Is it always necessary that the analyst accept at face value the validity of a patient's expressed need for a holding experience? What about the possibility that such statements reflect conscious or unconscious anxieties, conflicts about the work, or even an attempt to control the analysis or the analyst? Is it not possible for the analyst to work interpretively with the patient's declared need for holding, rather than simply to enact the experience? From a relational perspective, the analyst never "simply" chooses to move toward a holding position, but always first attempts to explore the meanings of the patient's expressed or implicit need as fully as possible. Ultimately, the shift toward holding emerges out of a combination of the analyst's clinical judgements and the element of enactment that is always present in the work.

Certainly, Alan's declaration that he "needed" a holding experience did not require that I provide it. Although I felt considerable pressure from Alan to do as he asked, my movement toward a holding position did not emerge organically out of Alan's request. I persisted for some time in trying to understand what it was about my more active presence that was so disturbing to Alan.

My attempts to explore the nature of Alan's experience of me generally met with an overtly cooperative response. Alan rapidly became the "good patient." He too quickly wondered whether he was being infantile in wanting such a high degree of responsiveness from me, whether he was manipulating me into doing something that he didn't actualy need. As I understood it, any investigation of the nature of Alan's need reactivated his identification with very depriving and somewhat sadistic parental introjects. Although Alan was able to recognize this process intellectually, he lost affective contact with his experience of need and its historical origins. He moved back into a false-self position in which he could treat his own experience from a dispassionate distance. Paradoxically, this retreat was a great relief to Alan: from this distance he no longer felt the level of pain associated with the regression. Yet the possibility for deeper levels of experience became increasingly elusive.

Despite (or perhaps because of) Alan's very well-developed capacity for insight, work around the sources and meaning of his need for holding tended to be integrated by him in ways that supported sadistic self-attack. Further work around this process resulted in either depression or detachment. It was only after many cycles of investigation into the source and meanings of Alan's need for holding that I came to feel increasingly convinced of the necessity for this kind of work. As we moved toward moments, and even longer periods of dependence, Alan became increasingly able to expose painful and shameful aspects of his self-experience, and he began to integrate these with other aspects of his process.

Despite this evidence of the positive therapeutic impact of work around holding, my emotional response to Alan's communications was mixed. On one hand, I felt enormously pressured to sustain a high level of affective receptivity and to bracket other aspects of myself, whereas on the other hand, I was encouraged by his rather clear progress in a way that validated my sense of what he needed. Also (paradoxically), I felt acknowledged by this indication that Alan knew it might be hard for me to tolerate maintaining a holding stance. Over time, I felt some but not an overwhelming degree of strain; I mainly was comfortable in our work and moderately convinced of its therapeutic effect.

It is clear that the analyst's own dynamics and her always subjective experience of the patient's process will together influence the analyst's perception of the "legitimacy" of the patient's need for a holding experience as well as the actual shape that such a process takes. Mitchell (1993) notes that these factors will influence the analyst's sense of the patient's request as "need" or, alternatively, as "wish," and therefore of its legitimacy. My response to Alan, and of course to all my patients, was influenced by my inevitably personal way of assimilating our interaction. To some extent, this was unique to me. Another analyst, for example, might have experienced Alan's request as enormously controlling. Such a response would hardly leave the analyst with the wish to meet the patient's need for a holding experience. Instead, the analyst probably would stay with more confrontative or interpretive interventions that explicitly addressed the control issue. Although my own sense is that Alan could not easily make use of interpretations around his unconscious attempts to control the analytic process, it is possible that a different sort of negotiation around the control theme could have evolved within another analytic dyad—with good therapeutic result.

The analyst's subjectivity, then, informs her experience of the patient's need, and thus impacts on her movement toward a holding process. In addition, the patient may unconsciously pick up aspects of the analyst's subjectivity in a way that results in implicit (though rarely explicit) mutual negotiations around the holding experience. In this sense, the patient may to some extent limit the need for a holding experience to what the analyst can tolerate. For example, despite Alan's expressed need for a high degree of emotional and concrete evenness from me, he was able to adapt without great distress to a number of appointment changes that I made each year. I was always especially careful to tell Alan about them early, and to reschedule if at all possible. Nevertheless, these changes were, from my perspective, nonnegotiable. Although I never explicitly said this to him, I am sure that I subtly let him know this was so through the way that I communicated. Alan's response to the changes did not seem to be simply compliant; he reacted with irritation and some complaints, but notably without a feeling of great disruption.

Alan's response can be understood in a number of ways. Perhaps he felt held by the firmness of my position vis-à-vis the appointment changes even while feeling disrupted. Alternatively, he may unconsciously have sensed that to fully contact his distress would break into the holding process in a way that he could not tolerate and/or that he feared I could not tolerate. He may thus have made something of an unconscious deal with himself and with me—to limit his need for evenness to areas in which he felt quite confident that I would not fail him. It seems likely that, within a different analytic dyad, these sorts of negotiations would take a different shape, resulting in a different sort of holding process.

I would further suggest that even the analyst who works confrontatively with the patient may know unconsciously about a particular patient's special sensitivities and may avoid confrontations around certain "hot" areas. In this sense, the patient may feel held even by the analyst who absolutely rejects the notion of holding as a viable therapeutic process! Thus, it is quite clear that the shape and texture of what constitutes holding is highly subjective, colored by issues of personal dynamics and style. Furthermore, it is probably always the case that the analyst's stance to some extent is influenced by a subtle negotiation between patient and analyst around the limits of both parties (see Chapter 8 for a discussion of issues of choice and negotiation around holding).

Evolution Toward a Holding Process

Within the treatment context, the analyst will recognize the shift toward a holding process in the patient's increased reactivity to analytic interventions, as well as in the analyst's spontaneous, often unreflective shift in the direction of a parental stance. That shift is usually made out of a mix of conscious and unconscious factors.

Sarah has been in analysis with me for some years. When she first entered treatment (following a halfhearted suicide attempt), she appeared quite schizoid, detached both from those affective experiences that had led to the attempt and from a sense of connectedness to others. Sarah made use of the first period of our work to address, in an emotionally remote way, the multiple meanings embodied in her suicide attempt. However, our work progressively led in the direction of her early history, and, to her amazement, Sarah contacted memories of a level of parental deprivation that was at times functionally equivalent to child abuse. These memories altogether disrupted Sarah's sense of her "perfectly normal" family context, and resulted in a period of enormous distress, not unlike the responses of patients who recover memories of childhood sexual abuse (Davies and Frawley, 1994). As I explored her emotional experience in the sessions, it became clear that Sarah needed a holding process in order to tolerate reliving her (previously dissociated) painful early history, and to address the depth and power of her self-hate. I responded to Sarah's distress with the desire to function as a parental object, and Sarah became intensely dependent on me and on my ability to remain attuned to her. During many sessions over a period of more than a year, her whole body shook as she talked about the level of neglect with which she had lived and about her repetitive enactment of a tortured life in adulthood.

What constituted evidence that this period of work included a holding process? First, the affective ambience of the sessions was overwhelmingly characterized by a powerful neediness on Sarah's part, to which I found myself responding in a reciprocal way. When Sarah seemed to feel the need for an empathic response, I usually felt like offering one. I was aware of my fantasy that Sarah was my vulnerable baby, and that I often waited for the opportunity to give to her. Without much forethought, I made a special effort to be even and especially available to her, to never begin a session a moment late, to make up hours missed because of holidays, and so on. I found myself frequently sitting forward in my chair out of a sense that she needed me to be as close as possible during our sessions and spoke to her in an especially gentle tone of voice.

It is noteworthy that I was unaware of much conflict about meeting Sarah's needs; I felt my responses to be natural, spontaneous, and appropriate, even when they exceeded what I would ordinarily consider to be within analytic boundaries. For example, when Sarah had a medical emergency, I responded without hesitation, making contact, at Sarah's request, with her physician in order to alert him to her vulnerability around certain physical interventions. What was unusual was not my willingness to make the call, but rather the absence of dialogue (internal or explicit) around the therapeutic pros and cons of that intervention.

Sarah responded extremely positively to the treatment; she progressively exposed the more painful and private aspects of her experience and for the first time allowed herself to cry in my (or anyone's) presence. She was able gradually to link the rather tortured position she maintained in her family with her current life situation. This allowed her to make palpable changes in her relationship with her husband and coworkers, and less obvious but perceptible shifts in her self-experience. During moments of holding, Sarah made her dependence on me quite clear. For example, she found any disruption in the treatment to be intensely disturbing, so that if my answering machine clicked on following a telephone call, she typically would fall silent for a time, feeling jarred. She often phoned over the weekend to make contact.

As my summer vacation approached, Sarah became intensely fearful about my approaching absence. Her desperation over being left alone and her inability to sustain our connection in the absence of contact were emotionally compelling. Sarah also struggled with such powerful feelings of shame at her level of need that it was frequently impossible for her to articulate what she wanted or needed. I also was concerned about my absence and its potential impact on her, and began to think about what I believed to be her need and, notably, also what I would feel comfortable offering her. I finally voiced what I guessed to be her wish—that she be able to have ongoing phone contact over the summer. Sarah was enormously relieved, and asked whether she could have regular phone sessions. I said that we could, but with some constraints; I could only be available at times that might not be convenient for her (I intended to be overseas). We agreed on a schedule of telephone contacts that felt comfortable to me and, I hoped, to Sarah as well. Sarah did phone me as planned that summer, and seemed to be carried through the separation by our contacts.

Holding as Enactment

To a significant degree, my holding response to Sarah involved an enactment around her need. Sarah "became" a helpless baby and I responded reciprocally, by spontaneously offering a holding response. The organic quality of our interaction, my relative lack of doubt about Sarah's need or my capacity to meet it represent clear evidence of the crucial ways in which this period of work involved an enactment around the illusion of parental attunement. That enactment was based both on Sarah's conscious and unconscious communication of need, and also on my (conscious and unconscious) identification with the parenting role.

The pivotal quality of enactment here surrounded the smoothness of our interaction—the near total absence of awkward moments, missed responses, conflicts, doubts, and so on. Although on one level I perceived Sarah's needs quite "objectively," on another level Sarah's state of intense neediness stirred up feelings in me that *propelled* me in the direction of a holding stance.

To the degree that our interaction was characterized by a high degree of affective synchrony, this period of work involved the bracketing of both Sarah's and my own dysjunctive subjectivities. It certainly seems that my subjectivity initially was experienced quite unidimensionally; I assumed a romantic posture vis-à-vis my baby/patient. Periodic interruptions in this idealized holding situation were crucial because they left an opening that could result in deepened meaning. It is the presence, however intermittent, of the analyst's questions and doubts about the holding process that limits the reflexive quality of such experiences in crucial ways.

Although I often responded to Sarah with parental, nurturing feelings, these were not my only reactions to our work. There was a paradoxical aspect to the holding illusion: When Sarah's session was over, I frequently felt quite tired—even on days when I did not feel especially depleted by my work with other patients. Further, although I felt little conscious conflict during the sessions, there were times between sessions when I found myself struggling with markedly incongruous and somewhat disturbing thoughts about our work together. How far should I go in meeting Sarah's needs? To what extent was I gratifying Sarah in ways that would subvert the analytic process? Where was my wish to be a good parent in this process? Should I override my own needs (e.g., for an uninterrupted vacation) in order to meet Sarah's dependency need? What about Sarah's capacity to tolerate the separation, and the ways in which it would be strengthening? I was not able to reach a clear conclusion about the absolute "rightness" of my work with Sarah, and instead periodically returned to these questions without finding a resolution. It is noteworthy, then, that although I succeeded in postponing my questions about the process in the treatment sessions, I had not in fact deleted them altogether. By excluding any sense of doubt or conflict during our contacts, however, I created a way of being that did not markedly disrupt the holding process, only to struggle with my dysjunctive subjectivity when we were not together.

The holding process surrounding Sarah's dependence, then, was characterized by an apparently high degree of emotional resonance between Sarah and myself. Nevertheless, the bracketed, but intermittent presence of my dysjunctive subjectivity was essential to the therapeutic effect of the holding process. By remaining peripherally aware of my questions about the process, I retained contact with its illusory or paradoxical component. This reduced the possibility of a permanently narrowed experience with limited therapeutic potential.

I was not alone in my attempt to bracket dysjunctive elements within the holding process; Sarah engaged in a similar sort of bracketing process in order, I believe, to maintain the illusion of parental attunement. Sarah did this by excluding from her experience any evidence of my inattentiveness or misattunement. A particularly stark example occurred during one of our summer phone conversations. At that time, I was staying in a house that had a cat. As I settled into a chair to speak with Sarah, the cat made a flying leap for me, landed on my shoulders, and slid down my back, inadvertently delivering quite a painful series of scratches. I spontaneously yelled when the cat landed, said something about what had happened, and briefly put down the phone. When I picked up the phone again, however, Sarah resumed talking without missing a beat, as if oblivious to the interruption. It was not until the period of acute dependence had passed that Sarah was able to talk about this experience and acknowledge that she was, in fact, marginally aware of the interruption, but simply too much in need to allow it to register.

A colleague who read a draft of this chapter commented to me that he could not have tolerated making himself available to a patient in that way—so why could I? As I thought about it, I was most struck by the fact that I really hadn't minded the calls, and mainly had felt concerned about the possibility that my children's voices would be overheard and would disturb Sarah, that is, that I might fail her. Certainly, my concern about Sarah's potential for suicide and the obviously positive effect of our contact impacted on my decision to make myself available in this way. Yet, it was crucial for me that *I* defined my availability to Sarah, and limited it in ways that suited my own needs. For example, in thinking about having phone sessions while on vacation, it felt central that our contacts not break the flow of my day. For this reason, I did not accommodate Sarah's desire to speak in the evening, but scheduled our contacts for the very early morning. In this sense, what appeared to my colleague to be excessive responsiveness felt acceptable to me because of the limit that I placed on my availability.

There are enormously varied and individual ways in which each analyst makes herself available and yet creates clear limits on her availability. At first examination, what feels excessively boundaried to one analyst may seem inappropriately unboundaried to another. Only a very careful examination of the complex ways in which we each meet and yet limit our capacity to hold the patient will elucidate the complexity and uniqueness of the individual analyst's holding stance. For example, it may seem paradoxical that although I do not usually feel intruded on by my patients' calls, my patients seldom call me. What should I make of this? Am I unconsciously communicating to my patients that they should not call me? Am I providing a sufficiently containing experience so that most people do not need extra contact? When I do receive such calls, do I not mind them because unconsciously I feel gratified, reassured of my importance to my patients?

My willingness to be used, and especially my comfort in being used by my patients in this way, is associated with a parental aspect of my self-experience, with my pleasure in meeting my children's needs. There is a way in which I simultaneously want to be needed and taken for granted, and there is something reassuring and sustaining in that experience. Yet, I also implicitly maintain a separate arena of action that I am not easily willing to abandon. It is, I believe, crucial that these two arenas remain potentially available to the analyst—that the analyst retain contact both with the state of "being" characteristic of the holding function and with her more differentiated "doing" self-state. When either position becomes a unitary need that pervades the treatment, ultimately the treatment may fail. If my need to hold dominated the treatment, my patient would come under its influence and would either rebel against that pressure or capitulate. Alternatively (and, paradoxically, similarly), if my insistence on the centrality of my own subjectivity predominated, my patient would respond to a sense of intrusion or impingement by either accommodating to me or withdrawing. Both of these scenarios essentially would be in reaction to my needs rather than to those of the patient.

Dangers Inherent in Holding Dependence

Did I have other choices in Sarah's case? Was it really necessary for me to make myself as available as I did? Had I truly been unable to be in contact, could Sarah have survived the separation without returning to false-self functioning? Although it is impossible to be certain, of course, it is my sense that although Sarah would have lived through such a disruption, a price would have been paid in terms of the internal depth to which she would have felt prepared to go with me. That is, although Sarah might have survived the break intact and even untouched, in a central way she would have withdrawn, hopeless about my capacity to understand her and her experience, and trusting only her defensively self-reliant posture. In this sense Sarah probably would have experienced my abandonment as a reenactment of her childhood experience—of being ignored by her parents when she was hurt or ill. For me to fail to recognize the danger inherent in her having revealed herself for the first time would have represented a profound abandonment.

Yet other dangers would have emerged had I met Sarah's compelling needs in a way that fully ignored my subjectivity. This might have happened if, for example, I failed to examine whether and how I *wanted* to be available to her during my vacation, and simply offered to be in contact. I might then have experienced my parental capacity and her helplessness as if that were all there was to each of us. By excluding the press of my subjectivity and of my ambivalence about setting it aside in the interest of protecting Sarah, the emotional risks inherent in my offer would have been increased for both of us. These risks were multiple. They included the potential for resentment and retaliation on my part, a narrowing of my experience of Sarah and of her experience as well. I would have deleted Sarah's potential to find her own way of managing the break and of negotiating with me around her neediness.

Only by choosing to bracket rather than ignore my subjectivity could I fully address the dilemma posed by Sarah's need. That is, my capacity to meet Sarah's need was enhanced rather than diminished by my willingness to experience and tolerate my own desire and also my unwillingness to offer a holding experience. In the same way, by simultaneously recognizing the absolute emotional reality of Sarah's dependence on me although both of us had the potential to relate in other, more complex ways, I was able to accept, enjoy, and privately challenge the illusion of attunement that characterized the holding situation.

Effects of Ruptures During Periods of Holding

Central to my thesis is that disruptions of the holding process, while to some extent inevitable, often have a potentially derailing effect, especially in work with dependent patients. Nevertheless, disruptions are unavoidable in the sense that they frequently emerge as a reenactment of the original parental failure. Despite the patient's need for a reparative experience, the emotional press of both conscious and unconscious memories of such failures inevitably find their way into the holding situation.

Winnicott (1963b) believed that at times the analyst's failures were central to the therapeutic process. It is most paradoxical that Winnicott, who historically is associated with the importance of provision, believed that ultimately it was the analyst's *failure to provide* that was pivotal to change. I address the centrality of the analyst's failure to the evolution of the treatment process in more depth in Chapter 10. Here, however, I would like to emphasize the implicit tension between the analyst's capacity actually to hold the patient in order to meet her needs, and the patient's ultimate need for the analyst to fail. The analyst's failures (which are, in any case, inevitable) create an opportunity for the patient to sort out those elements of her experience that are and are not projections and to place the object out "in the world." In this sense, I do not believe that the process of holding with dependent patients itself is sufficient to allow the patient fully to integrate split-off aspects of self-experience. It is, nevertheless, a pivotal step in that direction.

It is the experience of safety implicit in the holding process around dependence that facilitates the emergence of dissociated or repressed affective states. If the analyst's holding capacity fails in a major way during periods of regression, that failure may be anything but useful to the patient. The analyst's failure instead may represent a traumatic reenactment to the patient and may push the patient toward a more defensive level of functioning. Winnicott was well aware of this. He noted that at other times such reenactments carry an especially high risk and represent a serious failure that is not always analyzable. In contrast to the relational-constructivist position, which views "failures" to be enactments with therapeutic potential, I (with Winnicott) understand some analytic failures to be anything but useful to the patient. In a sense, the analyst sometimes must fail (to help the patient), and, at other moments, must not fail. The latter moments occur most often when the patient's need for the illusion of parental attunement is acute. Consider the following examples.

Sharon is a very anxious, middle-aged writer in a four-times-weekly analysis. She generally feels somewhat dependent on the treatment because she suffers from periods of debilitating anxiety. Yet she is also quite friendly and adult. We work in a rather straightforward way; I feel relatively free to offer my thoughts or interpretations when they occur to me, and Sharon seems reasonably able to assimilate and work with my input without losing contact with her self-experience. I feel no need for the highly attuned responsiveness characteristic of the holding work described above, nor does Sharon implicitly or explicitly ask for it.

It was in the context of this rather easy and positive working relationship that a breach occurred. As the winter descended in earnest, Sharon often arrived for her session with a cup of coffee, from which she typically took a sip prior to lying on the couch. She would then set the cup down on the rug next to the couch, where it wobbled a bit precariously as she lay down. I found myself watching the coffee cup with some discomfort, wanting to snatch it up before it spilled, remembering the day a patient accidentally spilled coffee on a new chair. I privately struggled with some discomfort about this personal concern, which overrode any interest I might have had in the dynamic meaning of Sharon's action. Feeling uncomfortable about reframing my concern as an analytic issue, I simply asked Sharon to put her coffee on a table.

Sharon complied, but as she lay down she spontaneously voiced a feeling of surprise and annoyance at my request, which she interpreted as reflecting my lack of faith in her (that I didn't trust her to be careful). For the first time in our work together, she began to question what I was like as a person, whether I was really interested in her, and whether I cared about her and valued her. As I listened, saying little, Sharon vented a fuller range of negative feelings toward me than I had heard from her previously. I indicated that I heard how angry she was with me, privately feeling a bit relieved that she had not simply complied with my request. Toward the end of that session, Sharon began to connect my action with her father's fastidiousness. For the first time, she associated me with her father and elaborated on her anger at him and her difficulty expressing it.

These themes pervaded our work for that week. Sharon periodically reiterated how angry and disillusioned she was with me. That anger, however, was expressed in the context of Sharon's readily available perceptions of my own subjectivity. She stated quite clearly that she recognized that I was a person too, and that I had a right to my "irrational concerns." She was disappointed in this evidence of what she called my "pet peeves," but not so derailed as to lose contact with the more positive aspects of our work. This week marked a shift in the treatment; increasingly, Sharon felt free to express her negative and critical feelings about me, and to make use of her own aggression in our work and in her life.

It is clear that my failure to meet Sharon's expectation initially had a disruptive impact on her, but one that she was able to work with and ultimately to make good therapeutic use of. Thus, this clinical vignette fits with what Winnicott considered to be the therapeutic effect of the analyst's failures. I believe, however, that this was possible largely because Sharon was not involved in a holding process with me.

In contrast to the positive therapeutic effect of this breach of expectation with Sharon, I would like to describe the impact of an analytic rupture with Sarah. During the winter I developed a particularly bad cough, despite the fact that I otherwise felt fine. For many of my patients, my cough was a cause for either concern (how sick was I?) or irritation (it was distracting and annoying). For Sarah, however, the cough produced quite a different reaction. I tried mightily to suppress my cough but without success. As it persisted, Sarah spoke with increasing hesitancy, becoming silent when my coughing interrupted her. When, after some minutes of silence on both our parts, I said quietly that it was clear to me that she was having trouble either ignoring or responding to the fact that I kept inadvertently interrupting her, she began to weep convulsively, unable to speak for some minutes. Finally she said, simply, "There is no room for me here." She could not hold on to the expectation that I would soon be better, be angry with me for impinging on her experience, or be concerned about me. At that point in the treatment, my containing function was so pervasive that its disruption had an unhinging effect that Sarah could not make therapeutic use of.

Despite several attempts on my part, Sarah made it quite clear that she could not talk about the session in a useful way, and instead needed to return as quickly as possible to the feeling of being soothed. It was not until the period of acute dependence had passed that Sarah was able to talk about her experience during that session, and about her distress at evidence of my misattunement.

That incident raises questions concerning the limits of the analyst's and the patient's capacity to bracket their subjectivity during a holding process. Should I have anticipated Sarah's reaction to my coughing and cancelled her session that day? Why *did* I choose to see her? To what extent did I act out of self-interest (wanting the income), anxiety (my awareness that she would feel disrupted and distressed were I to cancel) or concern (about maintaining the delicate state she was in)? Was I angry at her intense need or neediness (Winnicott, 1947)?

Tolerating the Holding Environment

The analyst who attempts to bracket her subjectivity is in a particularly tight spot emotionally. To the degree that the analyst's subjectivity is all too present, the requirement that the patient be protected from it represents an added emotional dilemma. That strain is likely to build up over time, and may result in unconsciously motivated disruptions in the holding experience. These are especially likely to occur when the analyst does not fully acknowledge her dysjunctive subjectivity during moments of holding.

My work with Sarah continued primarily to involve issues of dependence over a period of several years. Over time, I began to take the work for granted; I no longer actively considered my feelings about Sarah's need, but rather automatically did what I had been doing with her. However, I also was increasingly aware of a sense of pressure, largely as a result of factors in my own life that left me feeling overburdened and undersupported. It was in that context that I scheduled a meeting with a colleague during Sarah's session time. This colleague was someone with whom I could be fully myself, and thus I anticipated feeling supported (perhaps held?) during our meeting. I was aware that I would have to cancel or reschedule Sarah's hour, but somewhat guiltily decided that it would be all right because she would be able to see me later that day, whereas my colleague would not. I did, in fact, easily reschedule Sarah's session for the early afternoon. Although I of course should have anticipated it, Sarah's intense distress took me by surprise. She was not so much hurt as disoriented; this disorientation lasted for over a week and was quite severe. Sarah's recovery was gradual, in much the way that Winnicott (1964b) described his vulnerable patient's reaction to his own idiosyncrasies.

Why did I introduce this disruption into Sarah's analysis? Certainly, on one level, I knew better. I did so with full awareness that I had deliberately placed my needs ahead of hers. I was not, however, fully conscious of the likely effects of my actions, although certainly my guilt should have signaled this to me. Although one could speculate that I changed Sarah's appointment as an unconsciously motivated retaliation against her for the pressure I was under, I am inclined to view my behavior as more complexly motivated. Retrospectively, I understand my action as an unconsciously motivated attempt to renegotiate with Sarah the limits of my availability. I could no longer tolerate fully bracketing my subjectivity in the context of our work. I had "had enough," and despite my conscious intentions to the contrary, I rebelled against an ongoing experience of pressure and thus alerted myself to the limits of my emotional reliability. In doing so, I initiated a dialogue around the weight of our respective needs, and in this sense, I broke into the holding experience.

Paradoxically, this disruption was crucial for me. It allowed me to maintain a holding stance with Sarah by creating a space within which I could reassert my own limits. In the absence of any possibility for negotiation within the analytic relationship, it is inevitable that the analyst's ability to maintain a holding stance will break down in fairly dramatic ways. However, although it is possible that this disruption was somehow strengthening for Sarah (in that she ultimately lived through it with me and survived), my sense is that she paid too high a price and was far too unhinged for this possibility to represent more than a rationalization on my part. Sarah's traumatic response to the disruption was all the more evident because, in contrast, many of my patients use such incidents to expand and deepen their awareness and capacity to express their feelings about our relationship.

The Self-Holding Function

In hindsight, it seems surprising that unconsciously motivated disruptions of the holding process do not occur more often. Why not? How does the analyst tolerate keeping herself out? A pivotal aspect of the holding process involves the *analyst's capacity to hold herself*, that is, to provide a self-protective holding function during analytic work. This self-holding function involves the analyst's ongoing struggle to hold on to her affective state even when it must be largely excluded from the analytic work. This is particularly difficult with dependent patients because of the pressure on the analyst to respond in absolutely reciprocal ways. It is tempting for the analyst to persuade herself (as I did with Sarah during the period just described) that she *does* feel just what the patient needs her to feel. Yet it is clear that the cost of deleting her dysjunctive subjectivity will likely involve a serious disruption of the holding process.

Self-holding also involves the analyst's capacity to exercise her right to maintain her always arbitrary boundaries. This is a process that varies dramatically in form from analyst to analyst, but one that is always essential. I know that I automatically maintain rather clear boundaries around my sessions, especially with patients in a regression. These boundaries delineate my constraints literally, and also subtly, probably in partially unconscious communications. The effect of these boundaries is to limit my attunement to what I can tolerate. In addition, these boundaries establish evidence of my idiosyncratic presence. This process is largely subtle and symbolic. It involves the assertion of my subjective presence and implicitly establishes the limits of my willingness to adapt.

I would like to offer a concrete example of this. Some years ago, (after refurnishing my office and feeling pleased and somewhat protective of it), I became aware that on snowy or very wet days I felt irritated when some of my patients did not use the floor mat to wipe off their shoes and tracked mud into my office. After an internal struggle, I decided to ask people to leave their wet boots in the hall on bad days. I was aware that this was an unusual request, but after some initial apprehension about people's reactions, I felt relieved, and no longer uncomfortable working on those days. Those patients who were involved in a holding process did not particularly react to this request, because, I believe, of their need to exclude dysjunctive elements from the holding experience. However, more than one of my patients who were not involved in a holding process articulated a reaction to this request. Most typically the feeling was that I am excessively fussy about my office, and that I was asking my patients to accommodate me in this fussiness. In a way, I agree. It seems to me that this perhaps insensitive request symbolizes the reality of my subjective presence, and serves as a measure of self-protection. It is as if I say to the patient: "You can't mess up my space, at least in this way. I have one foot in a separate world, and I intend to keep it there." The explicit or implicit establishment of one's subjectivity is probably what allows the analyst to tolerate this work in general, and perhaps most especially with patients needing a holding process. I imagine that it is always necessary that the analyst make this statement (to herself, and probably sometimes also to the patient), either concretely or symbolically. It is absolutely crucial that it be made if the analyst is to undertake and tolerate the holding stance.

Reliability as Paradox

It seems, then, that the holding process with dependent patients involves an implicit paradox. While the patient is not a baby and the analyst is not the mother, both parties may partially suspend their awareness of the illusory nature of analytic attunement for a time. That awareness, however, hovers at the edges of the analytic experience, occasionally breaking into our contacts. Yet it is simultaneously clear that explicit evidence of the analyst's misattunement (i.e., separateness), whether through unconsciously motivated interventions or the inevitable unreliability of the setting itself (e.g., vacations and other interruptions), is in fact profoundly disruptive during moments of holding. These disruptions once again underline the temporary reality of the patient's need for a high degree of adaptation on the analyst's part. With most patients, this highly reactive state will be a transitory one. It will alternate with and ultimately give way to a more complex and mutual level of relatedness within which patient and analyst participate together in elaborating on the meaning of their interaction.

Holding Issues of Dependence in Ordinary Treatment

Although the holding process and especially the analyst's attunement are most pivotal when the patient is sufficiently vulnerable to require a regressive experience, the holding theme can also emerge at moments in other treatment situations. Here, the holding dimension is likely to be more symbolic than real, and to emerge in a form that is transitory rather than ongoing. Nevertheless, these moments may be crucial in that they permit the patient a more powerful level of overlapping affective experience. A brief holding experience may indirectly support a deepening of analytic interchange by allowing the patient a momentary dependence on the analyst. That dependence points to the analyst's capacity to hold, and thus may be reassuring for the patient in a way that deepens the process.

Charles, an anxious young man, entered treatment complaining of his difficulty in establishing relationships with women as well as his inability to complete his doctoral thesis. During the first five years of treatment, he worked quite steadily to understand the nature of his experience, and was able to complete his doctorate and to engage in casual dating relationships. His relationship with me was mildly positive, and he was able both to make use of our work and to reject my comments without marked distress when he found me to be off base. I felt fairly free to be myself with Charles, to interpret things as I saw them, and to work internally with my varied subjective responses to him when they did occur. Charles did not show the kind of reactivity to my separateness that is often associated with the need for a holding experience.

However, from my point of view, Charles's transference involvement remained very muted, and did not evolve over the years of our work together. Charles's response to my attempts to probe his experience within the transference were cooperative but markedly mild. He preferred to see me as a helpful mentor and was quite defended against the possibility that I could be the object of his intense emotions. Interestingly, I developed rather strong positive feelings toward Charles, very much respecting his capacity to work with his experience and his determination to change and make a better life for himself.

During the fifth year of treatment, Charles came to a session in obvious distress, and disclosed that his mother had suddenly and unexpectedly become seriously ill. As he spoke about his mixed feelings toward her and his fear of losing her, he sobbed with uncharacteristic abandon. I responded with feelings of great sadness, and a wish to comfort him as he faced this imminent loss. The session was characterized by a level of intensity and synchrony typical of a holding process around dependence; Charles expressed a need for highly resonant, nurturing responses, which I was able and eager to meet.

Although the emotional power of that session did not recur, it marked Charles's entry into a new treatment phase. Increasingly, he addressed me with some affective charge, and began to experience and express an array of transference feelings. Much later in the treatment, Charles spoke of that session and of his surprise and relief at the discovery that I could respond to him in such a full way.

In retrospect, it appeared that while Charles did not need a regressive treatment experience, he nevertheless carried a covert level of mistrust that prevented him from becoming fully engaged in the treatment. When reality stresses broke through his somewhat defended, highly autonomous style, he was briefly receptive to experiencing his own need and my capacity for responsiveness. The level of reassurance that he derived from a single holding experience was sufficient to move the treatment beyond our partial emotional impasse.

Conclusions: Paradoxical Elements in the Holding Experience

The analytic dyad does not often enter a holding experience easily or seamlessly. Paradoxically, this apparent seamlessness both exists and is simultaneously illusory. That is, an implicit negotiation between analyst and patient does take place around the holding moment. However, this negotiation is almost always tacit, never explicit. For a holding process to take place, the patient cannot challenge the boundaries of the analytic holding process. Instead, patient and analyst often wordlessly agree not to question the analyst's largely good intentions, her attunement, or her holding capacity. Yet the patient makes clear, through both conscious and unconscious communications, what is essential for *her* and the analyst also inevitably asserts the limits of her capacity to sustain this stance. These negotiations around both participants' needs and limits remain largely unarticulated in a direct way with the patient. This tacit negotiation stands in marked contrast to the very explicit bargaining that often takes place with patients who are engaged in more mutual analytic interchange.

Chapter 4

Holding and Self-Involvement

The Evolving Holding Metaphor

Central to my understanding of the holding metaphor is the assumption that holding describes a containing function that operates well beyond the bounds of infancy and also well beyond the needs and experiences of the patient in a regression to dependence. In the next two chapters, I extend the concept of holding in ways that explicitly address its therapeutic function, first in work with issues of self-involvement and then around problems of hate and self-hate. Despite the conceptual limitations of the parallels between mothering and psychoanalysis (see Chapters 2 and 3), I remain convinced of the usefulness of such comparisons. I believe that the origins of core affective experiences for both analyst and patient may be found in a careful examination of the complex subjectivity of mother and child. For this reason, before addressing the holding theme in the treatment setting, I once again return to early development and the evolution of the theme of self-involvement.

The end of infancy marks the close of the period associated with the classic maternal metaphor. As the baby becomes a toddler and an older child, her evolving autonomous capacities ordinarily diminish the frequency and intensity of her need for a holding experience in Winnicott's sense. To whatever extent it did exist, the period of primary maternal preoccupation passes; the mother fully reconnects to her own desires and her own life, and the child moves in the direction of an increasing capacity for independence. However, despite the ever-widening arena within which parent and child operate, and despite the child's progressively more complex experience, there continues to exist a theme related to the parent's capacity to hold the child in a dependent state. In this sense, the need for a holding experience around dependence represents a theme that pervades the life span, at times as "figure" and at other times as "ground." It especially tends to reemerge in moments of intense vulnerability or stress, for example, around loss or other trauma. Yet the need for a symbolic holding experience in moments of heightened dependence also may be needed everyday by the older child or the adult, as at bedtime or at other separations.

We nevertheless ordinarily do not associate childhood and adolescence with the infant's dependence on the holding function. This is not because holding disappears as a developmental theme, but instead because the predominant affective tone of the holding process shifts away from issues of dependence and toward the more complex issues of self-involvement.

The holding process around self-involvement describes the parent's ability to support the child's emerging autonomous functions by remaining a reliable but nonintrusive background presence. The developing child needs and depends on the parent's consistent yet unobtrusive presence in order fully to develop and exercise a sense of self—of separate, affectively alive, autonomous potential. The parents hold the child because their relatively silent, even, potential availability helps to sustain the child's evolving self-experience, even as the parents apparently are ignored or taken for granted. It is, in fact, their willingness to *be* taken for granted that is central.

Winnicott (1958) suggested that the child's experience of being alone in the mother's presence would form the backdrop for the development of a capacity to be alone. The experience of being alone in another's presence is ubiquitous, and takes many forms throughout the life cycle. The connection to a background holding presence may be taken for granted, but nevertheless supports a variety of adult experiences, including the essentially alone process of many forms of creative expression. Winnicott (1958) also viewed the experience of aloneness after intercourse to be a variant of the capacity to be alone.

Winnicott's notion of aloneness in the mother's presence represents, I believe, a metaphor for an essential element within the psychoanalytic situation. In this chapter, I would like to emphasize the *therapeutic* or *reparative* function of that experience. For those people who have sufficiently internalized a sense of whole aloneness, the analytic setting itself may create a space within which such aloneness may productively be used. However, for those individuals whose sense of self is especially vulnerable to external assault, a therapeutic holding process around self-involvement may become pivotal.

It is necessary here to distinguish the holding process with issues of self-involvement from Kohut's (1971) discussions of mirroring and also from Mahler's (1972) discussions of emotional refueling. Kohut used the concept of mirroring to describe the mother's capacity to respond to the child's achievements with joy and appreciation. As I understand it, Kohut's notion of the mirroring function characterizes the mother during moments when she is far more explicitly engaged with the child than she is during periods involving the child's more total self-involvement. The child in need of mirroring is intensely engaged in interaction with the mother, albeit largely as a selfobject. When the mother provides the child with emotional refueling in Mahler's sense, the mother functions as an affectively responsive base to which the child may return in moments of stress or anxiety. The mother of this rapprochement period is largely a background presence, but one whose primary function involves her willingness to receive and respond when the child does feel the need to reconnect.

Both the mirroring and refueling functions, then, describe an emotionally present and responsive maternal presence. In contrast, when the parent holds the child's self-involvement, she does so not by actively engaging with the child, but by her willingness to be physically present and yet to stay out emotionally. The parent who holds self-involvement creates a space within which the child can experience not so much her potential connectedness to the parent but instead the child's *own self*.

Winnicott (1958) made reference to the mother's importance as a backdrop to the child's evolving capacity to be alone, although he did not describe this as a holding function. I would like to explicitly tie the mother's background function to the holding metaphor. The mother's or father's ability to contain, unexpressed, his or her own affective processes is pivotal if the child is to have a full experience of self. Here, what is critical is the parent's willingness essentially to tolerate being useless in the child's presence without withdrawing or intruding.

Strain When Holding Self-Involvement

During those moments when the parent holds the self-involved child, a different sort of subjective strain may be experienced from that typical during moments of dependence. On one hand, parents may derive considerable pleasure from their facilitative effect with the self-involved child, especially insofar as the child thrives in their presence. There can be something enormously gratifying about being gradually discarded as an essential object. Parents may find a sense of confirmation in the child's growing ability to be and to do in the absence of their active support. At times, then, the parents may take enormous pleasure in being able to experience their own aloneness in the child's presence. When the child seems to want the parent to be physically present but is sufficiently caught up in her own activities, the parent may be able, for example, peacefully to read a book, sensing the potential connection with the child. Pleasure, not strain, characterizes this experience.

On the other hand, though, this background holding function is likely to leave the parent in something of an emotional quandary. An aspect of parenting that is not often talked about, but one which mothers and fathers sometimes confess to one another, surrounds a periodic struggle to tolerate incredible boredom, irritation, and even judgementality vis-à-vis the child who is increasingly becoming her own person, paradoxically less needy of the parents while still requiring their reliable presence. The nature of the child's needs may leave parents unable simply to withdraw into a self-focused reverie or to relate to the child in a full way. Long stretches of parenting may involve, for example, listening to a child's apparently incessant, self-referential chatter, playing seemingly endless board games, repetitively reading the same book (not necessarily one's favorite), and accompanying a child on outings during which one's function is largely to chaperone. Children are rarely in an emotional position that would allow them to experience, let alone acknowledge, their parents' subjectivity during such activities, and this is especially true during periods of self-involvement. There is sometimes little gratification for the parent in these contacts, and one can feel like a necessary body; needed, for example, to move the game piece, but not actually taken in by the child who is so intensely engaged in the mechanics of the game.

In addition, the nature of the child's or adolescent's concerns, interests, or values may leave the parent struggling with feelings of disappointment or criticality about, for example, their child's insensitivity toward peers, selfishness, ambitiousness or lack thereof, and so on. At times the child's intense level of self-involvement obliterates the parent *as a subject* in Ogden's (1986) sense.

Yet, ordinarily parents do not tell the child to snap out of it, grow up, make contact, select an activity that they would find more fun, or, at least, leave them alone. Instead, they more or less contain their irritation or boredom, knowing that this self-involvement is necessary for the child. Parents probably do so most easily when they are confident that the child will spontaneously emerge from this preoccupied state and again will relate in a fuller or a different way.

It is nevertheless rare that the parental response to feeling bored, judgmental, or irritated with the child is a neutral or accepting one. Instead, there is likely to be a sense of shame and inadequacy associated with such responses. After all, wouldn't good parents suspend their personal preferences and preoccupations and fully enter the child's world, that is, take pleasure in the child's self-absorption? The power of this conviction has been repeatedly made clear to me by the pain with which parents (and, interestingly, especially mothers) confess such feelings.

Holding in the Treatment Setting

Although the child's self-involved state may be quite difficult for the parent to tolerate, the narcissism that represents an adult variant of it is far more problematic. Those patients who struggle with serious narcissistic issues frequently present with a combination of difficulties; they are extremely sensitive to slights of any kind, and yet almost absolutely unable to work with the analyst's interventions around that sense of injury. With some narcissistic patients, virtually *any* intervention that extends, alters, or breaks into the patient's own narrative is experienced to be so assaultive that the patient reacts with a sense of profound injury. That injury sometimes is expressed in rageful attacks on the analyst, withdrawn periods of silence, or, not infrequently, abrupt terminations. Often, the patient is quite unwilling to acknowledge the analyst's impact, making dialogue around the injury virtually impossible.

As with dependent patients, holding creates an emotionally protective setting for self-involved patients (sometimes the first such setting) within which feeling states can be experienced without the patient being required to respond to the analyst as a discrete other. However, self-involved patients are far less affectively related during the holding process than are people struggling with issues of dependence. Modell (1975, 1976) described the narcissistic patient as being in a cocoonlike state that allows for a measure of omnipotence, of invulnerability to the analyst's presence. He suggests that the cocoon period permits the patient to experience an illusion of self-sufficiency. It gradually facilitates sufficient ego consolidation so that the treatment can move toward an active investigation of the patient's emotional experience. Bach (1985) similarly suggests that "the narcissistic state of consciousness . . . attempts . . . to establish or recapture an ego state of physical and mental wholeness, well-being and self-esteem, either alone or with the help of some object used primarily for this purpose" (p. 10). He notes that the narcissistic patient has great difficulty retaining a simultaneous awareness of herself and of the analyst.

Patients who present with powerful narcissistic issues as children frequently had to contend with their own parents' self-involvement. For these individuals, the analytic setting may offer an opportunity to reverse the experience of being the object of the parent's obliviousness. To the degree that the analyst understands such dynamics, she may be more able to tolerate being "wiped out." Sometimes it may also be possible to work with the patient around the dynamic meaning embedded in her annihilation of the analyst's impact; more often, however, it is not.

Strain During Periods of Holding

To the extent that a self-involved patient cannot examine her transference experience, the analyst must contain her own agenda—her wish to do "real" analytic work, to make contact with the patient's emotional experience, and to deepen the process. Tolerating a feeling of uselessness is not something that we have been well trained to manage, however. In fact, the primary means by which we derive and retain a relatively even level of self-esteem in the face of the inevitable vagaries of analytic work is disrupted by this sense of uselessness. It is through a periodic confirmation that we do understand our patients, and are capable of usefully communicating that understanding, that we are most easily affirmed as analysts. Even when working with a patient who is difficult to "get" at times, we may manage our frustration by renewing our efforts to clarify the meaning of the material's obtuseness! It is a considerable subjective strain for the analyst to continually tolerate a patient's narcissistic obliteration without at least inserting an interest in the nature and function of the need to screen her out. The difficulty of tolerating, unexpressed, feelings like boredom and irritation, is further intensified by the self-criticality that tends to be evoked by these feelings. When the analyst's subjectivity is utterly denied by the patient, there may be moments (or even longer periods) when the analyst becomes deadened to her own process and simultaneously to that of the patient. It is often the analyst's struggle against a feeling of internal deadness that results in a renewed (and useless) attempt to interpret.

Countertransference Resistances to Holding

The subjective strain with which the analyst struggles when working with narcissistic patients tends to create a sense of tension within the analyst about how little is happening in the treatment. On a less conscious level, the analyst may feel insufficiently valued by the patient and narcissistically injured herself. That experience increases the possibility that the analyst will retaliate via muted or indirect attacks on the patient.

Mr. J., an older attorney, was in treatment because of serious marital and work problems. He attended his sessions regularly, but, from his analyst's viewpoint, made little use of them. Mr. J. instead spent the sessions boasting to Dr. M. about what appeared to be largely fantasied personal and financial victories over his co-workers. Mr. J. seemed disinterested in his analyst's responses to his stories, and quite content to continue telling her about his professional prowess.

Dr. M. initially listened to Mr. J.'s stories empathically. She understood well the compensatory nature of the fantasies, and did little with the material other than to gently reflect on Mr. J.'s concern with his own potency. Mr. J. did not respond to her comments, but instead seemed to dismiss them in order to continue to elaborate his own stories. As weeks became months, Dr. M. felt increasingly uncomfortable with her therapeutic stance. She wondered whether the treatment might not be a sham because she could not find a way with which to work directly on the issues underlying Mr. J.'s fantasies. She increasingly began to worry that she was wasting Mr. J.'s time and money. Dr. M. repeatedly tried to engage Mr. J. in a dialogue around those issues that had brought him into treatment, reminding him that he was bothered by his failures and wanted help with them. Mr. J., however, evaded her inquiries, or, when pushed, denied that he had interpersonal difficulties. Dr. M., feeling increasingly impotent herself, decided to confront Mr. J. directly in order to move the treatment forward. She asked Mr. J. why he continued to come to therapy if he had no interest in working on his difficulties, and wondered whether she should discontinue the analysis since he was not willing to address any issues. Mr. J., not surprisingly, took offense at the challenge, and quit analysis precipitously.

Dr. M. felt badly about this and also was quite angry with Mr. J. It was not difficult to attribute the therapy's failure to the fact that her patient was simply too narcissistic and defensive a person to be receptive to psychoanalysis.

What was the therapeutic function of Mr. J.'s self-aggrandizing stance? As Modell (1975), Bach (1985), and others have made clear, Mr. J.'s vulnerability was so intense that the analytic situation represented an extraordinary threat to him. His rather transparently compensatory fantasies reflected a desperate attempt to ward off Dr. M.'s potential to disrupt his already precarious internal intactness, and probably also to render her as impotent as he felt himself to be. Dr. M. was well aware of this. However, what was less obvious was the therapeutic potential of maintaining a nonintrusive holding stance with Mr. J.

For Dr. M. to have maintained a holding position with this patient, she would have had to tolerate a prolonged period during which she was, in fact, quite impotent, in which no "analytic work," in the ordinary sense, was done. Mr. J. probably would have needed a considerable period of time during which the analyst made few interventions other than to listen to his (often unbelievable) stories without challenging or even commenting on them other than to reflect Mr. J.'s conscious communication. The purpose of this holding period would be to allow Mr. J. a highly protected setting within which he could elaborate on his self-experience. The hope is that very gradually, he would sufficiently consolidate a sense of his own boundaries and of the analyst's nonintrusive but receptive presence to develop tolerance for self-examination.

The strain involved for the analyst working in this way would include her boredom and irritation at Mr. J., but more importantly her anxiety about her uselessness as an analyst. This is the pivotal difficulty for the analyst who tries to maintain a holding stance with the self-involved patient. What makes holding with issues of self-involvement so uniquely difficult is, then, the analyst's profound doubt about the therapeutic leverage of the holding process. Because the therapeutic efficacy of a holding stance is rarely apparent until the patient begins to emerge from the narcissistic state, the analyst cannot rely on evidence of change in the way that she can during periods of holding with dependent patients.

Jane, a young woman recently graduated from college, entered treatment complaining of problems in her relationships with men and an inability to settle on a career for herself. In an early session, she declared that her aim in life was to marry a rich European and to live in a mansion. In subsequent sessions she elaborated on the centrality of this fantasy, which she actively pursued. In contrast to Mr. J., the patient described above, Jane was able partially to realize her rather grandiose fantasies in her daily life. She regularly dated wealthy foreign men, and told me in great detail about the elaborate parties, elegant gifts they brought her, and the trips on which they took her. Jane could spend an entire session describing her weekend in this way. As she lay on the couch, she would preen, stretching out an arm or leg, admiring it, adjusting a piece of jewelry or clothing as she spoke. She rarely expressed any interest in or concern about her internal life, or (most striking to me) her lack of sustained emotional involvement with these men or with anyone else.

I tried with little success to engage Jane in a way that would allow her to become interested in the meaning of her core fantasy, her relationships, or her working life. Jane responded to my questions undefensively, but perfunctorily, sometimes with mild surprise or annoyance at being interrupted. My attempts to explore her experience of me or of my efforts to probe were met with cooperative but strikingly disengaged responses. Occasionally she became involved in what felt to me like an intellectualized discussion that seemed to lead us nowhere.

Throughout this period, Jane's attitude toward me was friendly but superficial. I felt like a saleswoman whose product was being examined, but who was of no intrinsic use or interest to her. I periodically struggled with a sense of being obliterated, useless, and ineffective. Nothing that I said to Jane made an impact, as far as I could tell, and Jane seemed happiest when I asked her a simple, concrete question or did not speak at all. Although I had little sense of a genuine positive connection between us, Jane did not appear contemptuous, angry, or even particularly irritated with me. In fact, I found it increasingly difficult to believe that we were involved in anything approaching psychoanalytic process.

To further complicate matters, quite often I felt judgmental of Jane's life focus. Where, in this emphasis on money and objects, were people? Jane's fascination with playboys was repugnant to me—their abuse of alcohol and drugs and their conspicuous consumption stood in such contrast to my own values that I sometimes had the wish to intervene with a pseudomaternal lecture on what really matters in life.

Sometimes, Jane simply bored me. I found myself unable to keep the names of her many boyfriends straight. My mind wandered—to people and activities that would offer me some more genuine emotional contact. I caught myself anticipating a friend's phone call, planning my child's birthday party, focusing on sources of affective pleasure in the context of what felt like an emotional wasteland.

At other times, I tried more actively to understand why I felt so "dead" with Jane, and what the impact of my deadness was on her. As I recognized the nature of Jane's reactivity as well as my need to maintain a sense of aliveness, I attempted to contain my reactions, questions, and judgements silently. This did not mean that I was literally silent with Jane, but rather that the bulk of my responses reflected or elaborated on Jane's conscious communication. By tolerating my sometimes intense reactions to her and not attempting to manage them through the use of queries or interpretations that explicitly or implicitly *raised questions* about Jane's experience in her own eyes, Jane experienced a holding period during which she progressively elaborated on her process in (for me) a remarkably unreflective way.

It was not until several years into the treatment that Jane started to move out of this narcissistic position. The slow shift in her emotional stance vis-à-vis me and herself first became apparent when Jane began to ask me what I thought about aspects of her experience, and was able to think about my input rather than ignore or reject it. She gradually was able to tolerate examining her own life, and to think about her choices. Although she never developed an intense transference involvement, by the end of the treatment Jane regularly examined her affective process in a way that resulted in significant movement in her life. She ultimately became accessible to interpersonal interchange that felt real to both of us.

What happened that allowed Jane to develop a fuller capacity for affectively alive connections? Jane used my nonintrusive holding position as a space within which she could begin to "be." Over time, she became able to contain aspects of her internal process for the first time.

It was the elaboration of Jane's subjectivity within a highly non-intrusive space that facilitated the gradual build-up of a fuller sense of separateness and internal aliveness. Only within the context of that absolutely separate subjectivity could Jane begin to tolerate analytic process without an excessive sense of threat.

It is always easy to write about a difficult treatment at a point when the positive therapeutic impact of earlier years has become apparent. But what I would like to emphasize here is that throughout much of the holding process I had no real hope or expectation that Jane could change or that I had any therapeutic leverage. In this sense, I worked from a position of absolute *uncertainty*—not knowing whether I was doing the right thing or being emotionally dense or even lazy. Certainly, it is difficult to feel suffocated by a patient's need. It can be yet more difficult to tolerate feeling incompetent and bored, even when the analyst studies those feelings to deepen her understanding of the patient. Yet, paradoxically, it seems quite clear that with patients who suffer from powerful narcissistic issues, the analyst must *stay out* in order for a sense of self to consolidate.

Holding, Self-Involvement, and the Analyst's Attunement

What uniquely characterizes the illusion of attunement during work with narcissistic patients? With patients who struggle with issues around dependence, the analyst's attunement reassures the patient of the analyst's willingness to "carry" the patient, to evenly meet the patient's needs as she exposes her vulnerability. In contrast, the narcissistic patient is not able to experience, let alone express, her need for the analyst.

For this reason, the therapeutic function of holding here serves a rather different purpose. The analyst repeatedly demonstrates to the narcissistic patient that she can tolerate being obliterated without disappearing or intruding on the patient's self-experience. The analyst remains reliably alive, intact, and able to survive in a space that does not impinge on the patient's space. In this sense, the analyst's holding stance may permit the patient an experience akin to aloneness in the presence of another (Winnicott, 1958).

Does the self-involved patient remain oblivious to the analyst's emotional experience during the holding process, or is such awareness merely bracketed so that the patient may remain within the holding experience? For large portions of the treatment process, the narcissistic patient is likely to be quite unaware of the analyst's subjectivity. There may however, be moments during the treatment, and especially during breaks in the analysis, when the patient can articulate something of her impact on the analyst.

Margaret, an artist patient, returned for her first session following the summer break, and, quite characteristically, proceeded to tell me in great detail what she had accomplished during the month. It was clear that no response was required; instead, she was pleased to be telling me all that she had done in the absence of any response from me. Toward the end of the session, however, she paused and said, "Why am I telling you all this? I just want you to listen. I don't really want you to say anything at all. It's like I want to hear *me*, not you. I wonder if that bothers you, if you want to put your two cents in. Or if you're bored, if you really don't care how many paintings I finished. That's tough, though. I don't care. You're not here to be entertained by me." When I responded by asking her whether she really wanted to know what I thought, Margaret paused only briefly. "No way. One way or the other, you'll try to change something about me, and I only want you to know."

Was it necessary that I comply with Margaret's insistence on my silence? Could she in fact tolerate continued discussion of her experience of my input? I felt that her communication reflected the first evidence of some receptivity on her part to my separate subjective presence. I was able to pursue her experience of me for a bit here by addressing her anxiety regarding my potential impact and what she assumed would be its derailing effect. Underlying this anxiety lay a mostly unconscious assumption that I would not tolerate being "mistaken" any better than she could—that my narcissistic investment in my own ideas would require that she comply with me (as she had in childhood with her very narcissistic mother).

In a way, then, Margaret's insight about her unwillingness to receive my ideas was pivotal; the emergence of a sense of awareness that she needed me to "stay out" actually marked the first evidence of her capacity to allow me in. During the next months, although Margaret continued to present herself in a highly self-involved way, this was her first glimmer of awareness that I might have reactions to her need to shut me out. About a year later, she began to consider her impact on me and on the people in her life. As she did so, the treatment moved toward a more mutual interchange that included an explicit consideration of transference factors.

Dangers Inherent in Holding Self-Involvement

Whenever the analyst engages in a therapeutic process that involves the partial suspension of explicit dialogue around the patient's experience of the analyst and of analytic process, certain dangers present themselves. A clear possibility with a narcissistic patient is that the analyst may resort to what only appears to be a holding stance in sadistic retaliation for the patient's negation of her therapeutic potency. Here, the analyst's avoidance of interpretive responses serves not a protective function but a destructive one. The patient unconsciously may feel tortured, deprived, or judged, and may defensively withdraw even further into a self-protective position.

A beginning analyst presented a session early in his work with a narcissistic young man. The patient began the session by telling the analyst that he had begun to date a really beautiful girl. He described her appearance and their sexual encounter in great detail. He then mentioned that he had a photograph of her with him, and showed it to the analyst. The analyst, himself a young man who had not connected satisfactorily with a woman, was unaware of the degree to which he felt threatened by this patient's social success. He decided that the patient needed a quiet and even, nonreactive response from him. He looked at the photo without comment or expression, and remained quiet throughout the hour. The patient did not explicitly react to the analyst's nonresponse, but spent the rest of the session elaborating on the woman's beauty in increasingly hyperbolic terms. He did not appear for his next session and never returned to treatment.

The analyst's rationale for his silence in response to the patient's bid for admiration and possible unconscious wish to evoke the analyst's jealousy focused on the patient's need for a therapeutic holding experience. The analyst's lack of awareness of his intense countertransference response to the patient made the withholding element of his behavior particularly obvious and toxic; however, with more sophisticated analysts, such retaliatory responses also may take place, although in better camouflaged ways, embedded either in silence or interpretations.

Yet, at other times, an analyst may maintain a holding position out of a genuine belief in the patient's intense negative reactivity to self-examination. The possibility always exists, however, that it is the analyst's emotionally dense or awkward interventions that the patient is reactive to, and that a more sensitive study of the nature of the patient's experience might allow the analyst to find a better and more effective way to intervene. Insofar as the analyst settles too comfortably into a holding stance, a danger inherent in that stance involves the analyst's potential for complacency; that is, for progressive inattention to shifts in the patient's experience that might permit a different level of response. (See Chapter 7 for a discussion of stalled holding processes with self-involved patients.)

Effects of Disruptions During Holding

What effect do disruptions of the holding process have with narcissistic patients? In work with dependent patients, even small alterations in the analyst's even responsiveness can be highly disturbing. This is somewhat less obvious with narcissistic patients. Because dependence on the analyst is energetically denied, a self-involved patient is likely to show little overt response to the analyst's literal or emotional absences. Instead, an unconscious sense of injury may build, unnoticed by either party until it erupts, sometimes resulting in rageful attacks on the analyst or in the abrupt termination of treatment. Because the self-involved patient cannot listen easily to the analyst's interpretive interventions even when framed within the patient's subjective sphere, disruptions are especially likely and difficult to deal with. This may be particularly problematic for the analyst when the patient's self-involvement is somewhat less overt.

Lisa, a graduate student, was referred by a much admired older friend of hers for analysis with me. She began treatment with very positive feelings about the process, and engaged with me easily and with apparent receptivity to my interventions. The treatment proceeded reasonably smoothly for about a year. Lisa progressively explored and elaborated on the nature of her relationship with her parents; she did not appear to develop any particularly strong feelings toward me. I was aware, however, that Lisa did not easily experience her own impact or the possibility that there was more than one way in which a given situation might be assimilated. When I raised such issues, she appeared somewhat puzzled, and struggled to justify her position once again. I did not press these matters, and Lisa moved back into an insulated position from which she described her own experience, wanting little more than confirmation from me.

Then, one day, I received a phone message from Lisa, stating that she had a meeting with a professor and needed to change an appointment. I was able to offer her an alternate time. Over the course of that month, Lisa called on several occasions to reschedule her sessions, always for apparently good reasons, related to school meetings and family obligations.

In our sessions, I tried as tactfully as possible to raise questions about other meanings of Lisa's need to cancel sessions. I also attempted to explore her feeling about both my ability and potential inability to reschedule. Lisa responded by elaborating on the reasons for the cancellations, and assured me that there was no subtext involved in her need to change appointment times. She said that she understood that I could not always offer a make-up appointment.

Over the next few months, Lisa continued periodically to cancel an hour and ask for a make-up appointment. I became aware of Lisa's unconscious testing of my attunement and willingness to accommodate her, to allow her needs to override my own. I was also aware of the possibility that unconscious contempt was embedded in her treatment of me. Over time, probably both in response to her subtle contempt for me and in response to increasing pressure in my own life, my willingness to reschedule her sessions wore away. Somewhat at the end of my rope, I decided to try again to talk directly with Lisa about the nature of our interaction, although I was aware that in doing so I would reintroduce my subjectivity into the exchange.

In our next session, I told Lisa that I had the feeling that she would like me to accept her need for make-up appointments at face value, and not address it with her. I felt, however, that we needed to look at what she was saying about her needs and how she expected me to meet them. Lisa again responded by assuring me that the cancellations were all quite legitimate, and that she understood that I could not always make up the time. She was not willing or able to talk about any less rational feelings about our interaction. However, I received a phone message later that day from her. In it she said that she felt that it would be better for her to work with a therapist who had more flexible hours since her own schedule needs were so pressing. Lisa would not agree to return to treatment despite several contacts on my part.

In retrospect, it seems clear that Lisa was not yet ready to cope with the reality of my subjectivity or of her own unconscious motives. By raising those issues with her directly, I disrupted her unconscious experience of omnipotence so dramatically that she could cope with her sense of injury and rage only by leaving treatment altogether. The remaining question, of course, is whether there was a more tactful or less threatening way in which I might have addressed this issue, or whether only my willingness to tolerate and/or accommodate her self-involvement *without* inserting my subjectivity would have permitted Lisa to remain in treatment.

Tolerating the Holding Environment: The Self-Holding Function

Self-holding serves a somewhat different function when the holding process is dominated by issues of self-involvement. With narcissistic patients, analysts are often intensely aware of and involved in an ongoing effort, one not always successful, to retain a sense of confidence in the efficacy of the analytic work. At times, this requires some tenacity. Internal self-holding is necessary because of the ongoing absence of any clear evidence of therapeutic effect with these very difficult patients. In this sense, holding here involves the analyst's containment of self-doubt about her competence and about the treatment process itself. I would like to underline the importance of this self-holding function in permitting the analyst to *experience* rather than to deny the presence of self-doubt about the therapeutic process.

When the analyst's capacity for self-holding is diminished, for example, during periods of intensified internal or life stress, the analyst may have particular difficulty with a self-involved patient's need for a holding process. The analyst may feel unusually sensitive to the patient's disregard for her, and may struggle with the desire to break into the holding stance and to "make" the patient attend to her. This can be a common response on the analyst's part when, for example, the patient fails to notice a new engagement or wedding ring, advanced pregnancy, evident ill health, a new office, and so on. In situations like these, the analyst is likely to feel simultaneously somewhat guilty about wanting acknowledgment and resentful about the patient's obliviousness to explicit evidence of her subjectivity.

To the degree that the analyst's subjective response to a self-involved patient involves a sense of boredom, distaste, or irritation, a holding stance in part will protect the patient from the analyst's subjective responses. Yet, simultaneously, this type of holding process will allow the analyst to make use of some of these subjective responses. By *keeping out*, by allowing the patient to control the analytic space, the analyst can fully experience her own frustrated and anxious reactions without fear that she will make use of these through pseudoanalytic interpretations. Her interpretive silence in part will express her hate, in much the same way as the ending of an hour (Winnicott, 1947). While the analyst at times may experience her silence to be retaliatory, if the analyst can acknowledge these wishes, she will be far less likely to act them out. In this sense, the analyst's subjectivity is only partially excluded during the holding process.

Attunement as Paradox

The self-involved patient is as much in need of apparent analytic attunement as is the patient in a regression. Further, although the nature of the analyst's attunement places somewhat different strains on the analyst, the analyst's subjectivity again will occasionally break through the illusion of attunement, resulting in ruptures of the holding process. To an even greater degree than with a dependent patient, such ruptures are quite risky because they potentially can result in a unilateral termination on the patient's part. Yet the analyst's capacity to tolerate the holding position and to bracket her subjectivity is, paradoxically, enhanced when she attempts to renegotiate its limits.

Holding in Ordinary Treatment

The necessity for holding around issues of self-involvement and the analyst's momentary reaction to feeling irrelevant or emotionally obliterated can emerge in the most ordinary of treatment situations. When the theme of self-involvement does not dominate the treatment, the analyst is unlikely to struggle intensely with her subjective responses. Nevertheless, the analyst's capacity to tolerate the patient's cocoonlike state may be important at times within any treatment context.

I have found the patient's self-involvement to require a holding response when the patient's concerns appear absolutely to obliterate their awareness of, for example, major world catastrophes, serious family difficulties that do not affect them directly, and so on. I was once tempted to ask a patient preoccupied with the details of an apartment rental whether she was avoiding thinking or talking about her father's critical illness. I restrained myself, however, and focused on the concrete matters that she presented. Later that week, she voiced relief at having a space that was hers. She spontaneously returned to the subject of loss in a way that included an increased capacity to deal with the reality situation and with her very complicated feelings around losing her father.

It is therefore important to emphasize that holding self-involvement does not describe a stance of analytic silence or neutrality; instead, it addresses the analyst's struggle to contain her wish to communicate *understanding* and thereby to deepen the process. Holding may, for some patients, be reflected in a very active dialogue around the patient's experience; for others, the analyst will be fairly or even completely quiet. Holding always involves the analyst's acceptance of the patient *exactly where she is* (Bach, 1985), and in this sense it involves a suspension of nearly all that is ordinarily thought to describe analytic process.

Chapter 5

Holding and Ruthlessness and Hate

As we expand and complicate our understanding of the nature and meaning of holding processes, it becomes clear that the holding metaphor is a multidimensional theme that emerges and reemerges throughout the lifespan. In this chapter, I examine the relevance of holding to themes of ruthlessness and hate as they manifest in the psychoanalytic situation. Although the analyst's understanding of, and response to, issues of hate have many roots in clinical theory, I again begin by examining the parental metaphor as it develops around these issues. A careful study of the contemporary parental metaphor is particularly useful in explicating aspects of the analyst's subjective struggle when working with these issues.

Long after the period of early infancy, the child's need for moments of holding periodically surfaces. In part, these moments emerge from the dependent child's and adolescent's periodic need for a holding experience. However, as I discussed in Chapter 4, the increasing complexity of the child's self-experience results in a second holding theme related to self-involvement.

There is a third theme involving ruthlessness and hate that also surfaces during childhood and adolescence. As the child's capacity to experience and articulate complex affective states progressively develops, her responses will at times be hard for the parent to manage, and also discordant to varying degrees with the parent's own emotional state. Of particular difficulty are those moments when the child reacts with great negative intensity to internal or external stress. The parent may experience the child's distress to be puzzling, enraging, endless, and also not easily repaired. The child's tantrums, demandingness, incessant no-saying, or whining can create pressure on the parent for a reparative response. Yet even when the source of the child's need, frustration, or anger is relatively straightforward, a resolution may be far from simple for either parent or child.

Two developmental processes may be involved here, either alternately or in rapid fluctuation. One was described by Winnicott (1945) as ruthlessness, that is, the infant's (or, by extension, the child's) utter disregard for her impact on the maternal object. Ruthlessness does not reflect destructive intent toward the object, and may thus be differentiated from Klein's (1975) concept of destructiveness. Despite the absence of destructive intent, however, the ruthless child experiences the press of her own needs in a manner so intense as to effectively obliterate any potential awareness of the object's subjectivity. Thus, at times, the child's insistence that the parent "get it" just right may reflect the incredible power of the child's emotional experience and the consequent screening out of a second set of (parental) subjectivities. At other times, object-directed hate *is* embedded in the child's distress, and a core communication involves the child's rage at the parent for real or imagined failures.

As the infant becomes a toddler and then an older child, the progressive evolution of her emotional life renders such affective communications ever more complex from the parents' point of view. The source of the child's need or anger may, paradoxically, become increasingly murky as her internal life evolves outside of the parental relationship. Thus, the school-age child may leave home quite happily only to return from her day in a foul mood and explode at the parent; the adolescent's emotional variability may leave parents feeling that they have no idea whatsoever what it was about their apparently innocuous comment that resulted in a contemptuous, defensive, or nasty response. At other moments, the child's apparent insatiability and disregard for the parent's need may become more than a bit difficult to tolerate.

It is, of course, inevitable that the parent will react with a variety of strong feelings to the child's anger and distress. Yet if the child simultaneously is to sense the validity of her affective experience and of the parent's capacity to survive without retaliating or collapsing (giving in), it is sometimes necessary that the parent tolerate such expressions in a way reflective of the holding metaphor. This holding process involves the parent's struggle to accept and contain need and rage while neither retaliating nor submitting to the child's intentional or unintentional provocation. Holding here describes the parent's attempt to provide an affectively alive, safe setting within which need, rage, or distress can safely be expressed.

Of course, an important aspect of the parents' responses to the child's demands or anger often includes a willingness to *negotiate* with the child, to find a way to meet the child's demands or to alter their own position in response to the child's reaction. However, here I would like instead to emphasize a different theme. There will be times when the child or adolescent is enormously helped by the parents' capacity merely *to contain* their reactions to the child's anger, thereby creating an emotional limit. Holding may at moments include physical holding, a literal containment of the child's rage or distress. At other times holding will be symbolic and will involve the parents' *acceptance without action* of the child's experience in the absence of any attempt to insert their own, that is, to negotiate around their two subjectivities.

Strain in Holding Ruthlessness and Hate

The intensity of children's reactions to both minor and major frustrations, and to internal distress that has no discernable source, can be overwhelming to the parent. This is especially so when our children's demands, hostility, denigration, or rage are directed at us, at our real or not so real failures. It is unlikely that such difficult affective experiences can be tolerated by the parent without considerable self-doubt. After all, if we had done a good enough job, wouldn't our child be less angry or critical, or at least more easily soothed? To tolerate a child's intense distress quite often leaves parents with painful questions about their own capacity to nurture. It can be tempting to respond to the child's tantrums or the adolescent's denigration by withdrawing or retaliating, by blaming the child for her unhappiness, or by blaming ourselves for having been so insensitive to her needs. The possibility of remaining relatively firm but emotionally present, of accepting the child's misery or criticality without either privately abandoning our own beliefs and subjectivity or attacking the child, requires that we simultaneously experience and contain both our rage and self-doubt about our capacities as parents.

There is an additional difficulty for the parent who attempts to contend with the child's painful emotional states. Even during times when the ruthless or hateful child needs a holding process, at other moments it is crucial that the parents notice and respond to other, subtly expressed needs. That need may be for holding around dependence, or for an experience of omnipotence that requires parents to tolerate "staying out." In this sense, even when the holding process primarily involves issues of ruthlessness or hate, earlier themes related to holding dependence and self-involvement may persist, but on a more subtle and less pervasive level. And all of these will, of course, intersect with moments when negotiation, rather than holding, seems to be required!

Holding in the Treatment Setting

Analysts are familiar with the difficulties involved in work with patients who present with ongoing, sometimes unremitting expressions of frustration, distress, rage, or contempt. Tolerating the patient's periodic negative affect is something that we are ordinarily well equipped to do, and know is both necessary and useful; living with a patient who is relentless in her desperation and in her explicit or covert attacks on our analytic self or our personal characteristics is not. When our patients spend apparently endless sessions attacking themselves, the analyst, or analysis itself, it may become clear that ordinary interpretive interchange is relatively useless (Robbins, 1988; Gabbard, 1989). However, we are unlikely to receive such awareness with great pleasure; our relative therapeutic impotence, together with the distinct discomfort that we all have when subjected to unremitting hostility or subtle denigration, inevitably leave us contending with powerful subjective reactions to our patient. A central difficulty often surrounds the analyst's struggle with intense and negative countertransference feelings (Winnicott, 1947; Heimann, 1950; Little, 1951; Pick, 1985). There is considerable cross-theoretical consensus (although Kernberg [1975] disagrees) that in situations like these, the treatment is unlikely to be moved as a result of interpretations (Bion, 1962, 1963; Balint, 1968; Modell, 1976; Gedo, 1979; Poggi and Ganzarain, 1983; Horowitz, 1985; Carpy, 1989; Druck, 1989).

In a series of important papers, Epstein (1977, 1979, 1984) has elaborated on the therapeutic function of the analyst's stance in work with issues of destructive aggression. He especially addresses the difficulties involved in treating patients who regress as a consequence of their own abusive behavior toward the therapist and the setting. Because these patients arouse frustration and anger in the analyst, their primary impact is to leave the analyst feeling incompetent and enraged. In line with Winnicott (1947), Epstein (1984) suggests that the therapist's surviving of the patient's attacks is crucial to therapeutic movement. He proposes that by using "counterbalanced aggression," expressed mainly in feeling tones that counter the patient's aggression, the therapist will retain her viability as a therapeutic object.

> Those patients whose destructive aggression is expressed openly in persistent fault finding, denigration and undermining of both the therapeutic setting and the therapist ... [require] ... that the therapist understand that the severe emotional upsets to which he is being subjected by such patients are nothing more than the ordinary complement of the patient's ongoing primitive ego-splitting and projective processes and that this negative countertransference experience is a necessary part of the treatment ... that the therapist prove to be capable of fully acknowledging his ownership of the totality of this countertransference experience, and of riding out such intense feelings as hatred, self hatred, impotence and despair without acting them out, i.e., retaliating, emotionally abandoning the patient, or in one way or another getting rid of him ... that the therapist facilitate a corrective maturational experience by maintaining his own boundaries, setting firm enough limits, and, when under relentless and abusive attack, use enough of his own aggression—but only enough—to resurrect himself

from the denigrated state into which the patient has cast him, thereby, signifying aliveness and reestablishing the reality of the two-person situation [Epstein, 1984, pp. 652–653].

I propose that the apparent therapeutic stalemate with a hateful patient will be resolved precisely because the analyst can tolerate her own highly dysphoric subjective process while maintaining a steady holding position. The therapeutic holding stance here involves the analyst's attempt to tolerate her subjective experience *without* making use of interpretation as a way of managing the ongoing tension between her and the patient. It is essential that the patient be free to express a full range of frustrated, attacking, or denigrating feelings toward the analyst while the analyst demonstrates her capacity to survive intact through affectively toned but nonintrusive responses rather than through interpretations (see also Slochower, 1991, 1992).

What is the therapeutic function of the analyst's holding response to the ruthless or hateful patient? Certainly, the intensely uncomfortable position in which the analyst is likely to find herself does not easily fit with the notion of a therapeutic holding stance. It is, however, precisely the analyst's willingness to allow (and at times even to encourage) the patient to express a wide range of intensely painful affective states without attempting to impose an (external) understanding of these that provides a holding experience for the patient. The analyst thereby creates a space within which the patient may fully expose her ruthlessness, despair, and rage without risking the break-up of the relationship or the patient's self-experience.

Because the patient who continually expresses desperate or hateful feelings toward the analyst is likely simultaneously to fear her destructive potential, the analytic holding function in this situation contains an additional component; in order to feel held, the patient needs ongoing evidence that the analyst is surviving intact in the face of the patient's emotional discharge. For this reason, holding with a ruthless or hateful patient requires that the analyst continuously demonstrate her aliveness through affectively toned, but largely noninterpretive responses. The patient's intense and negative affective states are held when they can be both *acknowledged* (explicitly or implicitly) and *tolerated* by the analyst without the use of interpretations to detoxify the painful feelings that are inevitably evoked in these tense treatment situations. The analyst's responses serve to hold the patient by providing evidence that the analyst has confidence in both the patient's potential for change and her own survival.

Because the clinical picture tends to be quite different depending on whether issues of ruthlessness or of hate predominate, I will describe separately the evolution of a holding stance in each of these two treatment contexts.

Holding Issues of Ruthlessness

Sandra presented herself for analysis complaining of anxiety and volatile relationships with men. Although her initial appearance was both friendly and appropriate, during the initial months of treatment she rapidly developed an intensely anxious and dependent transference. Sandra exposed violently fluctuating emotional states that were accompanied by desperate requests for help with her own internal pain. Sandra cried hysterically throughout her sessions, speaking rapidly and with great distress about the crisis of the moment. She repeatedly phoned between our daily sessions, leaving long and anxious messages. The anxiety centered around a feeling that she was "falling apart" and could not manage her real life or her intense terror and need without either drugs (Quaaludes, etc.) or me.

Sandra's desperation was intense and emotionally convincing, and initially I responded to her with concern and empathy. Sandra seemed to be struggling with previously split-off feelings of dependence and rage (at herself and at the object of her dependent wishes). These feelings were evoked in the treatment setting with special intensity as I alternately became the nurturing and the sadistic object. For this reason, my soothing or interpretive responses did not make more than a brief impact on Sandra's distress, which continued to escalate. As Sandra pressed me for help, I became aware of her unconscious communication that I was her torturer. Sandra was reenacting with me a sadomasochistic relationship that had sources both in her own life and in her parents' history (they were war refugees). Sandra seemed to take in statements reflecting my understanding of her distress as well as her underlying anger at me for failing to meet her needs. I said that I imagined that she would like me to feel as tortured as she, if only so that I would more fully understand her plight.

Sandra responded with apparent relief to these interpretations, saying that she felt understood for the first time. However, her desperation rapidly escalated, and she articulated that she now knew even more acutely how much I was denying her. The intensity and ruthlessness of her demands increased. She continued to phone nearly every day, leaving long messages, and she began writing me letters as well. She begged to be allowed to move in with me, not altogether clear that this was not possible. Even more alarming, Sandra increased her level of exposure to real danger. She escalated her drug use and began to flirt with abusive men in sufficiently unprotected settings that I began to wonder whether she was toying with suicide.

Although I continued to feel concern for Sandra, I also was aware of the ruthlessness of her demands, that is, of her obliviousness to her impact as she left incredibly long messages on my machine or pressed me for extra time and extra sessions. Over time, the obvious deterioration in Sandra's emotional state raised both my anxiety and my anger about her capacity for self-destructiveness. I became increasingly aware that my attempts to communicate understanding to Sandra were doomed to failure, not because she was incapable of assimilating them, but because they aroused in her both intensified neediness and, on a more unconscious level, destructive envy of my apparently calmer, more knowing status.

Ultimately I turned to a holding stance with the idea that Sandra needed me to hold her ruthlessness and desperate demandingness as well as her more unconscious sense of badness. I explicitly spelled out the treatment's behavioral limits (for example, I told Sandra that she could not leave me messages that were longer than a minute in length. I did not, however, address the dynamic meaning of those messages in ways that went beyond her own understanding). I also persistently but rather flatly (i.e., not especially empathically) commented on the objective dangers to which she exposed herself. I attempted to maintain an extremely matter-of-fact stance vis-à-vis Sandra's demands and anxieties, accepting their intensity without interpreting the meaning embedded in them except when she herself did so. I tried to maintain a posture in which I expressed a full, nonanxious recognition of the power of Sandra's needs and potential self-destructiveness while containing my sometimes considerable anxieties and anger about these. At the same time, I let Sandra know that I was aware that she was enraged by my failure to meet her needs fully, but that neither of us would be destroyed as a result.

Although I did not often offer interpretations about the meaning of this material, it is clear that there is an implicit interpretive message embedded in the holding stance. I indicated that I recognized the intensity of Sandra's affective process, was not overwhelmed by it, and had confidence in her capacity to survive intact. By not explicitly interpreting the destructive wishes directed toward me, I partially contained Sandra's self-hatred in a way that I could also tolerate.

In order to maintain a holding stance with Sandra, I was forced to confront and to live with what felt like an impossible mix of feelings about her and about our interaction. I was, at moments, intensely frightened that Sandra would land herself in a life-threatening situation or would overdose on drugs. I felt like intervening in a variety of concrete ways to stop her, to save her. Yet the intransigence of her desperation was always frustrating and sometimes enraging, especially when Sandra's ruthlessness overrode what she knew about me in particularly jarring ways. For example, when Sandra left a desperate message on my answering machine, I was immobilized as I struggled with my anger at the length of the message and my concern about her obviously real distress. In order to hold here, I had to hold onto both my own impotence to protect her and my anxiety and anger about her behavior.

During the next year, Sandra gave up drugs, stopped going out with dangerous men, and gradually became calmer both in and out of our sessions. Slowly, the telephone calls and letters stopped, and Sandra was able to use the sessions in a way that brought her more lasting relief. By the end of the third year, our work together became ordinary in that we were able to collaborate around the meaning of Sandra's experience.

In what way did this process permit Sandra to move out of a position of such powerful self-destructiveness? In the context of our work, intense underlying feelings of need and self-hatred had been rather rapidly released. By holding Sandra, I recognized the power of her affective experience, yet indicated my own as well as her capacity to tolerate it. Within that frame, Sandra could more safely elaborate on her own process without fear of intrusion or reprisal on my part. The discovery that she could not destroy herself or me altered in a basic way her unconscious fears (of the power of her destructiveness), and allowed her to integrate a fuller range of her own affective processes. Ultimately, this sufficiently strengthened Sandra's capacity to experience affect such that relatedness became less dangerous.

The holding process that appeared to be pivotal in facilitating a shift in Sandra's experience of herself placed some strain on me as I contended with contradictory feelings of concern, anxiety, helplessness, and anger. The holding process with patients who present with unremitting rage is still more difficult to manage.

Holding Issues of Hate

Karen[1] was a recent college graduate in her mid-20s when she was referred to me by another analyst who had met with her several times but felt unable to work with her. Karen was reasonably friendly during our first encounter, but spoke in a low flat tone and described herself as depressed. Karen did not volunteer any information about

---

[1]This case is also described in Slochower (1992).

herself, but responded to my questions cooperatively. She ascribed her depression to her recent breakup with a boyfriend of five years. The relationship ended because the boyfriend would not change in the ways that she needed him to. She spoke bitterly about her sense of betrayal by him.

Karen described her relationship with parents and siblings to be fraught with conflict. She had a handicapped sister who took up most of her parents' time and energy. Her brothers were boisterous, and filled the house with literal and emotional noise, leaving, she felt, little room for her. Karen functioned in her home as a mediator, attempting to defuse parental or sibling conflicts. Although she had friends and a job, neither pleased her, and she saw herself as a loner. She felt quite pessimistic about analysis, but also felt she had little choice. During these early meetings, Karen typically looked down, allowing her hair to fall in front of her face. That action, coupled with her long bangs, made it nearly impossible to make eye contact with her (subsequently, she moved to the couch with relief at not having to be "looked at").

The initial months of treatment were taken up with descriptions of the failures of her former boyfriend, family, and friends to meet her needs. Characteristically, she would provoke a confrontation filled with accusations against the other person and would then withdraw, feeling bitter and bewildered when the relationship faltered or ended. Karen always concluded that the other person had failed her irredeemably. She was quite unaware of her contribution to these interactions, and became extremely defensive at any suggestion from me that perhaps there had been some input on her part in the conflict.

During the first year of treatment, Karen very gradually became more openly irritated and irritable in our sessions. She would wait for me to begin each hour, and could be silent for the entire session if I did not. When engaged, she described her many conflictual relationships flatly, without obvious affect. Much of the material centered around her ex-boyfriend, about whom she was obsessed. She showed no apparent interest in understanding why she had been so easily angered by him or why she was so unhappy without him.

My initial response to Karen was one of mild sympathy and curiosity about her apparent disengagement from her own pain. I repeatedly attempted to communicate my understanding of her experience, and, when possible, to deepen our sense of its emotional threads. This was not difficult in that Karen was willing to answer my questions about her history. At times there were apparently clear connections to be made between her marginal position in her home and her current emotional experiences. However, although I was not yet especially frustrated with Karen, I was puzzled by the apparent pointlessnes of these interchanges, in which I inevitably ended up failing her. The following typical exchange occurred after Karen described an ongoing obsession of hers concerning whether to send her ex-boyfriend a Christmas card.

Karen: I don't know what he'd do if he got a card from me.

J.S.:   I guess the hope is that he'd accept it and call you and the worry is that he won't.

Karen: I guess [long silence]. Anyway, it's all a game.

J.S.:   What's the game?

Karen: If you don't know by now what's the point of talking?

J.S.:   You really want me to know exactly what you mean by a game.

Karen: I suppose. But then shrinks only tell you what they feel like telling you.

J.S.:   Why would I want to withhold information from you?

Karen: Who knows. God knows you'd never tell [long silence].

J.S.:   [feeling on solid ground conceptually and ignoring a growing sense of futility about communicating my understanding to Karen]: Is it possible that -sending the card would be a bit like trying to get him to finally act like you can't get your father to?

Karen: Obviously. So what? How much mileage can you get out of that one? And what difference does it make anyway? This is a waste of time.

Actually, from my point of view, the material was quite new, and far from integrated. However, in pursuing this line of inquiry, I had unconsciously attempted to override my developing sense that Karen absolutely was not interested in deepening her understanding of her own process. By offering my understanding, I appeared to be doing my job and I was able to relieve a growing sense of helplessness about the state of our work; I did not, however, seem to help Karen in any discernable way.

Over the next few months, my sense of helplessness increasingly transformed into one of alarm. Karen remained indifferent to her plight. She continued to provoke new conflicts with friends and relatives with no apparent memory of their painful effects. She acted unconcerned about the deterioration of several important relationships. She quit her job, staying at home for long periods. She showed no curiosity or concern about herself and continued to ignore or belittle all my interventions. Yet her response did not seem simply to reflect depression; there was an unmistakable undercurrent of active dismissal in her tone and manner. When I identified this and inquired about it, she responded with apparent disinterest, saying only "that could be."

Toward the end of the first year of treatment, Karen gradually became more engaged with me. This engagement was first evident in her request that I describe my theory of therapy to her, so that she could compare it to that of her friend's therapist. I responded internally with a sinking feeling that there would be no good outcome to this one, that nothing I could say would be satisfactory or helpful to her. I again tried to override that feeling, however, and asked Karen what in particular about my way of working concerned her. She reacted to this slight with rage, and attacked me for wanting to understand rather than simply to respond.

The next few weeks were solely taken up with this issue. Karen persisted in attacking my idea that her request needed to be understood. She dismissed with scorn my efforts to explain why I felt that understanding should precede action. She mocked my attempts to communicate that I understood how frustrated she felt at my unwillingness to simply answer. Her rage at me escalated. She refused to cooperate in investigating her ideas about her therapy or her friend's, or about anything else. She attacked me with increasing vigor for my withholding stance. She accused me of being a fraud, of exploiting her financially, and of hiding my knowledge about her in order to have power over her. After weeks of unremitting sessions like these, I felt that a stalemate had been reached. Again, overriding my sense of the futility of a response, I decided directly to address Karen's question about how I viewed the treatment process.

Karen: Apparently you don't know how treatment works since you won't answer my question.

J.S.:   I guess that's one possibility. Actually, I'm not sure what purpose answering would serve. But I guess I'll accept your conviction that you need to know and give it a try.

Karen: [sarcastically] Finally. My goodness.

J.S.:   Well you know that I prefer to understand before acting. My idea is that if we could get to better understand what Sam means to you and how he evokes old feelings in your life now, that you might get to feel less like your life stopped when you broke up. Talking about your ideas and feelings in the present and the past gives us a way of helping make some of those connections. I see that as a first step in getting rid of the awful feelings you keep complaining of.

Karen: My, what sophistication, what insight. Are you taking as long as possible to do this?

J.S.:   Why would I want to do that?

Karen: Obviously, to get as much money from me as possible.

J.S.:   So my goal as a therapist is to rip you off.

Karen: You got it. And if you knew all this before, why not say it before, except to string me along.

J.S.:   So I'm not only incompetent, I'm manipulative.

Karen: [mockingly] So I'm not only incompetent, I'm manipulative.

Karen's scornful response to my attempt to answer her question was followed by further rageful attacks on me. She continued to express her fury with me, now both for having held out so long and for the stupidity of my ideas. Her hateful and contemptuous feelings dominated the sessions. She scrutinized and sarcastically attacked my every action or inaction, so that my behavior and not hers became the sole focus of the treatment. For example, she used a watch with a second hand to time our sessions, elaborately consulting it as she lay down on the couch and again as she sat up at the end. At the end of the month I received a check from which two dollars had been deducted for a minute that she had been "cheated out of." It is noteworthy that I was not altogether certain that I had not, in fact, cheated her out of a minute, given my wish to end our sessions as early as possible.

Karen was consistently unwilling to consider the meaning of our interaction, or its possible relationship to other interpersonal conflicts. We were at war and retaliation was her only possible response. Each session continued to address one or another of my failures. She met my attempts to understand the source of her rage at me with sarcasm. Even when I felt fairly certain that she had felt understood by a statement I made, she bitterly complained that I was retracing old ground and was wasting her time for mercenary ends. My silence was met with sarcastic comments about my laziness. When I inquired about her silence, she would mockingly repeat my inquiry and then lapse into further silence.

My experience with Karen gradually shifted away from any sense of genuine interest or empathy with her emotional plight. I began to despair of the possibility of communicating my understanding of her rage and underlying unhappiness and their sources. Increasingly, I dreaded our sessions and questioned the efficacy of my work with her. I was both furious and puzzled by the relentlessness of her sarcasm. I entertained fantasies of retaliating. (I imagined bashing her head with a pencil. I continued to hold the pencil in the vain hope that by taking notes I would divine some useful meaning from the material that was eluding me.) I entered our sessions girded for an onslaught, hoping more to survive her attack than actually to be of use to her.

It was only when the intensity of my own fury and helplessness had escalated, however, that I was able to move in the direction of a holding stance with Karen. That stance helped me find a way simultaneously to tolerate and contain Karen's ongoing aggressive attacks while refraining from an active use of interpretation or even empathic statements as a way of coping with the strain of such attacks in an apparently hopeless treatment situation. However, such silent containment alone carried with it the risk that Karen would feel that she had injured or destroyed me. Thus, it was essential that I find a way to make use of my feelings through contained yet affectively toned communications. Those communications would, I hoped, confirm my aliveness and my capacity to bear attack without injury, and in this sense would represent an implicit interpretation to Karen about the limits of her destructiveness.

To the extent that Karen's underlying unconscious conviction was that she could not, in fact, make an impact on me (or any object), my neutrality would tend to confirm that fear. In contrast, by meeting her rage with a very modulated aggressive stance, I might provide evidence that Karen did affect me but would not destroy me. To that end, I began to limit my interventions to concrete questions, responding to Karen only when she engaged me directly, and meeting her attacks with dry or mildly annoyed responses.

Karen:	[enters, silent]
J.S.:	[after 3 minutes] So, what's on your mind today?
Karen:	[mockingly] So, what's on your mind today?
J.S.:	[dryly] Annoyed, are you?
Karen:	Why should today be different? You never have anything to say that's new.
J.S.:	[using a tough tone] You've really got yourself a lousy analyst.
Karen:	True enough. God knows why I stay. [silent for 5 minutes] No brilliant new ideas today?
J.S.:	Brilliant new ideas about what?
Karen:	Well, last time you made another stupid comment about my father. You could have said that a year ago.
J.S.:	Stringing you along again, huh?
Karen:	Yeah, waiting to raise my fee.
J.S.:	By the way, is it true, about your father?
Karen:	You think I'd tell *you* if it were?
J.S.:	Question withdrawn.

At other moments, Karen's attacks lacked even this slightly playful quality.

Karen:	[enters, glowering with fury, silent for 10 minutes despite several queries from me] You think you know everything.
J.S.:	What do I know?
Karen:	Why the hell should I tell you? You are a pathetic example of an analyst.
J.S.:	[dryly] Well, this pathetic analyst would like to know what the hell I said that bothered you.
Karen:	And give you more ammunition? In my next life [long silence].
J.S.:	So should I try to get you to talk or not?
Karen:	[mimicking] So should I try to get you to talk or not?

Karen left these sessions in a fury, slamming the door behind her. Although she did appear to feel less depressed than when she entered, the therapeutic efficacy of my interventions was rarely immediately clear to me. Nevertheless, Karen's overall response to this shift in stance was striking. She persisted in attacking me and my theories of treatment and she countered my every remark; however, her silent stance was replaced by a caustic but lively one. Her engagement with me became far more active; silent periods decreased in frequency and length. Karen obviously enjoyed her considerable cleverness in challenging my statements during the exchanges that she termed our "fights." When I retreated into silence out of fatigue or real anger, she became increasingly vicious and arrived at subsequent sessions depressed, perhaps unconsciously convinced that I had been injured by her, and fearing retaliation.

My emotional response to Karen during this period shifted only slightly. I felt somewhat more alive during our exchanges, and occasionally I even enjoyed the rapid banter that characterized them. However, I continued to doubt the therapeutic value of a treatment based in such acrimony. I responded to Karen's persistent nastiness with a feeling of defeat, and finally asked her whether I should consider referring her elsewhere for a consultation. Karen sarcastically refused, and then offered, in a most offhand way, the first evidence I had of improvement in her external life. She had made up with a friend, and had in fact made the first conciliatory overture. She had also obtained a new and possibly better job. This was all said in passing. She would not speculate about the source of these changes and quickly returned to her attacks on me. Her response nevertheless suggested to me that Karen had perhaps been helped by our work, and that her dependence on the treatment, though rarely visible, was real, and had been aroused by my indication that I was prepared to give up.

Karen continued to focus the sessions on me and my failures throughout the next year. However, she made an increasing number of oblique references to her outside life that indicated a marked decrease in the intensity of conflict in her important relationships. During the third year of treatment, the relentlessness of these attacks slowly diminished, and Karen occasionally told me about the people in her early and current life. She began to consider the notion that other people experience conflict and act on the basis of their feelings, and she speculated about how conflict operated within her family. My sense of dread prior to her sessions diminished, and I began to feel slightly freer to function with her on the basis of my understanding.

Throughout this period, however, Karen rarely addressed her own experience or feelings directly; instead she remained safely on the emotional exterior of her speculations, only toying with the idea of self-examination. Any attempt on my part to investigate her experience of her parents' behavior brought on a renewed phase of sarcasm and silence. Karen was now sufficiently secure within the analytic frame to introduce her world of real objects, but not to address her internal experience of them. This nevertheless represented a significant step in the direction of a capacity for self-reflection.

During the subsequent years of our work together, Karen slowly developed some tolerance for contact with me. Her outbursts of rage subsided, and were replaced by expressions of annoyance that were more appropriate and directly reactive to my failures in understanding.

It seems, then, that the holding process served a therapeutic function by creating a sufficiently contained space within which Karen could fully elaborate on her most painful affective states. When I held these states, Karen was able to discover her own resilience as well as mine, and that discovery ultimately altered her self-experience in a way that permitted some movement beyond issues of hate toward self-examination.

Of course, it is not always possible for the analyst to provide the patient with implicit reassurance that the analyst is surviving the patient's attacks. This can be difficult when the analyst herself is not so sure that she *is* surviving, or when the patient cannot easily integrate the reality of the analyst's intactness. Active attention to these issues will be crucial to the therapeutic effect of a holding process.

Countertransference Resistances to Holding

It is difficult for the analyst to retain a position of conviction about the therapeutic efficacy of a holding response to a patient's ruthlessness, and close to impossible with a hateful patient. Such attacks inevitably touch off our anxiety, vulnerability, self-doubt, and defensiveness, sometimes to such an extent that we may give up, and choose literally or indirectly to terminate the treatment, often quite unilaterally. Even if we refrain from so drastic a move, in such situations it can be most tempting to break into the patient's distress or rages with interpretations that actually function as disguised attacks (Epstein, 1979, 1987). The purpose of these attacks is to rid the analyst of the intense anger and/or helplessness that tend to be evoked when one is subjected to a relentlessly tense analytic situation. It is only with ongoing internal work that the analyst can maintain a holding stance here.

An experienced analyst came for a consultation regarding a patient with whom he felt utterly "derailed." Ms. A. had subjected him for months to a barrage of complaints about, criticisms of, and muted and overt attacks on his analytic acumen. His attempt to interpret the source of her rage and dissatisfaction had only intensified the patient's unhappiness. The analyst felt prepared to admit defeat, to refer Ms. A. elsewhere in the hope that another analyst (perhaps, he thought, a woman) would find the right touch with Ms. A. The only hesitation he felt about making this move came from Ms. A.'s apparent disinterest in looking elsewhere for help; in fact, when he suggested such a referral, she became quite upset with him and indicated that she did not want to end the analysis. He was, he felt, up against a wall; his choices were to unilaterally terminate the analysis or to continue to work with her in a seemingly hopeless treatment context.

What the analyst had not considered, I felt, was the possibility that the therapeutic task with Ms. A. involved precisely that dimension of their relationship that he found unbearable; that Ms. A. needed him to tolerate massive feelings of hopelessness, helplessness, and rage— without retaliation or interpretation. The purpose of this holding stance would be to help Ms. A. experience the safety of the analytic setting and of the analyst as she elaborated on these painful affective states. Because of the power of her own self-hatred, it was only within the context of the analyst's absolutely even, nonretaliatory survival that Ms. A. could test out and discover the limits of her destructiveness. Yet for the analyst to continue working with her, he would have to be prepared to hold onto that knowledge in an emotional situation that absolutely negated it. That is, the work with Ms. A. would be unlikely to shift rapidly in a more positive direction, and his engagement with her meant that he would inevitably feel more frustrated, angry, and hopeless than otherwise.

In this sense, holding work here required that the analyst find a way to sustain himself without retaliating against the patient through the use of apparently neutral interpretations that effectively place the "badness" back into the patient (Epstein, 1979). Even then, it was likely that the analyst would feel intensely uncertain that the patient was experiencing sustained internal change, and he would instead continue to struggle periodically with overwhelming doubts about the therapeutic efficacy of the work.

Holding Ruthlessness or Hate and the Analyst's Attunement

What is the therapeutic function of holding with ruthless or rageful patients? The analyst's reliable containing function provides the desperate patient with a set of powerful reassurances that ultimately may result in heretofore absent therapeutic action. These reassurances concern two pivotal issues. First, the patient receives evidence of the analyst's capacity both to tolerate and to survive the patient's emotional impact. That evidence is provided by the even steadiness of the analyst's boundaries. The analyst survives intact, and, by not retaliating (literally or via interpretation), reassures the patient that she is not capable of destroying the analysis or the analyst.

At the same time, however, the holding stance provides the patient with the experience of making an emotional impact on the analyst. Because the analyst makes use of her emotional responses to the patient in her affective tone, the patient derives steady evidence that she is, in fact, impacting on the analyst. For many patients, this may be the first such experience—the first evidence that their affective communications are neither warded off nor retaliated against. It is the patient's simultaneous experience of having feelings of ruthlessness or hate *received* and *tolerated* that is pivotal to a therapeutic effect in these treatment situations.

Because the analyst uses her subjectivity to some degree, the holding function here is somewhat more inclusive of the analyst's affective experience than with patients needing holding around dependence or self-involvement. The analyst does not fully bracket her subjectivity, but instead allows it partial expression through the emotional tone of her interventions. The analyst and patient consequently may feel less of a need to fully set aside aspects of their knowledge of the other during the holding process.

Dangers Inherent in Holding Ruthlessness and Hate

The risks involved in the suspension of interaction around the patient's affective impact are similar to those which characterize holding issues of self-involvement. The analyst may resort to what appears to be a holding stance in retaliation for the patient's overt or covert sadism. This retaliation will become quite evident because it is likely to result in a rapid escalation of the patient's distress and/or her attacks on the analyst.

Alternatively, it is possible that the analyst's abandonment of explicit interpretive work will be experienced by the patient as a withdrawal and/or an expression of the analyst's impotence. This is especially likely when the analyst *is* feeling undermined and resorts to a holding stance in order to protect herself.

An analyst reported that she had moved toward a holding stance with an especially difficult, provocative patient. The patient, however, responded with an escalation of her attacks on the analyst. As we began to examine the nature of the analyst's subjective experience of the patient, it became clear that the analyst's voice conveyed a measure of what she was feeling, mainly, a sense of hopelessness about being of help to the patient. That affective tone belied the analyst's tough words, and made the patient intensely anxious. The patient's attacks reflected her unconscious attempt to test the analyst's potential for both aliveness and destructiveness.

Effects of Disruptions During Holding

Although disruptions of the holding function will always impact on work with ruthless or hateful patients, that disruptive effect is likely to be less devastating than it can be with dependent or self-involved patients. When the patient's capacity to express rage is accessible, there is a possibility that the patient will be able to articulate her reaction to the analyst's failure. However, to the degree that the disruption of the holding function exposes the patient's hidden dependence on the analyst, the patient is likely to respond intensely, often by abruptly truncating the treatment or threatening to do so.

Steve, a patient with whom I had worked for some years, presented a nearly monochromatic picture of bitterness and hopelessness, within which I rarely if ever "came up to snuff." I struggled with anger at his treatment of me, but tried to maintain a relatively even, somewhat tough stance vis-à-vis his contempt.

During a particular session, Steve presented a difficult work situation to me in what felt like a straightforward (i.e., nonprovocative) way. I spontaneously responded without thought, saying "God, that's awful," and then asking him whether he had considered the possibility of responding to his boss by taking account of the envy that appeared to lie behind his boss's attacks. (I was not conscious at that moment of the implicit connection to Steve's own behavior.) Steve seemed to appreciate my suggestion, and left with an easy, almost friendly good-bye. However, he returned the next day in a quiet fury. I had, in his words, "acted out," and become controlling. He did not connect his fury to the content of my intervention, but rather to the fact that I had commented in a practical way about his outside life. This meant that he could not trust me. He wondered whether he should leave the analysis, and whether I had any boundaries at all.

Steve's rageful reaction to my intervention seemed to emanate from several sources. My suggestion was probably assimilated in terms of Steve's own (disavowed) envy of and dependence on me and my potential "helpfulness." I had penetrated Steve's rigidly autonomous stance and thereby evoked a complex of feelings of destructive envy and energetically denied dependency wishes with such intensity that Steve could restore his sense of emotional intactness only by attacking me.

It was with some difficulty that I engaged him again within a holding frame that was sufficiently bounded to restabilize the treatment.

That frame involved two key elements. First, I maintained the treatment boundaries in an especially clear way; I virtually never commented or otherwise responded to him with spontaneous reactions, suggestions, or the sort of relaxed comments that sometimes mark the beginning or ending of sessions. Second, I attempted to increase Steve's feeling of safety by dealing with his contempt with a firm but noninterpretive response. Interpretations aroused his envy and rage, and silence confirmed for him that I had been injured by his attack.

I do not mean to imply that from this point forward, the treatment evolved in an easy or a straightforward way. On the contrary, I continued to struggle with Steve, with his anger and contempt, his bitterness and periodic hopelessness. However, within the solid reassurance of a holding context Steve began to tolerate the always implicit dependency intrinsic to analytic inquiry and the analytic relationship.

The Self-Holding Function

How does the analyst need to hold herself with ruthless or hateful patients? Here, perhaps more than in any other treatment context, the analyst holds herself by holding onto the complexity of her feelings toward the patient, and most especially her own rage. It is primarily when that rage becomes dissociated (often because it does not fit the analyst's self-image as a knowing, even presence) that the holding process is likely to break down.

Holding in Ordinary Treatment

How are ruthlessness and hate held in ordinary treatment contexts? Often quite easily. It is only when such emotional factors take over the treatment that the analyst is subjected to intense strain. Nevertheless, the analyst's capacity to accept and live with such feelings without retaliating against the patient can be crucial in any treatment context. It becomes difficult for us to do this primarily when we feel implicated, to some degree, in the patient's accusations.

Bill has been in twice weekly therapy with me for 3 years. Following a session during which he received his bill, he returned with his bill in hand, looking quite angry. He noted that I had misspelled his name, and expressed disgust at my not knowing who he was. He was somewhat uncharacteristically furious, and blasted me for the duration of the hour. I struggled with my wish to explain myself, to get myself off the hook. I wanted to tell him that I periodically do make such errors in writing names, that he should not take the error personally. I also felt the wish to work interpretively with both his response and my own, with his quick assumption of being forgettable, and with his ideas about why I made the error. (I was also aware that I needed to examine more closely just why I had made this error with Bill.) It was with difficulty that I accepted Bill's anger and neither explained myself nor worked interpretively with his upset.

Why, then, did I not further explore with Bill the meanings of my error? Certainly, Bill would have been able to accept and work with an interpretation around his assumption of his being forgettable. However, that work was ongoing anyway. In making use of my failure to interpret Bill's affective response, or by speculating with him about my process, I would have short-circuited an opportunity for Bill to express, untempered, his anger and clear view of my real failure. In that sense, I would have inadvertently redirected the "pathology" toward Bill, gotten myself off the hook, and, most importantly, deprived Bill of the experience of safely and fully expressing rage toward an object who could both receive and survive it.

Chapter 6

On the Edge:
Working Around the Holding Process

In the preceding three chapters, I have tried to delineate the core emotional situations that may require a holding process in psychoanalytic work. None of these experiences is likely to be easy. When, however, patient and analyst find their way into a holding process and can tolerate its uncertainty, that experience may alter the progression of analytic work in a dramatically different and more positive direction.

In this sense, all varieties of holding processes carry with them a hope—that the analyst's very capacity to tolerate her subjective experience without explicit expression ultimately will facilitate increasingly complex emotional processes within the patient, a deepened level of self-understanding, and also a new possibility for mutual dialogue.

Yet there are moments with some patients, and protracted periods with others (or with some analyst–patient pairs), when interpretive work fails and a holding experience also does not result in a gradual build-up of confidence in the analyst's affective attunement, or in the patient's internal resources. There are patients who seem to remain on the perimeter of the treatment experience, forever returning to states of mistrust and despair about themselves as well as the analytic process.

Although these individuals may hope for the analyst's attunement, and thus toy with the possibility of intimacy and deeper self-exposure, they simultaneously are extraordinarily skittish in a way that makes a holding experience elusive. Here, the analyst's reliability is never satisfactorily assessed, so that a relaxation of strain on the patient's part inevitably is followed by its intensification. Most paradoxically, what is desperately needed is precisely what the analyst so often fails to provide from the patient's point of view. Unlike the rageful reactions described in Chapter 5, the primary response to analytic process here involves a cycle of hope and despair.

To the degree that it is the object's capacity for attunement that is most untrustworthy, the analytic situation may evoke not only hope but also fear of a particularly poignant sort. *If only* the analyst could be trusted, the patient could relax in a situation where real self-exposure is possible, perhaps for the first time. Yet the analyst's very power as a potential reparative object heightens the danger that trust will be misplaced, and that, willy-nilly, the patient will find herself painfully rejected, misunderstood, or impinged upon. For these patients, interpretations about the process rarely make much lasting affective impact. Even when they do, that impact tends to dissolve in the face of the more convincing "evidence" embodied in the analyst's actions, for it is only the latter that usually are felt to really count.

In situations like these, even the most emotionally resilient analyst is likely to feel an enormously complex set of reactions. These include confusion about what went wrong just when it did; distress at the patient's distress; anger at the patient's apparent "ingratitude"; and frustration or inadequacy at her inability to get it right. The analyst's capacity to tolerate ongoing feelings of failure may be worn down, resulting in increasing hopelessness, despair, anger, and even moments of abuse on the analyst's part. It is the *insolubility* of the satisfaction-distress cycle that is so difficult here, and that tends to leave the analyst in such a quandary.

What emotional position is left for the analyst who is repetitively experienced as misattuned in precisely those functions so apparently essential for her patient? To the extent that the psychoanalytic dialogue does not deepen the patient's sense of confidence in the emotional reliability of such interchange, each moment of intimacy becomes a danger signal. No illusion of certainty characterizes these situations. Instead, the analyst may feel as if she is endlessly on an emotional tightrope, destined to fall off at any moment.

If the analyst is not to despair altogether, or to turn against the patient in anger, she will have to find some way of both surviving and making therapeutic use of the patient's inability to tolerate the paradoxical nature of analytic process, that is, of the ways in which she simultaneously does and does not meet the patient's needs. Certainly, this process leaves the analyst no solution and no real expectation of one. Yet, if the analyst can retain an affective memory of the moments during which she *has* been found to be satisfying as well as the ultimate elusiveness of that experience, she may be more able to tolerate her repetitive failures. Ultimately it may be her capacity to tolerate failure *without* giving up hope in the patient or herself that will bring about a shift toward a more even level of positive relatedness on the patient's part.

Failures in Holding as an Enactment

What makes it simultaneously crucially important and yet absolutely impossible for the patient to trust the analyst's affective attunement?

Because those patients who are highly reactive to the analyst's failures repetitively play out a painful cycle of hope followed by despair, it is likely that the process itself represents an enactment based on early cyclical patterns of hope followed by unexpected parental failure.[1] For some people, a history of unreliable caretaking has too powerful a press for any current object to easily dislodge. This is perhaps the simplest of situations, because here, a build-up of experience wherein the analyst demonstrates her trustworthiness in conjunction with interpretations about the repetition eventually will act to move the treatment. I occasionally have found this shift to take place rather dramatically when I somehow managed symbolically to demonstrate my capacity to meet the patient's wish for a consistent response of a particular kind. It is noteworthy that the patient's need to assess my emotional reliability before settling into a holding process can be quite intense, whether the central holding theme involves dependence, self-involvement, or ruthlessness and hate.

With some patients, then, an apparent impasse eventually is resolved as sufficient evidence of the analyst's attunement breaks through the patient's defensive despair. With others, however, the analyst's attunement is not so easily assessed. Here, it would seem that the patient's experience of the analyst's emotional reliability *inevitably* is disrupted in a way that reflexively reenacts early disruptions. It is the "repeated" (i.e., unsatisfactory) rather than the "needed" relationship (Stern, 1994) that dominates the treatment and interferes with therapeutic movement. The patient's sense that self-disclosure is enormously dangerous is thereby reinforced in a way that does not allow for its working through. The analytic process stalls. It repetitively addresses the analyst's successes *and* failures as a reliable object and the patient's pervasive experience of herself as unlovable or even repellent. What characterizes the stalled process is the patient's inability to work with her experience of self or object in a way that expands the space around her experience.

In this situation, the analyst is truly "up against it"; her very reparative capacity is what the patient associates most closely with imminent failure. At times, an analysis of this cycle may break into the patient's experience in a way that moves the dyad beyond the stalled holding process; at other times, however, no such movement is evident.

Like the negative therapeutic reaction, the patient's inability to integrate and make use of apparently good therapeutic moments may carry a variety of meanings. These failures are frequently understood

---

[1] A wide array of emotional processes can account for these negative therapeutic reactions. These include destructive envy, rage, guilt, etc. I emphasize the centrality of the patient's despair at parental failures because the clinical scenario that I am describing is dominated by this cluster of affective responses.

as a form of splitting (where the patient cannot integrate good and bad aspects of the analytic object). The pattern may be seen to be defensive, that is, to protect the patient from the risks of self-disclosure by repetitively refocusing the treatment on the analyst's failures. Additionally, that focus may represent the patient's unconscious attempt to get the analytic object to make reparation for early (parental) failures, and/or to test the resilience of the analytic object, especially its capacity to retain hope and/or to withstand attack. The patient's difficulty integrating her own hateful and loving feelings or her need to expose and address a deeper level of suicidal despair also may be involved.

To the extent that the patient can join with the analyst in an active investigation of these or other such dynamic processes, the treatment has not stalled; when such interpretive investigations fail to move the work, however, a stalemate may ensue.

Amy was 35 and a partner in a major law firm when she came for analysis because of a longstanding depression. Despite that depression, Amy was quite successful professionally and had a few close friends. She was unmarried, had no children, and said that she wanted none; she did not, she thought, have enough "good stuff" inside to offer a baby.

Amy consulted with a number of people, sensing that she needed a particular kind of emotional responsiveness from her analyst. Amy chose me because of what she described as my "no-nonsense steadiness and warmth." She said that she needed an analyst who could stand her very strong feelings. She was very hopeful that I would be able to help her.

Having been aware of how intensely Amy had looked me over prior to making this decision and of how hopeful she felt, I entered the treatment cautiously but optimistically. Although I anticipated that Amy would be highly sensitive to my emotional position and might become quite reactive to me, Amy's initially positive response left me unrealistically sanguine about the outcome of our work together.

During the first half year of treatment, Amy was simultaneously open, affectively alive, and extremely sensitive to my state. She made rather intense and direct eye contact, often leaving me with a sense that she was carefully examining me for evidence of something, although I was not yet clear as to what. As the end of our first half year of work approached, Amy let me know with some discomfort that she found the gap between our sessions quite difficult (she was coming three times weekly). As we began to talk about what felt so difficult, it became clear that Amy was quite unable to experience or to retain a sense of the potential reliability of our relationship. Amy found it impossible to believe that I was genuinely interested in her, no matter that I cared about her. So, when she did feel understood in a session, her "antenna went up," as she put it, and it was sometimes only moments later that disillusionment followed. Thus, for example, if I failed to smile or smile warmly enough, especially when I ended the session, Amy could carry, over a whole weekend, a powerful sense of worry about how my feelings toward her had changed. That worry would effectively "ruin" the weekend.

Amy and I investigated in great depth the historical sources for these feelings and seemed to arrive at a partial if not a total understanding of their origins. Amy had experienced her parents to be so caught up in their own concerns and so emotionally detached that there was no sense of safety at home for her. Amy had a very early positive relationship with a nanny who cared for her during her first year, but who left abruptly, never to be satisfactorily replaced. It seemed as if Amy repetitively reexperienced the cycle of intimacy followed by abandonment—as soon as she felt that she "had" me in some way, the certainty that I would leave increased, and Amy guarded against that possibility by vigilantly scanning me.

For several years our work focused largely on investigating the nature and history of Amy's desperate need *and* inability to relax in my presence. Not surprisingly, Amy's state of tension persisted even after we moved to a four-session-per-week schedule.

Amy was quite conscious of her wish that I "hold" her (her words), which to her meant that I remain emotionally accessible in a way that reassured her that she could count on me. Most paradoxically, though, that reassurance was extraordinarily elusive and was disrupted as rapidly as it was acquired. Amy spent a great deal of our time together talking about her place with me. Did I care about her? Could I? Should she trust me or was I in it for the money, or worse, for my own self-enhancement? If she let herself need me, she would feel intensely humiliated, and she imagined that I would humiliate her further. Yet in not trusting me, she could not fully be herself, could not allow me to help her, and so stayed in a perpetual state of self-protective mistrust and isolation. Evidence that I did understand her and was emotionally *with* her therefore was simultaneously reassuring and terrifying, and Amy permitted herself only the briefest moment of relaxation before returning to a state of either worry or conviction about the danger she was in.

During these years of work, the bulk of analytic time was spent focused on the transference. In that context, we addressed Amy's rage at her parents for their obliviousness to her needs, her wish to punish them and even to destroy them as parents, her refusal to allow them (me) to "fob her off" by accepting anything positive from them, her fear that were she to be satisfied even momentarily, they (I) would abandon her—that her hold on the object took the form of intense neediness. Occasionally, Amy was able to link her focus on me to its implications for her own powerful feelings of unlovableness, self-hate, and rage. We then reached a deeper level of understanding that Amy would briefly hold onto; during those short periods, she would bring in other issues (e.g., her sexual difficulties) that she could only talk about when she felt a sense of confidence in my emotional reliability. Paradoxically, though, as Amy exposed more of her vulnerability to me and allowed me to work on it with her, she scanned me with increasing intensity for evidence that I was repelled by her. Inevitably, she found that evidence, and the cycle would resume.

Here is an example that is notable only in that it occurred so regularly. The third of our (now) four weekly sessions tended to feel the best to Amy. By then she was partially relieved of the mistrust that had built over the weekend break, and she was not as yet anticipating the subsequent interruption in our work together. If all went well, Amy presented herself in a sufficiently candid and nondefensive way that I found it easy to understand her experience and to communicate that understanding to her. It was on those occasions that the material shifted from the question of my emotional reliability to issues in her own internal life that were *not* primarily derivatives of the former question.

On one Thursday, Amy spent the session describing her very painful and unsatisfying relationship with her father. I was well aware that she felt deeply understood by me. That feeling was evident in a variety of ways, none perhaps more telling than in how her body relaxed for the first time that week, as she allowed her hands to fall loosely by her side instead of remaining folded across her chest in symbolic self-defense. I was conscious of the riskiness of her state, and it was with some trepidation that I (as usual) sat forward in my chair a few moments before the session's end to signal that fact. Amy reacted with a whole body jerk, obviously shocked by my movement. She nearly jumped off the couch, and then made for the door. Before she exited, I was able to say that I knew she felt my ending to be a complete rejection of her. Amy acknowledged this but said that my understanding of my impact did not in any way mitigate its negative effect on her.

On one hand, my response to Amy's reactivity might be considered its own form of holding; I neither withdrew nor retaliated against Amy, but rather attempted to maintain a position of even responsiveness. Yet Amy's reaction indicated that she did not in fact feel held—instead, in signaling the approaching end of the session, I disrupted her feeling of safety, symbolically reminded her that she is a patient (with all that represents to her), jolted and rejected her, and returned her to a state of mistrust. Yet endings are inevitable, and so then is evidence of the transitory or at least paradoxical nature of emotional safety. What made this process so difficult was the fact that Amy's experience of my emotional failure was absolutely pervasive. Her inability to tolerate more *complicated* (that is, less unitary) experiences of me propelled her in the direction of hopelessness again and again, because hopelessness protected her from the more complex, uneven, and uncertain nature of relatedness. As such interactions occurred over and over again for months, I became aware that every ending, every disruption, each bit of evidence of my lack of attunement or of my separate needs *absolutely* undid the very feeling Amy needed to have if she were to allow herself to be fully known. Despite many sessions during which we spoke together about the meanings that this pattern had for her, it retained its emotional potency in a particularly frustrating way.

Amy's reaction was linked to a painful and familiar self-state, in which she felt essentially unloved and unlovable. That subjective state felt so core and so toxic that Amy despaired of finding a way to mitigate its effects or to integrate it with other (temporarily dissociated), more positive aspects of self-experience. Instead, Amy sought to undo it in interaction with me. It was only within the context of the absolute (momentary) reassurance provided by my perfect responsiveness that Amy was able to retain a more positive sense of her own impact. This reassurance was, of course, inevitably transient.

Despite Amy's clear awareness of this process, we remained stalled around the double issues of my emotional reliability and her lovableness. This pattern continued with only small shifts over several years, despite multiple attempts on our part to talk about it in different ways. Amy did not often reject my exploration of these issues; she was willing, for example, to consider the possibility that she was angry with or envious of me and thus needed to spoil anything good that I seemed to offer. We spoke about the way in which this return to hopelessness was self-protective, that is, warded off a bad surprise, the way in which it recapitulated aspects of the emotional abandonment that she had experienced in infancy and childhood. I wondered with Amy whether she felt that she needed to protect me from her anger by attacking herself for my failures. However, such possibilities, although meaningful at other times, remained absolutely removed from her experience in the moment, where all that felt real to Amy was how *wrong* she had been to trust me. My work with Amy was enormously frustrating, as good moments were predictably followed by bad. I found myself tempted to try harder, to find even gentler ways of ending sessions, to search for just the right words from which she might derive a more lasting sense of confidence in our connection.

Ultimately, however, that search proved elusive, as I reached the limits of my own capacity to tolerate what felt like the repeated spoiling of good experience. I came up against my own despair, against the feeling that I could not be "right" for her; that I, or the treatment, was a failure.

Although it is not unusual for the analyst to become enraged with patients who maintain a position of dissatisfaction, I felt more sadness, helplessness, and frustration than rage with Amy, probably because Amy was rarely attacking and never denigrating of me. I also could be momentarily angry with Amy, as we returned over and over to the same emotional place. Over time, I became progressively more aware of the limits of the holding process and of its potential for repair. (A colleague suggested to me that Amy had "cured" me of my own theory in this way!)

It is possible that had Amy wished to leave treatment, I would have agreed. For long periods it was quite difficult to hold onto a sense of forward movement of any kind, as I apparently succeeded mainly in retraumatizing her on a regular basis despite my best efforts to do otherwise. Notwithstanding the difficulties, however, Amy never seriously considered leaving treatment and has stuck with it and with me for some time. I gradually came to accept as inevitable my failure to be good enough with Amy. Increasingly, I settled into a feeling that we would remain together because we needed to work over these moments, *not* in order to repair them per se, because they were not in fact reparable. Paradoxically, I believe that my eventual reconciliation with the ongoing nature of these disruptions was crucial because it allowed me to stay with Amy through the cycles without losing all hope.

As Amy and I returned again and again to moments of closeness followed by their disruption, we both came to know that the sequence was quite inevitable. It seems to me that there may be a different kind of holding process implicit in that knowledge. To the degree that I could hold here, it was crucial that I hold onto a memory of Amy's capacity to feel held in the face of her more pervasive feelings of disappointment *and* also the unreliability of her momentary sense of absolute trust. In a sense, I needed to retain an awareness of the paradoxical nature of the holding experience when Amy could not. By holding onto those moments of closeness *without losing contact with their illusory quality*, I began to do what Amy could not yet do; carry an expectation (usually not articulated) of her potential to integrate good and bad aspects of the parental object. That affective memory served to sustain me through periods during which I had to tolerate disappointing or hurting Amy and was feeling hopeless or angry with her.

In this sense, I held the repetitive hopelessness that came out of Amy's constant spoiling of good experience while holding onto hope.

An additional factor was central to my ability to retain hope in my work with Amy; that factor concerned the build-up of evidence that Amy's external life was gradually improving, albeit slowly. Amy reported increasing freedom in her social and professional interactions, reflecting a new sense of comfort in her own skin. In the face of the near absolute absence of such evidence within the treatment context, I "held on" to Amy's reports of these external changes as a pivotal way of retaining confidence in the therapeutic potential of our work together.

I was not particularly expecting a shift in Amy's experience to occur when it did. The shift, as far as I can tell, did not follow a new insight or intervention on my part. Instead, Amy came in one day and said with considerable surprise that for the first time since she began analysis, she had me "inside" all weekend long in a way that left her free to be involved in her own life. Amy went on to say that, although she knew that she was not as important to me as she would like to be, what she had with me was pretty good.

From my perspective this reflected an enormously symbolic shift in Amy's treatment. Amy had internalized a capacity to retain confidence in her own self-worth and in our good-enough connection. That confidence no longer rode solely on the outcome of our interaction. Further, the relief that Amy experienced was not based on a fantasy that she finally did "have me" in a perfect way; this was crucial, for such fantasies inevitably resulted in profound disruptions because sooner or later that illusion was dispelled. Instead, Amy recognized, unhappily, but not with despair, the limits of our relationship; it was good enough, not perfect, and therein lay its hope.

Holding and Illusion

How was Amy able to develop a capacity to elaborate on her own experience within a relationship that *was and was not* real (Winnicott, 1951; Ghent, 1992; Pizer, 1992). That is, how did Amy acquire an ability sufficiently to suspend disbelief in order to tolerate the paradox of psychoanalytic work? For Amy, the question of whether our relationship was *real* rendered its boundaries intolerable and made her incapable of living with paradox. There was no way in which the holding experience contained within it an element of play for Amy; instead, I either *did* or *did not* care enough about her, and this could be proved or disproved at any moment. In this sense Amy could not sustain a holding experience precisely because she found illusion to be toxic. A core task for her involved finding a way to integrate and to tolerate my variability. Amy needed absolute (not relative) proof of my trustworthiness *not* because she lacked the capacity for concern (i.e., an ability to tolerate hating and loving the same object [Winnicott, 1963d]), but because she deeply mistrusted the reliability of emotional relatedness. Any evidence of the relationship's limitations was excessively threatening in a way that ultimately destroyed it for her.

Two possibilities exist as my work with Amy continues to unfold; one is that Amy slowly will acquire a further build-up of trust in my emotional reliability and will ultimately be able to relax within the treatment setting. The other, which I feel to be more likely, is that Amy will continue to integrate the sequence—to tolerate and work with the inevitable fluctuations in affective charge and closeness that characterize all relationships, while *holding onto* both aspects of me and of us rather than only to one. In that sense, it may well be the work *around* holding that is critical here, and not the holding process per se.

In what way was this work different from that which is needed by patients who can tolerate a holding process? For a patient to enter even a momentary holding process, there must be sufficient capacity to experience the object's attunement in the face of the inevitable fluctuations therein. That requires an ability to tolerate and enjoy the illusion intrinsic to the analytic relationship without raising questions about its essential affective vitality. Adler (1989) underscores a similar point when he notes that the patient's ability to tolerate ambiguity in the analytic situation is pivotal to the treatment process. Patients in a holding process especially tend to *exclude* those aspects of the analyst's presence or of the treatment parameters themselves that are disturbing in order to maintain the illusion of attunement (of whatever sort). However, the patient who cannot trust the analytic object is highly reactive to issues of deception in a way that makes such exclusion dangerous. It is possible that this sensitivity reflects repetitive early experiences in which the patient was, in fact, taken by surprise by the parent's failures.

For these individuals, what is most central is not the ongoing holding process, but instead the patient's ability to retain an affective memory of *moments* of holding. Over time, that affective memory creates a structure into which the object's failures can be integrated.

Strain During Work Around Holding

I find the strain connected with work around a holding process to be rather different from that which occurs during actual moments of holding. When patients find themselves unable to experience what they nevertheless say they need, the struggle between us is explicit rather than implicit. Rather than feeling as if I need to *be* a certain way, I am involved in studying the emotional space between us in order to figure out what it is that keeps going wrong. I am more likely to know how I feel because there is sufficient emotional space (difficult though it is) between myself and the patient to do so. The strain involved here centers around my difficulty tolerating and working with my ongoing failure to do it right, that is, to find a place to be with the patient that "works." The danger is that I will lose hope—in myself and my patient, and that, like my patient, I will affectively forget those moments during which something powerful and positive happens. Further, the emotional dysjunctiveness that characterizes the work makes it likely that frequently I will be taken aback by the patient's reactions and may have to work quite hard at understanding and negotiating my repetitive failures to satisfy if I am not to attack either myself or the patient.

Countertransference Resistances to Staying "On the Edge"

The emotional intensity and the rapid fluctuations characteristic of patients who need and yet are allergic to a holding experience makes this a situation fraught with countertransference dangers for the analyst. These range from an absolute abandonment of the analyst's subjectivity in an attempt to finally satisfy the patient to an all-out attack of the patient. Such patients are likely to repeatedly experience failures in treatment, and yet to return to try again. The following vignettes describe the cycle of failure in treatment that is typical for these patients.

Mr. S. is a middle-aged man with a history of severe deprivation. He entered his first analysis eagerly, and contacted and expressed a core feeling of being unlovable, along with a need for the analyst to mother him in a variety of ways. The analyst responded with feelings of empathy and warmth partially out of a conscious desire to meet Mr. S.'s needs and to symbolically repair the deprivation. Mr. S. experienced these moments of closeness with enormous relief; however, that relief was short-lived, and rapidly turned to despair as he felt the analyst inadvertently rejecting him, often in the next moment. When the analyst communicated his understanding of his hurtful effect, Mr. S. felt relieved again, only to be taken by surprise at the analyst's next failure. Mr. S. became increasingly despondent as the analyst's very sensitive understanding of him only intensified his hurt when he felt abandoned.

As that cycle intensified, Mr. S. placed increasing pressure on the analyst to meet his needs in concrete ways. After much thought and discussion with Mr. S., the analyst decided to try in varying ways to offer something concrete to the patient in the hope that such reassurance would help him move beyond the apparent analytic impasse. Thus, for example, he gave Mr. S. a symbolic birthday gift, phoned him over a weekend break, and offered him tea. Although the analyst had some misgivings about this "acting out," he felt that Mr. S. was a person for whom action was essential because words did not carry reliable meaning. However, the analyst's own concern for Mr. S. and his wish to finally provide evidence of his emotional availability progressively became infused with his wish to actually become the parent and with an intolerance of his own emotional limitations. Increasingly, the analyst overrode his awareness of his limits and of the inevitability of his failure to satisfy. The analyst became filled with rage and anxiety as he disregarded his own boundaries in response to Mr. S.'s demands. He knew intellectually that this enactment around Mr. S.'s neediness and his reparative capacity was doomed to failure. Mr. S. ultimately left treatment with a feeling of hopelessness about his own capacity to be satisfied. The analyst was only slightly less distressed about his inability to parent Mr. S.

An alternate danger for the analyst involves the all-out projection of badness into the patient who cannot be satisfied: Because Mr. S. continued to struggle enormously with self-hatred, he sought out treatment again, laying out the history of his failed analysis in the hope that this time it would be different. The second analyst initially was able to maintain an empathic, boundaried position with Mr. S. that did not seem to arouse his sense of intense neediness. However, by the end of the second year of treatment, Mr. S. once again found himself in a process that felt alternately satisfying and torturous. His responses to the analysis resulted in a deterioration in his outside life as well. The analyst, determined not to repeat the first analyst's mistakes, "held the frame," refusing all of the patient's requests for extra contact or gratification while actively interpreting the underlying destructiveness and self-hate attached to the pattern. Frequently she would remind him that he *had* felt understood by her but had then spoiled it. Initially, Mr. S. seemed to quiet down in response to the analyst's more even, less anxious stance. However, his sense of need and hurt remained a constant feature, and gradually he found himself again in what felt like a repetition of his deprived early life.

The analyst, probably feeling frustrated and inadequate as Mr. S.'s hopelessness became acute, moved from a holding to a withholding position while simultaneously interpreting to Mr. S. her determination not to be destroyed by him. Increasingly, she attacked him as she insisted on the rightness of her interpretations and her stance in a way that was at times overtly sadistic. For long periods, she insisted that Mr. S. needed her to be absolutely rigid with regard to the frame because otherwise Mr. S. would feel himself to be destructive. Mr. S. responded with a sense both that he deserved this punishment and that something had gone terribly wrong with the treatment. The analyst remained unwilling to address this second possibility with him, however. Mr. S. became aware that they had reached a stalemate but felt unable to leave the treatment because of the power of his conscious determination to undo that painful relationship by getting the analyst to change (and because of the unconscious attachment to the bad object). It was not until the analyst herself "acted out" and rejected him in an especially flagrant way that Mr. S. was able to quit the treatment. Even then, despite much support from a consulting analyst, he carried with him a paralyzing sense of failure that resulted in a major depression and hospitalization, and, ultimately, a search for yet another analyst.

It seems, then, that these analysts both failed Mr. S. by attempting to resolve the dilemma they faced. The first analyst did this by becoming the good object in the hope of providing sufficient reassurance to allow Mr. S. to trust him. The second analyst dealt with Mr. S.'s pressure by unconsciously rejecting his experience of her as a depriving object and attacking him for not being satisfied. Clearly, neither of these two stances is likely to be successful because both short-circuit the dilemma rather than addressing it directly.

Ultimately, Mr. S. sought out a third treatment. In that analysis, Mr. S. continued to address issues related to his difficulty believing in the analyst's emotional attunement. However, in contrast to his first two experiences, he began to address his own affective reactivity with the analyst in a way that felt helpful to him, and for the first time he felt a sense of internal change. It is certainly likely that this third analyst was himself in a better position to work with Mr. S. in a way that avoided either of the problematic choices made by the earlier analysts. Nevertheless, the possibility remains that the potential success of this treatment partially rested on subtle yet progressive changes on Mr. S.'s part; that is, it seems likely that his own capacity to tolerate treatment boundaries, and thus the paradoxical element inherent in the analytic relationship, had actually built up, albeit slowly, over the course of his previous treatment experiences.

It has been my experience that many patients who find treatment very difficult do go through a number of failed analyses before finally settling into a satisfactory treatment experience. The process whereby such failed treatments help is rarely clear. It is likely, however, that the aborted treatment contains within it a possibility for change, if reflected only in the patient's determination not to repeat the previous failure.

To the extent that a treatment becomes stalled around the edge of a holding process, neither patient nor analyst is likely to retain a sense of confidence in the process or in its potential for resolution. What may ultimately be pivotal is not the achievement of a holding experience per se. It may be the analyst's willingness to actually stay on the edge that matters, because the key therapeutic task for the patient involves an integration of the object's attunement with her potential for misattunement. There thus will be moments of genuine contact that on one hand speak to the patient's need and capacity for deep affective experience, and, on the other, forecast an imminent breech of trust. It seems to me that the analyst's task here involves her ability to retain a sense of hope in those better moments without reminding the patient of them. By holding onto that hope (i.e., to the illusion of the attuned analyst), the analyst may be able to live through what is often an extraordinarily long and frustrating period during which the patient moves from hope to despair without any apparent build-up in a sense of the object's emotional reliability. For the analyst to stay with the treatment without losing hope, she must retain an affective memory of the patient's (and her own) capacity for moments of contact. The analyst's ability to do this will be facilitated to the degree that she can make use of evidence of positive external changes in the patient's life as a way of holding onto hope. Additionally, it will be essential that she remain aware of frame issues within the treatment, and that she be able to explicitly negotiate around these with the patient.

Chapter 7

When Holding Fails

Despite the crucial importance of the holding experience with some patients, and the ubiquity of the holding metaphor at moments in virtually all treatment situations, there are times when the holding process stalls or even fails absolutely. Here, despite the analyst's ability to tolerate her subjective experience, and despite the ways in which the patient apparently settles into a holding process, that process does not evolve. Patient and analyst remain stuck within the metaphor, and no deepening is evident in the patient's self-experience or in her capacity for mutual relatedness.

These situations are characterized by an apparent stalling of the analytic process within a holding metaphor. During the holding process, patient and analyst do not fully elaborate on their subjective experience in a way that permits the therapeutic dialogue and its effects to be fleshed out. At times it thus can be difficult to differentiate between a process that is evolving, albeit slowly, and one that is in some way frozen or disintegrating.

Often, the clearest evidence of positive analytic effect with patients involved in a holding process is externally derived. At these times, despite the apparent lack of forward movement within the treatment itself, the analyst observes progressive or intermittent shifts in the patient's outside life. That evidence is especially reassuring to the analyst when the treatment itself appears stalled. In the absence of such evidence, the analyst may be at a loss with regard to the treatment's impact. Here, the possibility exists that in fact the process has failed.

Because there are such a multiplicity of factors that contribute to treatment impasses, my focus is exclusively on how holding processes stall or fail. Even here, a complex intermixture of elements must be considered, including the analyst's and patient's separate contributions, as well as the ways in which the particular dyad somehow fails.

The Analyst's Contributions to a Stalled Process: The Collapsed Illusion

Holding processes always contain within them at least an element of enactment (see Chapter 2). That enactment surrounds the illusion (at times shared and played out by patient and analyst) of parental attunement and of patient as baby or child. One of its consequences is that other aspects of the patient's and analyst's experience of themselves and of the other are temporarily excluded from awareness because they behave "as if" the metaphor were all-encompassing.

To the extent that holding processes represent an enactment of the parental metaphor, a pivotal aspect of the holding experience requires that the analyst retain access to her awareness of the element of metaphor within that process. It is the analyst's capacity to make use of metaphor that allows her to tolerate and sometimes to enjoy the experience of holding without needing explicitly to challenge its reality. Similarly, the patient who can enter into a holding process does so by *setting aside* what she knows about the analyst in order to engage in the illusion of attunement characteristic of holding. In fact, when the patient cannot engage in such an illusion, the holding process is quite intolerable (see Chapter 6).

It is my proposition that the analyst will be most likely to fail the patient during a holding process when she *ceases to recognize the ways in which holding represents a metaphor.* When holding fails, the analyst (as well as the patient) has lost contact with its metaphoric dimension, and in this sense, the holding process is actually *failing to hold.* What may look like holding instead represents a *collusion* between patient and analyst that goes beyond the bounds of a metaphor. That collusion protects the analyst as well as the patient by deleting a core affective dimension rather than by creating a space within which it can be experienced. The collusion may protect patient and analyst from experiencing a full range of feeling about the other, or it may provide a therapeutic rationale that covers over the analyst's personal investment in seeing herself or the patient in a particular way.

On one hand, then, in the holding moment, patient and analyst share a highly overlapping experience of the process. What Ogden (1994) has called the "analytic third" narrows because the patient cannot tolerate much evidence of the separateness of the analyst's subjective experience. It is nevertheless absolutely essential that the analyst retain a capacity to experience her subjectivity between if not within the sessions. That capacity reminds her that the holding process is, in part, illusory. In this sense, although the analytic "third" narrows dramatically during holding, it is crucial that it remains an *idea* in the analyst's mind; it cannot actively be used, but it also cannot altogether be forgotten.

Holding must thus remain a paradoxical experience for the analyst, even when it feels real in the moment. The holding process is most vulnerable to failure when the analyst as well as the patient completely lose contact with the nature of illusion inherent in holding.

Here, the power of the holding process is no longer balanced by its illusory quality. Instead, there is an absolute *collapse* of the holding metaphor, which becomes a simple reality to both parties. The analyst experiences the patient not *as if* she were, for example, a needy baby, but instead *as a baby*—as if that were all there were to the patient, and the analyst becomes the parent.

Although there are probably moments, even sessions, in many treatment contexts where an enactment takes over the process, ordinarily the analyst recovers sufficiently between sessions to recontact other aspects of the treatment experience, and especially the paradox of the parental metaphor. If the holding moment remains a fixed reality, however, that enlarged space (or the analytic third) no longer exists even as an idea in the analyst's mind. Such a process is doomed to fail because it so totally excludes each party's subjectivity that it cannot allow for the integration of this narrowed internal picture with a larger and more complex level of self-experience.

A critical dimension of the analyst's experience during holding involves her intermittent capacity to recontact her own dysjunctive subjectivity. As that capacity is lost, so is the analyst's freedom to think as an autonomous agent. Symington (1983, 1990), responding to Bion's (1962) work, has underlined the importance of the analyst's act of freedom within therapeutic process. He suggests that the analyst's capacity to think is destroyed when it becomes too closely linked to the patient's subjective constructs. Within this context, the patient's process gradually gains a stranglehold on the analytic interchange. As we examine the factors that contribute to failures in the holding metaphor, it will become clear that one important element surrounds the analyst's inability to retain contact with her dysjunctive subjectivity, that is, to think.

The Stalled Dyad: Collusive Reenactments

The analyst's inability to retain contact with the illusory element within a holding situation at times may primarily reflect the analyst's emotional limitations, especially her difficulty living with uncertainty. It frequently appears, however, that holding processes stall as a consequence of a mutual collusion between analyst and patient. To the degree that the patient's need for a particular kind of holding process fits in with the analyst's own emotional preferences, little tension may be generated between the two around the meaning or the limitations of the holding process. It therefore becomes a process vulnerable to a collusion around certainty.

In this sense, the stalled treatment may represent a mutual playing out between patient and analyst of a fantasy that the two share—that a certain type of experience is all that the patient needs or can tolerate. For example, the analyst with a powerful need to be idealized may only too easily succumb to the patient's conviction that she needs to be mothered. The analyst may be impacted on by her own fantasies, the patient's projective identification, and the meshing of these two elements. Similarly, the somewhat preoccupied analyst who is highly sensitive to intrusion may quickly move into a containing position with a narcissistic patient. In these situations, the highly overlapping nature of two separate subjectivities interferes with the analytic pair's tolerance of strain and uncertainty within the holding process. That collusion ultimately contributes to the failure of the holding process because of the near absolute absence of questions about the nature of the process on patient's or analyst's part.

The Stuck Patient

Although the patient is, to a greater or lesser degree, always dependent on the analyst's capacity to manage the holding situation, and especially to retain contact with its illusory quality, the patient nevertheless may contribute her own resistances to a holding process in a way that ultimate results in its failure. While it is always possible that such issues would have been better managed by a different analyst, it does seem as if there are patients whom no one helps—who return for treatment repeatedly, always ultimately dissatisfied with its outcome.

Stagnant treatment situations at times may reflect the analyst's inability to sustain illusion or the collusion of patient and analyst around the holding metaphor. But the treatment may also fail because of the patient's inability to tolerate analytic work, or even her unconscious need to destroy the process. There are patients who do seem to go through analysts—always expressing the need for a particular kind of experience and inevitably disappointed. For some of these people, a very subtle but gradual build-up in the capacity to sustain affective contact eventually may result in a more successful treatment outcome (see the case of Sam in Chapter 6); for others, however, it does not.

I am here referring particularly to those patients whose stalled treatments involve an intense need for what appears to be a holding process, which devolves into an enactment without indication of therapeutic movement, ultimately resulting in a ruptured treatment. Although one can never be absolutely certain that the patient is, in fact, not helpable within the analytic context, there are people for whom it appears that the commitment to staying stuck—in Joseph's (1982) apt term, addiction to near death—ultimately overrides hope and obliterates the possibility of change.

The holding process is most vulnerable to failure, then, to the degree that it acquires a fixed, locked-in quality that does not arouse doubt of any kind in the analyst's mind. When the analyst's experience of pressure leaves room for little choice, the analyst may feel quite clear that the patient cannot tolerate interpretive work or any investigation of her impact, and she may move toward a holding stance. Although the analyst frequently is under considerable strain during these moments, that strain tends to surround her difficulty in bracketing her subjectivity and does not always include her doubts about the viability of the therapeutic process per se. For that reason, there is a danger that analyst and patient will somehow settle in the holding process in a way that does not reflect a therapeutic potential.

Failures in Holding Dependence

Because of the intense need expressed by extremely dependent patients, there is a danger that use of the holding metaphor will stall when issues of dependence are involved. Patient and analyst may become stuck in a view of the patient where all that is seen is her absolute dependence. Balint (1968) called this evolution a malignant regression. Here, the dependent patient does not feel satisfied as the analyst symbolically or literally meets her needs; instead, satisfaction leads to an intensification of felt need, heightened demand, the analyst's eventual failure to satisfy, and a subsequent increase in suffering and/or demands of the analyst. Balint (1968) likened this to an addiction-like state, in which the wish for gratification overshadows all else:

> In the one form the regression is aimed at a gratification of instinctual cravings; what the patient seeks is an external event, an action by his object. In the other form what the patient expects is . . . a tacit consent to use the external world in a way that would allow him to get on with his internal problems [p. 144].

Balint made clear that even in cases of benign regression the analyst may need to create a setting in which she really does carry the patient. That process is not only verbal, and may involve physical contact, and so on. However, despite the "libidinous" or charged dimension of such concrete holding, Balint believed that in a benign regression the patient is able to establish a relationship of mutual trust in which the regression facilitates internal movement. In contrast, the patient involved in a malignant regression remains unable to trust, perhaps like the patient on the edge. Balint did not, however, view this difficulty to reflect a *shared* process, but rather placed the "malignancy" squarely in the patient's lap.

I prefer to think about such a dilemma in terms that include the analyst's participation. It seems to me that a malignant regression nearly always describes a process that includes an element of collusion on the analyst's part. For example, although the analyst may be experienced as quite satisfying by the patient, on a subtle level the two may unconsciously maintain the patient's need state in a way that does not permit it to evolve or to promote deepened self-experience. The patient remains permanently dependent on the analyst, grateful for her support but always unable to do without it. Both parties may too fully delete aspects of their subjective experience from the process. Ghent (1992) has suggested that what appears to be a malignant regression may in fact act to protect the patient from the yet more poignant threat inherent in a benign regression. He emphasizes the defensive function of the malignant regression in protecting the true self from being reached.

Another key factor characteristic of this defensive "malignant regression" involves the absence of any awareness of paradox—the very paradox so central to the evolution of a deeper sense of self. Instead, the emotional reality of the regression becomes so intense that it absolutely obliterates other aspects of each person's subjectivity. One can speculate, for example, that the analyst may be someone who needs the adoration of her patient, and/or that the patient is vulnerable to self-deprecation in an unconscious attempt to prop up the maternal object. If both patient and analyst remain unaware of the dysjunctive aspects of their experience in an unconscious attempt to protect the other from core affective states, the patient will become a baby, and the analyst will be reluctant to challenge the reality of the holding situation.

The analyst is especially vulnerable to a sense of intense pressure when working with regressed patients who appear to know what they need. Under the pressure of the patient's certainty about her needs, the analyst may lose contact with her freedom to think—with a sense of her own mind as a separate source of ideas and action. Here, the analyst may progressively lose confidence in her capacity to understand the patient differently from the way the patient sees herself, until the analyst has little choice but to go along with the patient's prescription for cure.

Dr. D. sought a consultation regarding his work with Ms. J., an extremely disturbed schizoid young woman with a history of sexual abuse. As Ms. J. contacted memories of abuse in response to the analyst's sensitive work with her, she gradually emerged from a state of virtually total isolation. Ms. J. attached to Dr. D. in a total way that left him feeling that he was literally responsible for her survival (Davies and Frawley, 1994). The recovery of memories of abuse increased Ms.

J.'s state of helplessness, which became acute; she was at suicidal risk and quite alone in the world. Ms. J.'s suicidal wishes intensified on weekends, when she remained at home, usually without seeing or speaking with anyone. Dr. D. felt that Ms. J.'s extreme vulnerability during this crisis period necessitated that he see her daily, and at times for additional weekend sessions. Ms. J. often phoned in the evening in a distraught state, and the analyst allowed this, although he limited the length of the phone contacts.

Dr. D. initially met Ms. J.'s needs with a feeling of concern and willingness, believing the crisis to be a temporary "phase." However, after more than a year, he noted with dismay that despite ongoing work around the recovered memories, Ms. J. continued intermittently to be suicidal. She became actively suicidal in response to her analyst's periodic attempts to engage her in an investigation of the nature of her transference experience, and especially of how the analyst had become responsible for her survival. Ms. J. insisted that these were simply realities, and felt wounded by the analyst's attempts to investigate her experience of need. When Dr. D. pointed out to Ms. J. that in even raising these issues, he became a sadist, torturing her once more, she agreed, but was unable to work with that awareness as a *dynamic*. Increasingly Dr. D. found himself to be stuck in a position where his patient's needs felt overwhelming. He came for help because of his conviction that were he to refuse her, he would be responsible for a suicide.

Although on one level Dr. D.'s fears regarding Ms. J.'s vulnerability were well founded, in another way he had altogether lost contact with an awareness that he could never fully meet Ms. J's needs. That is, he gradually gave up his very sophisticated understanding of the nature of Ms. J.'s conflicts and vulnerabilities and allowed his view of her to narrow until all that he saw was her dependence. Simultaneously, he lost contact with any awareness of the ways in which he was unwilling and unable to meet all of Ms. J's needs, and in this way he abandoned the holding metaphor altogether. Instead, he became the parent, and in doing so lost hold of any peripheral knowledge that his emotional reliability was partially illusory. He thereby joined Ms. J. in an collusive enactment around dependence[1] that contained within it no element of paradox.

The collapse of the illusory nature of the holding experience can be quite difficult to discern. First of all, Ms. J. did, in fact, need the analyst to provide a variety of parental functions for her; she had a minimal capacity to retain a sense of her own viability in the absence of concrete care on the analyst's part. In this sense, the analyst was the par-

---

[1] The analyst's narrowed experience might be viewed to reflect a powerful projective identification on the patient's part.

ent, as Winnicott (1963) suggested. However, the analyst's own resistances to experiencing his emotional limitations protected him from retaining an awareness of the ways in which he enjoyed and preferred not to challenge the reality that he was a parental object. The patient's need for him reassured Dr. D. of the depth of his own emotional resources, making it more difficult for him to experience the complexity of his response to the patient's needs.

Because of Dr. D.'s need to rescue his patient, he was relatively insensitive to the limits of that possibility. That insensitivity was further intensified because his wish to become the idealized object dovetailed so closely with Ms. J.'s own wishes. The dyad thereby colluded to exclude from their interaction any questions about the process.

It was only when Dr. D. was able to acknowledge to himself his inability to fully meet Ms. J.'s needs that he was able to question aspects of her neediness and of his response. Ms. J.'s suicidal potential was so real that Dr. D.'s awareness of their collusion led him to wonder whether to suggest hospitalization to her. As he considered this option and his own need for treatment limits, he began to address other dimensions of Ms. J.'s experience of him, notably her conviction that he would abandon her altogether were her need for him to be less than total. In that context, Dr. D. made explicit his inability to absolutely protect Ms. J. from suicide, and wondered aloud whether they should consider hospitalization. By introducing this element of reality here (that the analyst could not in fact save her), Dr. D. partially broke into the illusion of analytic attunement, once again rendering the treatment a partially symbolic process rather than a simple actuality. Ms. J. responded with a mixture of anxiety, lest she be abandoned to a hospital, and relief, perhaps because she was able to reintegrate aspects of a more competent self-state. Interestingly, Dr. D.'s ability to acknowledge the limits of his holding capacity had the effect of sufficiently containing Ms. J. to permit their work to go on outside the hospital setting.

Although Ms. J. continued to experience intensely difficult periods within the treatment, Dr. D. found himself to be progressively more able to retain a sense of the limits of the holding process. He was consequently less anxious about Ms. J. and freer to work with her around the coercive aspects of her neediness. The treatment, now in its sixth year, remains a difficult one. However, the shape of those difficulties increasingly resembles the pattern described in Chapter 6, with patients on the edge who need to find a way to tolerate illusion within the analytic setting. In this sense, it seems as if the analyst's recognition of the illusory nature of his savior function shifted the treatment in the direction of more explicit negotiation around the patient's communication of need. Although this hardly represents a full resolu-

tion of Ms. J.'s difficulties, the quality of the treatment is such that neither analyst nor patient feels frozen within a hopeless situation.

It is important to distinguish the analyst's capacity to recognize the
illusory elements within the holding situation from the ability to set
limits with the patient. On one hand, the analyst's ability to set boundaries can be crucial with patients in a regression. These boundaries
may protect the patient from an emotionally dangerous or seductive
situation in which it would appear that all needs can be met. Such
boundaries may also demonstrate that the analyst has limitations, and
thus implicitly underscore the illusory aspect of analytic attunement.

On the other hand, a danger exists to the extent that the analyst sets
limits with the patient on the basis of a conviction that such boundaries are what the patient needs, that the patient is manipulating or
testing the analytic setting. Certainly, this is sometimes quite true.
However, to the degree that the analyst sets limits out of a feeling of
certainty that she knows what the patient needs, she may inadvertently perpetuate the parental illusion in a way that excludes its paradoxical qualities. Had Ms. J.'s analyst set limits with her out of a position of emotional certainty, he would in a sense have confirmed Ms.
J.'s fantasy that the analyst was all powerful, perhaps extending that
boundary to include the hospital itself. I do not believe that this would
have been unambiguously helpful to this patient. She and the analyst
would have remained stuck within the parental metaphor, that is,
within the absolute reality of the patient's helplessness and the analyst's omniscience and omnipotence.

Failures in Holding Self-Involvement

In work with issues of dependence, the analyst is vulnerable to
experiencing the patient in a narrow way. However, at least some
dialogue is likely to take place between patient and analyst around the
nature of the patient's needs and the analyst's ability to meet these
needs. Both patient and analyst acknowledge the patient's dependence, and there is usually some degree of explicit negotiation around
the nature of the patient's experience. In contrast, holding periods
involving issues of self-involvement lend themselves to a different sort
of stalled process. Here, the patient's apparent impenetrability on one
hand, and her negative reactivity to analytic interventions of any kind
on the other, may leave the analyst increasingly impotent and potentially numb. The analyst eventually may succumb to a near trancelike
state of boredom, having abandoned any real hope of contacting the
patient in a deeper way.

Although it often seems clear that a self-involved patient needs a holding process because she cannot tolerate evidence of the analyst's separateness, the analyst is unlikely to feel especially gratified during this kind of holding. Instead, the analyst frequently is under considerable strain surrounding her doubts about the viability of the therapeutic process per se. The strain of living with those doubts is sufficiently intense that there is a danger that the analyst unconsciously will give up on the patient, and will settle into the holding process without therapeutic potential.

A self-involved patient is often not at all in contact with her inability to tolerate the analyst's interventions. Instead, the patient frequently is quite oblivious both to her own impact on the analyst and to her experience of the analyst's interventions. Here, the analyst works in an emotional vacuum; although she may have evidence that the patient experiences her input to be toxic, it is not at all clear that anything is happening when the analyst refrains from such interventions. How, then, can she hope to know whether or not the holding process has stalled, or gradually will build up the patient's capacity to tolerate more ordinary analytic interchange? Since the analyst's subjective experience is more than likely to surround a feeling of immovability, how is she to distinguish that subjective response from a realistic assessment of a truly stuck treatment process?

I do not have an answer. It has been my experience that with some extremely narcissistic patients, literally years may go by before real movement is evident in the direction of an increased tolerance for self-examination. Sometimes I have found myself to be taken by surprise when this shift is effected, when the patient shows a willingness to look at herself and to allow me to help her do so. It has been my sense that a subtle build-up in the patient's capacity for emotional experience preceded this shift, but could not be talked about (see Chapter 4). However, since this shift can rarely be addressed in any explicit way, it frequently is impossible altogether to differentiate a hope that something subtle is happening from that reality.

At other times (or with other self-involved patients), no such happy resolution presents itself. Instead, the near absolute absence of dialogue during the holding period leaves the analyst in a deadened position that increasingly excludes the possibility of change. Both patient and analyst may unconsciously give up, remaining in a lifeless process that tends only to confirm the patient's underlying sense of hopelessness. Not infrequently, this impasse is resolved by the patient's termination. That move may be accompanied by the patient's declaration that she is satisfied—that she feels better and has had enough. At other times, the patient may leave disgruntled and unsatisfied. In both situations, however, the holding process fails in at least one major respect—it does not help the patient move toward a deepened capacity for intersubjective dialogue.

Sharon had been in treatment with me for about three years. She was an actress, quite beautiful, and utterly self-involved and inaccessible from my point of view. She presented in a way that left no room for me to question or wonder about her process; if I tried to do so, she simply ignored me and went on with her own stories. My attempts to address the nature of our interaction failed so miserably that I gradually moved toward a holding position with a clear sense of Sharon's fragility. Over time, our work increasingly settled into a holding process in the way described more fully in Chapter 4. I felt settled too—relatively comfortable in the knowledge that Sharon could not tolerate a more actively probing stance on my part. Although sometimes I found the work to be quite boring and wondered when Sharon would be able to look at herself, I had no real question that for the moment, a holding process was the only viable choice.

One day, Sharon appeared for her session and announced that this week would be her last; she had, she said, "gotten a lot" from her treatment and now understood herself "so much better," but needed the money for other purposes. Sharon maintained a friendly manner, but utterly stonewalled all of my attempts to inquire about whether I had hurt her feelings or insulted her, whether she was disappointed in the treatment or angry with me, and so on. She maintained a friendly stance that left no space within which I could at least examine what had happened. In fact, she was surprised that I would in any way question her reasons for terminating.

There are a multitude of questions that may be asked here. What did happen? Had I failed Sharon by allowing her to avoid investigating her process, that is, by colluding with her around her narcissistic defensive structure? Did I excessively threaten her extremely fragile sense of self-esteem in a way that I was not aware? Alternatively (or in addition), was Sharon simply too narcissistically defended to tolerate the treatment process? Had we gone as far as we could go? Did Sharon and I together enact something here? Or did Sharon leave because in fact she did sufficiently assimilate a self-holding function to allow her a means of obtaining relief while avoiding the vulnerability inherent in self-examination?

Although it appeared that Sharon had accrued some benefit from the treatment, I feel nevertheless that in central ways our work failed to deepen both Sharon's experience of herself and her capacity to be related. In retrospectively considering what my contribution to the treatment's failure may have been, it seems possible that I too fully accepted the reality of Sharon's need for a holding experience and thereby abandoned the illusory element within this treatment. Because work with self-involved patients is often characterized by a quality of stagnation from the analyst's point of view, it was easy for me to settle into a position with Sharon from which I did not try to interpret or otherwise to introduce my subjective thoughts. Sharon seemed to me so much like a China doll—her narcissism and self-aggrandizing style were so painfully evident—that I may have abandoned any hope that Sharon had broader emotional potential—that the process could be deepened. That is, during our sessions I may too completely have accepted the reality of Sharon's intolerance of subjective interchange and thus rendered the holding process a complete reality. Had I been able to experience those parts of her that were at least potentially resilient, perhaps I could have opened up a dialogue around Sharon's need for a holding experience in a way that would have left room for questions about how we might deepen the process despite Sharon's fragility. An element of personal repetition for me was probably important as well; Sharon's extreme remoteness evoked memories of my inability to contact certain others (in my own childhood) and per-haps led me to give up on Sharon. In addition, Sharon's expectation that she be accepted at face value and not challenged, that I function largely as an admiring object, intensified the collusive element within the treatment. Sharon seemed to both need and expect exactly what I delivered. There was virtually no tension, and thus no irritant to shake up the holding process. It is probable that the treatment's failure was consequently furthered by the subtle pressure that Sharon exerted throughout the holding process.

It is also possible that Sharon simply could not tolerate the treat-ment experience. Sharon's negative reactivity to emotional contact was so intense that she may not have been able to remain even when my input was minimal. She may have left, therefore, in order to avoid facing her own emotional limitations. Leaving the treatment also probably reenacted some version of Sharon's relationship with her disconnected mother. As so often happens with patients like Sharon, I was unable even to investigate how the treatment failed, and so I am left primarily with a series of questions about it.

Failures in Holding Ruthlessness and Hate

It is less likely that this sort of stalling will occur during treatment periods involving issues of ruthlessness and hate. When patients struggle with these issues, the level of strain for analyst and patient is so high that the analyst usually is unable to settle into any comfortable state. Here, the patient's ruthlessness or anger creates such pressure that either the analyst or the patient will tend to disrupt the process in one way or another. As a result, it is far more likely that the analyst will be unable to tolerate a holding process for as long as is necessary. The failures in holding here will therefore tend to follow the pattern described in Chapter 5, where the analyst inadvertently attacks the patient in an attempt to relieve herself of the enormous strain inherent in the process.

The paradox of the stalled holding process, then, concerns the transitional nature of illusion; on one hand, it is essential that both patient and analyst experience and enjoy it; on the other hand, if that illusion loses its metaphoric quality, it will fail altogether to move the treatment. When the analyst, as well as the patient, loses the ability to think or to play with the idea of analyst as holder, there is virtually no room for process within the treatment frame. Instead, perhaps like the transitional object that has the potential to become a fetish, the holding process is subverted or even perverted.

Chapter 8

The Holding Function in Mourning

To the degree that the holding metaphor originates within the parent–child matrix, it is essentially one that psychoanalysis has borrowed from life. Perhaps because of the apparent purity of the treatment context, the holding theme is especially easy to parse out within a therapeutic interaction. This does not mean, however, that the holding process is invisible elsewhere. To the contrary, the human need for the illusion of parental attunement is ubiquitous. It pervades the life of the individual and the culture. Holding processes take a variety of forms, always reflecting individual need as well as sociocultural idiosyncrasies with regard to the interface of individual and group needs. What nevertheless binds these experiences together is the pervasive presence of a need for a particular sort of illusion. That illusion concerns the parental object's capacity to reliably receive, meet, and tolerate the individual's need.

A holding theme often is embedded within sociocultural responses to the individual during periods of crisis, at least insofar as the social frame remains intact and the individual's crisis does not threaten it. I would like to offer an example of such a holding process that is derived from a personal experience. That experience involved the loss of my father within the context of Jewish mourning observance. It was not until I directly experienced a mourning process that I came to recognize the therapeutic value of a set of prescribed rituals that had heretofore seemed to me to be somewhat puzzling and of questionable emotional use. Detailing the traditions involved in Jewish mourning illustrates what I believe to be the holding function of a very particular cluster of rituals. I hope, however, that this discussion has meaning that extends beyond the particulars of my experience of loss and mourning within the Jewish tradition, and that it may represent a model within which to examine a variety of such nonanalytic experiences (see also Slochower, 1993).

Loss and Mourning

Individual need is perhaps nowhere more poignant than during periods of acute loss. Although emotional losses occur in many forms, death is certainly an especially palpable one. Most of us know only too well that the death of close loved ones, whether dreaded or wished for, is a profound and wrenching experience. This is especially so when we lose a central and irreplaceable relationship—a parent, sibling, spouse, or child. Deaths like these affect our lives in profound and not necessarily temporary ways. Our immediate experience of loss reduces our capacity to be involved in the world of real relationships or activities, and may permanently alter our sense of our place in the world.

The mourning process itself is a complex one. Freud (1917) believed that mourning, a "normal" variant of depression, involved feelings of painful dejection, a loss of interest in the outside world, lost capacity to love, and an inability to engage in everyday activities. He understood mourning as allowing the libido to detach slowly and painfully from the loved object. Abraham (1924), in contrast to Freud, suggested that normal mourning and (neurotic) depression are similar in that both result in lowered self-esteem and can involve ambivalent feelings toward the lost object. Abraham further noted that the mourner deals with the pain of loss by introjecting rather than detaching from the loved object. The importance of the mourner's yearning for the lost object was also underlined by Bibring (1953) and Jacobson (1957).

Klein (1975) emphasized the inevitable sense of guilt and fear of retaliation following such loss. She related this to the work of the infant in the depressive position.

> The poignancy of the actual loss of a loved person is . . . greatly increased by the mourner's unconscious phantasies of having lost his *internal* "good" objects as well. He then feels that his internal "bad" objects predominate and his inner world is in danger of disruption. . . . Fears of being robbed and punished by both dreaded parents—that is to say, feelings of persecution—have also been revived in deep layers of the mind. . . . I would say that in mourning the subject goes through a modified and transitory manic-depressive state and overcomes it [p. 353].

Klein believed that the mourner must contend with grief, guilt, hatred, and self-hate, and also feelings of triumph over the lost object. Winnicott (1963c) similarly believed that mourning, like depression, required a resolution of guilt and the sense of responsibility for the death. He understood the source of these feelings to be the destructive feelings that inevitably accompany loving.

Bowlby (1960, 1980) described several emotional responses to the death of loved ones, including a focus of thoughts and behavior on the lost object; feelings of hostility that may be directed in a variety of ways; appeals for help; feelings of despair, withdrawal, regression, and disorganization; and, finally, reorganization of behavior toward a new object. He noted that in normal mourning, anger is in fact inevitable, and may be directed toward the lost object. Bowlby (1980) questioned

the centrality of the identification process in the resolution of mourning and emphasized the varied emotional responses involved: "Loss of
a loved person gives rise not only to an intense desire for reunion but
to anger at his departure and, later, usually to some degree of detachment; it gives rise not only to a cry for help, but sometimes also to a
rejection of those who respond" (p. 31).

Clearly, then, the mourning process is a powerful one, as the
mourner sorts out memories and mixed feelings about the death, and
lives through a temporary depression. Ultimately, the work of
mourning is aimed at helping the mourner to give up the lost relationship as a real, alive one, while forming and preserving an internal relationship to the deceased person in all its complexity (see Siggins, 1966,
for a review of this literature). There is some disagreement concerning
the degree to which mourning is analogous to or different from neurotic depression. Certainly, the mourner differs from the neurotic in
that the lost object is absent both symbolically and in reality. Further,
mourning, unlike depression, is at least ideally a circumscribed process, and is spontaneously curative.

The intensity of an individual's mourning will always depend on
the nature of the mourner's relationship to the deceased, the circum-
stances of the death, and the relative emotional health of the mourner,
especially the mourner's capacity to tolerate and work with painful
affective states. The affective tone of the mourning process is
inevitably varied, depending on whether the mourner's reactions to
the loss primarily involve feelings of abandonment, relief, guilt, sadness, rage, and so on. What I would like to emphasize, however, is that
whenever the loss is a significant one, the individual's need to integrate it remains a powerful and constant feature. During the period of
mourning, the mourner suffers from a significantly diminished capacity to be involved in the world of real relationships or activities.
Instead, the mourner is taken up with the task of avoiding, experiencing, and expressing grief about the loss; of sorting out memories and
conflictual feelings about the person; and of living through a temporary depression. That depression always concerns in part a sense of
having been abandoned by the deceased.

Death and Jewish Tradition

All cultures recognize the mourner's need to express respect for the
deceased individual and grief at the loss (see Mandelbaum, 1959, for
a discussion of the social function of funeral rites in some other

societies). Jewish mourning traditions create a remarkably detailed structure within which to address death. Some aspects of Jewish law pertaining to death and mourning (*shiva*) have their origins in the Biblical period (Genesis 50:15, Leviticus 10:20, Amos 8:10); many were developed during the Rabbinic period. These laws are quite complex; they address not only the mourner's and community's behavior during the week of *shiva*, but also during the days before burial and for 11 months after the death as well. I will attempt not to detail these laws fully but instead to highlight the major elements of traditional Jewish observance (see Lamm, 1988, for an excellent discussion of all aspects of Jewish mourning and references to relevant Jewish texts).

The laws of *shiva* describe traditional mourning observance for a parent, sibling, spouse, or child, that is, for the most central and irreplaceable of relationships. The first stage of mourning begins with death and lasts until burial. Most of the laws concerning this period involve honoring the deceased. From the moment of death, the body is watched, and shortly before burial it is bathed, dressed, and placed in a casket, preferably by members of the mourner's own community. Burial itself is designed in such a way that its impact is stark—an unadorned wooden casket (or, in Israel, a shroud without a casket) is used, and at the cemetery the coffin or shroud is covered with earth by the mourner and members of the mourner's family and community. The emphasis on honoring the deceased may provide a much needed activity for the mourner who is too shocked by the death to begin the actual work of mourning. During this phase (*aninut*), all social activities as well as most positive religious requirements (i.e., laws pertaining to religious acts of ritual observance such as reciting prayers) are suspended for the mourner. Every attempt is made to shorten this period by arranging that burial take place as soon as possible and that mourning itself begin. This is considered both respectful of the deceased and in the best interests of the mourner.

The mourner first concretizes her loss in the custom of *Keriah*. At the moment of death or at the funeral, a tear is made in the mourner's outer garment. This will be worn throughout the week of *shiva*, which formally begins when the mourner returns home from the burial. The mourner washes her hands prior to entering the home (this symbolizes a cleansing following contact with death). All mirrors (traditionally associated with vanity) are covered. A symbolic meal of condolence is then eaten. It is traditionally provided by the community, not by the mourner, and includes foods associated with life, such as bread and hard-boiled eggs. A memorial (*yarzeit*) candle is lit; it will burn for the seven-day *shiva* period.

Traditionally, *shiva* (which means seven) lasts for seven days (although *Shabbat*—the Jewish Sabbath, interrupts *shiva*, and major holidays either interrupt or actually supersede the *shiva* period). Throughout *shiva*, the mourner remains at home unless the *shiva* house is elsewhere and the mourner cannot reside there for the week. The laws of *shiva* alter virtually every aspect of ordinary social behavior for both mourner and visitor. The mourner's grief is concretized in a variety of ways. Leather shoes (traditionally associated with comfort and vanity) are not worn. The mourner neither bathes nor changes clothing, especially the rent garment (exceptions are made for those who find this restriction very difficult). The mourner does not use cosmetics, cut her hair, or engage in sexual contact. The study of *Torah* (Bible) is also forbidden, as such study is believed to bring joy. The mourner is free to walk, stand, lie, or sit but only on a low stool or chair.[1] Contrary to popular belief, the chair need not be hard or uncomfortable. Instead, the low seat symbolizes the mourner's lowered emotional state. The mourner does not rise to greet visitors; in fact, the front door is left ajar in order to free the mourner from this obligation. The mourner is excused from all household tasks (cleaning, laundering, etc.) and does not prepare or serve food for others or for herself. Thus, the mourner is freed from all social obligations and distractions and is expected to be involved solely with the task of mourning.

A *shiva* caller operates under similarly unusual rules. A *shiva* call is considered its own good deed and obligation (*mitzvah*). In traditional communities such calls are paid by most of its members, whether or not they personally knew the deceased. Callers generally come unannounced at any time during the day or evening. The purpose of the *shiva* call is explicit: to support the mourner in her grief by offering an opportunity to speak about the loss and by sharing with the mourner memories of the deceased. *Shiva* callers are not permitted to greet the mourner; instead, they wait until the mourner notices and greets them. Conversation must be initiated by the mourner, who may choose to speak of the deceased or of other matters, or to remain silent. The caller does not, however, attempt to distract the mourner unless the mourner indicates such a need. Thus, at times, the caller may simply sit silently with the mourner, while, at other times, the caller may be engaged in conversation of more or less emotional depth. The caller, who is not expected to stay long, does not say good-bye, and instead utters a traditional phrase, "May God comfort you among the mourners of Zion and Jerusalem" or a somewhat formalized alternative, "May we meet again on a happier occasion." The mourner does not

---

[1] Actually, these proscriptions originally prohibited wearing shoes of any kind and sitting anywhere other than the floor. The ancient mourner was thus placed in close emotional and literal proximity to the deceased (*Tractate Semachot*, 6:1).

rise or respond to this farewell greeting, but remains seated and silent when the caller leaves.

At the end of the seven days, the mourner gets up, that is, in most respects resumes daily activities. However, during the subsequent 30 days (*shloshim*), certain activities designed to bring joy (such as attending parties) are curtailed. Many male mourners refrain from shaving throughout *shloshim*. This represents a most powerful and visible expression of bereavement. In the case of a parent's death, the mourner continues to limit social activities and festivities for a full 11 months. In addition, the male mourner (and, in some communities, the female as well) is expected to acknowledge this loss concretely by saying *Kaddish* (the mourner's prayer) daily.

The Emotional Function of Shiva

The laws of *shiva* are most complex, and in large measure derive from ancient religious tradition and beliefs about death. Clearly, *shiva* serves a variety of religious functions for the community and for the mourner. Further, because *shiva* is a social and not an analytic interchange, the intrapsychic function of the *shiva* experience, and how it is assimilated by the individual mourner, will be variable, and frequently obscure from an outsider's point of view.

In fact, the emotional meaning and function of these highly detailed rules governing behavior are rarely obvious. It is mainly within religious Jewish communities that the laws of mourning are scrupulously observed. Although secular Jews have incorporated some aspects of *shiva* ritual into mourning observance, these rituals are often followed in a truncated or perfunctory way. This should not be particularly surprising. Death continues to be a subject that is treated gingerly by contemporary culture, very much reinforcing our natural discomfort with facing such pain. It often seems easier to simply get on with life, and to relegate traditional mourning observance to the antiquated customs of grandparents. The mourner may view as excessively restrictive and time consuming the requirement to set aside a full 7 days during which to withdraw from the world and face the loss, particularly when the emotional function of *shiva* is obscure.

The Holding Function of *Shiva*

My own father died several years ago. That loss, though not altogether unexpected, was inevitably a traumatic one. It was also my first exposure to *shiva* observance from the inside. I did not anticipate the *shiva* process to be a reparative one. I had paid enough *shiva* calls to know quite well how emotionally awkward and/or difficult the process can be. The idea of being the object of such visits, of being invaded by visitors with whom I was not especially close, of having no privacy and no easy escape from social contact, was not especially appealing. I anticipated being forced into perfunctory interactions at a time when I felt absolutely unable to do so. More superficially, I was not thrilled about wearing the same clothes day after day, or about sitting on a special chair—being identified as a mourner whether I wanted to be or not.

I was thus quite surprised to find that *shiva* was an extraordinarily reparative experience. As I worked over that experience for myself, it became clear that the very structure of *shiva* observance was pivotal to the mourning process. The customs of *shiva* created a therapeutic holding environment within which I was simultaneously comforted and allowed to mourn fully.

From the moment of my father's death, I derived comfort from the knowledge that his body was cared for by my own community rather than by strangers. As I arrived at the funeral home to make arrangements, I was overwhelmed at the sight of three members of my community who were there preparing the body. Their presence and warmth transformed a traumatic process into one of comfort, wherein I felt not utterly alone but symbolically protected by people who were not themselves grieving but who were aware of my grief. At the cemetery, I found something simultaneously raw and essentially real as the unprettified pine casket was covered by my family. The possibility of denying death was absent, and its shock was intense.

I returned home to the comfort provided by my community. I was both protected from and deprived of the external distractions that might be viewed as relieving the pain of loss. I did not work, shop or cook for myself or my family. Yet I was far from alone; a stream of *shiva* callers appeared who set aside their own concerns and allowed me to talk about my father when I needed to and about other things when I did not. They came and left unrequested, and so freed me from the burden of having to ask for the company that I did not always know I needed; at the same time, they made it possible for me to remain silent when I wished to do so. Many *shiva* callers brought food; few ate mine. Some were close friends or relatives, many were more casual acquaintances, yet most made it possible for me to talk, to stay with the feelings of loss as long as I needed to. Their farewell greeting offered the comfort of community ("May God comfort you among the mourners. . . ."), reminding me that I was not alone in this experience. I felt held by these visits, by the fact that I could count both on my family and a close friend to turn up each day and the visits of people I had never been personally involved with (including someone I never met before!). I had often hesitated to pay *shiva* calls to people I knew only superficially. Most paradoxically, I found these "superficial" visits to be extraordinarily moving in that they made me aware in an immediate sense that I was part of something larger than myself and my grief. I emerged from this very intense week of remembering exhausted but relieved. My recovery did not end there, but was steady, and at the end of that year of mourning I found myself largely at peace with this loss.

How did *shiva* help? These laws alter virtually every aspect of ordinary social behavior for both mourner and visitor in ways that make the denial of death nearly impossible. In fact, *shiva* deprived me of those distractions that are ordinarily thought to relieve the burden of loss. I was forced to express my grief in multiple concrete ways, such as in my shoes and clothing, my lowered chair, and so on, which underlined my state of mourning and interfered with the possibility of "putting on a face" (false self) to the world. Yet the community's visits, even people's farewells, required no request or acknowledgment from me. The *shiva* custom that I speak first, for example, facilitated a direct response to me and to death by making it harder for the caller or for me to escape into social convention. The prohibition against ordinary greetings and farewells was awkward for many of us, yet it served as a compelling reminder of the visit's other-than-social nature.

What at first appeared to be merely many rigid rules, taken together, created a setting designed to facilitate mourning. It seems to me that *shiva* facilitates mourning by establishing an emotionally protective setting—one reminiscent of the analytic holding environment. In *shiva*, the caller, like the analyst, brackets her subjectivity in order to provide a large emotional space for the mourner. In *shiva*, the community of *shiva* callers joins together to collectively provide this hold, creating an illusion of parental attunement. The *shiva* setting involves holding insofar as it makes a demand on the mourner's community that the mourner be permitted to use people within that community without regard for its needs (i.e., ruthlessly).

Subjective Aspects of the *Shiva* Call

The holding function of *shiva* addresses a particularly important aspect of the mourning process. The provision of this holding space may, however, obscure the fact that the caller also functions as an observer or as an "enmeshed observing-participant" (Fromm, 1964; Hirsch, 1987) in the *shiva* situation. The *shiva* caller is a subjective participant to the extent that the mourner or the mourner's loss makes an emotional impact on the caller. *Shiva* calls often evoke in the caller memories of related losses (or of anticipated losses), or feelings associated with other dimensions of the mourner–caller relationship. The caller's personal reactions may result in a fuller understanding of the mourner's experience, or may become an interference, much as the analyst's subjectivity impacts on the patient. If the caller chooses to share her personal memories or reactions with the mourner, the mourner may experience a direct sense of connection to others at a time characterized by acute loneliness. Alternatively, such revelations may be disturbing and distracting, reflecting an impingement from the mourner's point of view. Although the caller's ability to make use of her subjectivity in communicating with the mourner has the potential to enhance the therapeutic effect of the visit, the structure of *shiva* is largely designed to discourage such mutual interchange. It is instead the holding function of *shiva* that predominates. Thus, the caller is expected to contain her subjectivity in order to provide the mourner with an emotionally protective setting.

The Caller's Response to the Mourner

Even those who are familiar with the "rules" of *shiva* frequently struggle with the obligation to pay such calls. It is far from easy to tolerate the tension and social awkwardness associated with death, and also to encounter what may be an unfamiliar set of people and traditions. To enter a *shiva* house and not to greet anyone, to sit in silence (often among a group of strangers) waiting to be acknowledged, can be an intensely uncomfortable experience. It can leave the caller wanting to fade away, to leave as quickly as possible, even not to have come at all. To further complicate matters, the interpersonal nature of the *shiva* call means that the caller inevitably will be affected by variations in the mourner's own emotional state.

The *shiva* call is probably simultaneously easiest and most difficult when the mourner's grief is palpable. Here, the caller's sense of emotional responsibility for the mourner is considerable. At the same time, however, the mourner's appreciative response is likely to be both gratifying and reassuring in that the *shiva* caller inevitably doubts the usefulness of the visit. The caller who facilitates the mourner's expression of intense and painful feelings may provide the deeply grieving mourner with a powerful opportunity to work through earlier painful feelings about that relationship. This requires, however, that the visitor tolerate the difficult feelings generated by the subject of loss. These feelings can be quite intense. To the extent that the caller has failed to assimilate her own feelings about death, such a *shiva* call may be acutely stressful. Even, however, the caller who has dealt directly with death must now set aside these personal experiences to be there for the mourner, who may have quite a different response to loss. The caller's availability and willingness to bracket her own subjectivity are evocative of the illusion of attunement associated with holding dependence. Here, the caller may feel moved by and care about the mourner but is nevertheless strained by the weight of this task.

For other people (or at other moments), death represents a shock too great to assimilate with overt grief. To the degree that a mourner is defended against the experience of loss, grief may emerge in a diverted form or may be apparently absent. At times, grief appears as a flat focus on the self accompanied by an apparent disinterest in and imperviousness to the *shiva* caller. Here, the mourner's self-preoccupation may tend to leave the caller feeling emotionally obliterated. When the mourner is someone with little tolerance for emotional intensity, a powerful need not to experience grief may be communicated. The mourner may behave as if nothing is wrong, as if the *shiva* call were, in fact, a social visit. In this context, the caller may feel relieved, puzzled, bored, shut out, even judgmental of the mourner's apparent lack of grief—much like the analyst in response to the self-involved patient. Although the caller may be tempted either to join in the social atmosphere or to sit silently as if it were she who was grieving, *shiva* custom requires that the caller neither introduce nor distract from the subject of death. That is, *shiva* tradition indicates that the caller must remain with the mourner *as she is* and not demand that the mourner change—in this context, express real feelings. This stance gives the mourner both space and potential contact and may permit her eventually to feel safe enough to confront, and connect to the loss in a fuller way.

To the extent that the mourner's own feelings about the death are complex, and involve guilt about past actions or inactions, or feelings of hatred toward the dead person (Klein, 1975), the mourner is likely to experience expressions of concern ambivalently. The caller's very presence may intensify the mourner's guilt over perceived failures vis-à-vis the deceased. At other moments, the caller's concern may frustrate the mourner by its inadequacy in the face of loss. The mourner may react with irritation, or respond with anger or guilt to expressions of sympathy that inadvertently evoke guilt. To say the "wrong thing" during a *shiva* call can be chillingly uncomfortable; an irritable mourner is not likely to relieve such feelings. Yet *shiva* custom suggests that the caller needs to tolerate being unappreciated, unhelpful, or even hurtful to the mourner. It requires that the caller not withdraw out of annoyance or anxiety about the usefulness of the *shiva* call. By remaining emotionally present but not intrusive, the caller communicates confidence to the mourner about the mourner's ability to survive the difficult feelings generated by the grieving process.

The holding function of *shiva*, then, creates a structure within which the mourner's need to express grief (whether complicated or simple) or temporarily to avoid, deflect, or transform grief can be met. The therapeutic function of *shiva* refers to the ways in which the laws of mourning together create an emotionally protective setting within which the mourner can experience and express a wide range of affective states in the presence of a reliable, nonimpinging, holding object.

The Paradox of *Shiva*

The paradox of the analytic relationship is similarly evident within the context of *shiva* observance. The rules of *shiva* create an extraordinary social and emotional situation. In this setting, which represents a sort of transitional space, the relationship between mourner and caller is also characterized by paradox. For a limited and circumscribed time and in a fixed setting, the *shiva* caller functions in a highly specific, rather artificial way with a person temporarily in need. Within that context, the *shiva* caller provides a therapeutic presence for the mourner. Yet the caller, even more than the analyst, cannot possibly know what the mourner's internal world is like, and may not even be personally involved with the mourner. Further, the boundary around the *shiva* experience is quite rigid and artificial; at its conclusion, the caller's responsibility toward the mourner ends absolutely.

Yet the mourner and the caller do not ordinarily challenge the meaningfulness of *shiva*, despite these realities. Instead, there is an implicit agreement not to challenge the illusion of attunement created by the *shiva* setting. It is within this space that a therapeutic process may take place. Intrinsic to this paradox is the willingness of mourner and caller not to challenge the artificiality of the *shiva* setting, and, instead, to tolerate its ambiguities.

When *Shiva* Fails

Like any therapeutic process, *shiva* sometimes fails to provide a holding function for the mourner. At times, *shiva* fails because either the mourner or the community absolutely cannot tolerate the emotional strain of the holding process. This is particularly likely when the mourner's community is unaware of or uncomfortable in following *shiva* ritual. I vividly remember a *shiva* when those present (who were unfamiliar with these traditions) sat in strained silence interspersed with small talk and self-conscious political comments as they ate a meal provided by the family. The mourner's grief had no place in this context, and *shiva* provided no relief at all. Instead, the mourner and callers colluded to avoid addressing death and thus prevented the loss from being integrated. The caller who is well versed in *shiva* ritual also may be unable to tolerate its impact, and may inadvertently interfere with the mourner's need to express grief.

At other times, however, it is not the community's emotional limitations that fail the mourner, but instead the laws of *shiva* themselves that fail to hold. *Shiva* observance is interrupted by *Shabbat*. In addition, when the death coincides with a major holiday (*Yom Tov*), the *shiva* period is either cancelled or postponed (depending on precisely when the actual mourning began) until the holiday's conclusion. In these situations, the mourner's need to grieve is overridden by the community's need for ritual observance as well as by religious beliefs about the obligation to celebrate the holiday with joy. To the extent that this failure in adaptation to the mourner's needs was preceded by a period of good-enough holding, however, it may be strengthening rather than traumatic. A break in the *shiva* experience may actually begin to draw the mourner back into life, much as a small disruption in holding may facilitate an integrative process in a patient.

At other times, however, these interruptions in *shiva* fail the mourner in a more major way. This is especially likely when *shiva* is cut off in its earliest stages. How can the deeply grieving mourner be expected to suspend or to end *shiva* in order to participate with the community in a holiday's ritual observance? The mourner often will not be able to bracket her grief simply because a holiday interferes. Holding fails here, and the mourner is left to cope with being dropped in ways that may leave her traumatically unprotected. The suspension of *shiva* observance will sometimes delay or profoundly interfere with a full working through of the loss. I have worked with several patients who had this reaction to a death that was not marked by *shiva* observance, in contrast to their fuller mourning process where death was followed by *shiva*.[2]

---

[2] It should be noted that the custom of reciting the Mourner's *Kaddish* daily, is, as with all public prayer, traditionally viewed as an obligation incumbent only on men. In recent years, however, many women have taken on this ritual in both more and less traditional communities. The recitation of *Kaddish* during the 11 months after a death represents for some a powerful symbol of the ongoing nature of the mourning process, even as the mourner progressively returns to everyday activities. To the extent that a female mourner feels herself to be denied the opportunity to pay tribute symbolically to the deceased through this act, it is possible that a mourning process may thereby be truncated.

Protection of the Caller in *Shiva*

It is nevertheless clear that, overall, the laws of *shiva* are designed for the protection of the mourner, and make powerful demands on the caller. To require that a person who may have little psychological sophistication tolerate the range of feelings evoked by a mourner and by the *shiva* situation itself is a considerable demand. *Shiva* laws do, however, take into account both the caller's and the community's vulnerability. Interestingly, the *shiva* caller is protected in ways similar to the way the analyst is protected by treatment boundaries. *Shiva* calls are short, ordinarily paid not more than once by any individual. Instead, the mourner's larger community is expected to take on this obligation. The holding function of *shiva* is thus shared by the community, falling lightly on its individual members. Although the mourner sets the tone and content of the conversation, it is the caller who typically determines the time of the *shiva* call and of its termination—retaining, perhaps, the potential to express hatred in this way.

On the seventh day of *shiva*, the mourner must "get up," whether she is emotionally ready to or not. The caller is thereby automatically freed from further obligation at the end of the *shiva* week. Further, it is precisely because *shiva* is interrupted by *Shabbat*, and cancelled by major holidays, that the community's need to remain involved in life, in joyous or religious events that supersede even the needs of the individual mourner, is reaffirmed. Like the analyst who ends sessions and takes vacations despite the patient's need for treatment, *shiva* laws place the mourner's needs within a larger context—that of the needs of the community.

It seems clear, then, that while Jewish tradition views the mourner's needs as great, they are not always paramount in that they do not consistently override the needs of the *shiva* caller. It may be that the limits placed on the mourner's needs are actually what permit the community to tolerate the very great demand that is made of it during the period of *shiva* observance. It is, of course, not uncommon that the practice of *shiva* fails to hold the mourner, because either the mourner or the community cannot tolerate the discomfort generated by such an experience. Clearly, *shiva* cannot provide a holding experience in the absence of some degree of cohesive community, yet this is absent for too many. What is nevertheless compelling is the power of *shiva* ritual to meet an individual's temporarily intense need for a holding experience in its varied aspects, while still protecting the larger group. These laws are in many ways a brilliant prepsychoanalytic adaptation to universal human need, reflecting the capacity of society to temporarily hold its members while at the same time ensuring that the community remains a going concern.

Chapter 9

Holding in Context

At this point, I would like to pause and examine some of the issues raised by an emphasis on the clinical centrality of holding processes. Although I believe that the holding process very much includes the analyst's subjectivity, and is thus relationally derived, the notion of holding has met with considerable opposition from some relational theorists. In addition, although my emphasis on the analyst's containing function parallels aspects of both Freudian and self-psychological views of the analytic task, there are points of clear divergence between those perspectives and my own.

In this chapter I address the role of holding processes within a relational framework and directly take up the relational critique of holding. In addition, I briefly consider some of the differences between my perspective on holding and those of both Freudian psychoanalysis and self psychology.

Holding and the Relational Critique

Central to my thesis is the assumption that although many patients respond to evidence of the analyst's subjective presence in ways that dramatically open up the treatment process, for others at other moments, this same subjective element is derailing (see also Slochower, 1996). It is precisely when intersubjectivity and mutuality are so problematic that I believe the holding metaphor offers a crucial therapeutic alternative. However, there also may be moments when most patients need protection from those aspects of the analyst's experience that put into question the reality of the analyst's attunement.

As I understand it, the analyst's stance during holding processes implicitly describes her capacity to engage in a way that protects the patient from aspects of her impact. That stance is inherently asymmetrical, tilted in the direction of the analyst's relatively clearer sense of the patient's needs and of her ability to meet those needs.

In what way does this perspective fit within relational psychoanalytic models? As we abandon a positivist, rational model of the analytic function, we find that the analyst is anything but an objective observer in this process (Casement, 1991; Jacobs, 1994; Fosshage, 1992). Those relational theoreticians writing from a constructivist position (see especially Aron, 1991; Hoffman, 1991, 1992; Mitchell, 1991b, Burke, 1992; Stern, 1992; and Tansey, 1992) acknowledge the dissimilarity in patient's and analyst's experiences, but challenge the analyst's emotional superiority, her relative removal from the psychoanalytic dialogue, and her affective omniscience. This perspective has been enormously freeing for both analyst and patient because it opens the possibility for more mutual contact between the two.

However, the constructivist emphasis on mutuality makes clear that the analyst's capacity to tolerate a holding position is far from immutable. Instead, the analyst is understood to be constantly vulnerable to her own idiosyncratic responses to the patient.

The relational analyst, then, can hold only imperfectly, and sometimes not at all. As we study the analyst's subjective process more closely, we come up against the limits of the implicit idealization of the holding analyst. Although Bollas (1987), Bromberg (1991), and Casement (1991) have included the concepts of both mutuality and dependence in psychoanalysis, many take issue with the notion of holding and its implications. Winnicott and others who emphasize the patient's dependence on the analyst's maternal functions have been criticized for their positivist, quasi-authoritarian perspective. In fact, some relational theorists feel that the holding concept is so severely limited that it should be abandoned altogether. Mitchell (1988, 1991a) questions the idealized position in which the analyst/mother is placed by "developmental tilt" models, and notes that the patient is consequently infantalized. He further suggests that these models sidestep the question of whether the patient's *wishes* (conflicts) or *needs* (deficits) are the central therapeutic issue. Aron (1991) believes that the "analyst as holder" deprives the patient of a complex and adult type of intimacy. Stern (1992) points out that the "analyst as mother" has limited freedom, and that her patient will be similarly restricted. He notes that the patient/baby metaphor implies that the patient is relatively unable to see the analyst in ways that are inconsistent with the empathic, mothering position. From the baby's perspective, the patient could not easily communicate such perceptions to the analyst, and the resulting therapeutic interchange would thus address a rather circumscribed area of exchange between the two.

The relational-constructivist position raises questions about the viability of the "maternal tilt" that is built into the holding metaphor. It makes quite clear that the press of the analyst's subjectivity sometimes results in its unintentional expression, even within a holding frame. Further, the relational emphasis on the inevitability of enactments suggests that the analyst is not sufficiently "outside" the analysis to offer a holding experience in a seamless way. Instead, the analyst is in an ongoing struggle with her own (sometimes dystonic) experience, with her not always successful attempt to bracket it from analytic interchange. These realities put into question both the viability of a holding process and its therapeutic efficacy.

If the analyst provides the patient with a holding experience from a position of absolute emotional certainty about her patient's needs and about her desire and capacity to give, both analyst and patient will be forced into a rather narrow and rigid relationship with one another. This relationship may seem to be so limiting that some would prefer to abandon the maternal metaphor altogether.

Nevertheless, it is my conviction that the relational emphasis on mutuality within the psychoanalytic frame, although often pivotal, does not address treatment issues raised by those clinical contexts in which the patient cannot *bear* to know the analyst and therefore finds mutuality noxious. The relational-constructivist position (like some interpersonal models) implies that the patient often already knows the analyst but cannot say so, because of her personal historical constraints and the analyst's resistances to being seen. It takes for granted that the patient will be both relieved and helped if the analyst allows for mutual interchange.

Mutuality and Collaborative Psychoanalytic Work

The relational-constructivist position assumes (paradoxically, at times with apparent certainty!) that the patient is capable of collaborative[1] analytic work (or, in Winnicott's [1969] terms, has achieved object usage). The patient who works collaboratively with the analyst can both tolerate and integrate the sometimes marked contrasts between her subjective experience of the analyst and the analyst's external, objective existence. Given a solid capacity for collaboration, mutuality represents a potential enrichment of the analytic interaction rather than a threat. However, as I have detailed in the preceding chapters, not all our patients can tolerate and make use of intersubjective process.

The current focus among relational-constructivist theorists on analytic mutuality does not address the treatment issues raised by those patients whose emotional experience requires that, temporarily, the analyst *not* be known as a subjective source of either affect or under-

---

[1] Winnicott (1969) used the term object usage to describe the patient's evolving awareness of and tolerance for the separateness of the analytic object. For reasons that will become clearer in Chapter 10, I prefer to use the term collaboration to describe the patient's capacity to tolerate the analyst's separate subjectivity.

standing. It is primarily for these very vulnerable (yet not necessarily dependent) patients that the holding experience is therapeutically necessary.

I believe it to be unfortunate that some relational theorists view this metaphor to be inextricably associated with an analyst who is complacent, omniscient, potentially authoritarian, and out of contact with her own (dysjunctive) subjectivity. It is my conviction that the holding process is in fact compatible with an intersubjective position that views mutuality to be a therapeutic goal. As I see it, the relational experience represents a hard won analytic achievement for many of our patients. It parallels the transition from the holding environment and tolerance for a single subjectivity toward collaborative interchange. When the patient can tolerate collaboration as well as holding, a new level of relatedness will emerge, for then analyst and patient can explicitly address and ultimately integrate dependence and mutuality within the psychoanalytic setting (see Chapter 10 for a discussion of that evolution). The bracketing of the analyst's subjectivity during holding is usually only necessary temporarily. It is with that caveat that I would like to address the implications of working within a holding frame for the relational psychoanalyst.

Containment and the Analyst's Subjectivity

It is not surprising that the notions of regression to dependence and of holding are associated with a Renoiresque image of the analyst/ mother, gratified by her capacity to give and evenly available to her patient/child. Superficially, the analyst/mother metaphor does suggest that the patient is a passive recipient of good-enough care, and that the analyst functions in a comfortable, even way as maternal provider. The analyst/mother may, in this sense, be viewed as an empty container, ready and willing to receive the patient's experiences.

From an intersubjective perspective, this view of the holding analyst raises serious questions regarding the fate of the analyst's dysjunctive subjectivity (see Bass's, 1996, critique). Does the holding analyst maintain the containing position by splitting off or dissociating aspects of her emotional responses to the patient? Does the analyst "become" the parental object in ways that are potentially dangerous because of the presence of dissociated or disowned countertransference elements?

Certainly, many early descriptions of the holding function did imply that the analyst's holding response is embedded in the patient's need in a highly organic way. Thus, for example, in Little's (1985) description of her analysis with Winnicott, Winnicott is described as if he always felt like doing what Little wanted him to do. Winnicott was angry with Little's mother when Little needed him to be angry; he cried with her and mourned her loss when she was ready to mourn. Winnicott's emotional presence was powerful, but idealized, at least in Little's account. There is little evidence here of Winnicott's struggle— of what happened when, inevitably, Winnicott did not feel like being, or could not be, the way that Little needed him to be. Little implies that the press of her needs was responded to unambivalently. In fact, the one time Winnicott clearly became angry with Little (when she broke his vase), Winnicott left the office for the remainder of the hour, apparently unable to find a way either to use or to contain his anger at Little in her presence.

Frequently absent from early descriptions of the holding process is an explicit consideration of how the analyst's subjectivity could be so perfectly responsive to the patient's. Many theorists either failed to address, or actually excluded from their models, aspects of their dysjunctive experience, as well as the interplay of analyst's and patient's separate subjectivities. It might plausibly be inferred that these dysjunctive elements were not addressed because they had not consciously been experienced and dealt with.

A central theme of this book is to make explicit the complexity of the relational perspective on holding by focusing on the nature of the analyst's subjective experience in work with very difficult, emotionally reactive patients. I believe that it is inevitable that the holding analyst cannot simply feel what the patient needs her to feel, and yet it is sometimes essential that she *not* use her experience directly in the work. The analyst's struggle within the holding frame leaves her in anything *but* a dissociated state. Instead, the holding analyst remains affectively alive and present precisely because of her intense struggle with all aspects of her emotional experience.

The relational critique of the holding analyst seems to assume that she stops *thinking*; that she enters into an enactment in a relatively unconscious, dissociated way. Precisely the opposite is true. The holding position requires, if anything, more active thinking than does "ordinary" analytic interchange because of the absence of explicit intersubjective dialogue. My perspective on holding does *not* describe the "unconscious" analyst who unilaterally obscures or eludes affective process; it describes the *coconstruction* by analyst *and* patient of an illusion of analytic attunement that temporarily puts into the background certain dysjunctive aspects of each party's experience. The holding position describes a complex, enriching, yet strained set of emotional experiences that involve the analyst's struggle to be both affectively present and "even" while containing the considerable tension that this can involve. Analytic holding involves *active* affective engagement. By holding, I use my response but—and this is pivotol—without explicitly addressing certain aspects of my understanding and process with my patient *for the time being*. It is most useful with those patients whose hyperalertness leaves them extremely susceptible to derailment in the face of the analyst's separate input.

From the social-constructivist position, a serious problem exists insofar as the holding analyst does not fully *experience* elements of her dysjunctive subjectivity in the moment. In the absence of such consciousness, the analytic position may become an enactment of a more serious order. First, even an explicit intersubjective exchange does not preclude the possibility that the analyst brackets or dissociates aspects of her response. This sort of dissociation might occur because, for example, the analyst needs private time and space to process, or because a particular reaction to the patient is disturbing and cannot be tolerated in the moment. Even the most relational analyst probably at moments does not introduce her subjectivity into analytic process, but instead "holds on to" aspects of her response, studying and containing them for a time, more or less along the lines I have been delineating. Although the holding analyst temporarily may bracket part of her response (for example, her discomfort in holding a dependent patient), she continues to struggle with it between sessions in a way that prevents its full dissociation or exclusion. Further, in work around issues of self-involvement or rage, the analyst is unlikely to be able to exclude fully her dysjunctive subjectivity even *in* the session and, instead, struggles to hold herself in order to hold the patient.

The Coconstructed Idealized Analyst

The extraordinarily complex nature of this bracketing process must be underlined. This complexity reflects the fact that the patient most often *participates with* the analyst in excluding aspects of the analyst's response (for example, the dependent patient may bracket *her* awareness that the analyst feels controlled). In this sense, the illusion of analytic attunement is a *coconstruction* by patient and analyst. It reflects the patient's need to experience the analyst in a certain way as much as the analyst's need to hold on to aspects of her process for the moment. I certainly agree that holding contains an element of enactment; from an intersubjective perspective, however, so do all analytic interventions. Of course, the possibility always exists that the restraint implicit in a holding position may be toxic on some level and that the very nature of the holding process may make this especially difficult to talk about. In the same way, though, efforts at mutuality, at interpretation, or any other analytic intervention have toxic potential that may become masked by the process.

It should not be surprising that the illusion of analytic attunement is central to the experience of the patient in a holding process. In fact, a central fantasy that patients often express during periods of holding involves an idealized version of the analyst.

An extremely vulnerable patient who was involved in a holding process with me said, "You are always *with* me. I count on that. This is the only place in my life where I am safe, and what makes me feel safe is that I know that you don't let me down." When I questioned this (I think I said "Really, never?"), she replied, "Yes, never. Even when you get it wrong it's not by much, and you stay here until you get it right."

What is the consequence—for me and for my patient—of maintaining this emotional position? Clearly, there is a cost for both of us. On one hand, by bracketing, rather than using my dysjunctive subjectivity within the analytic framework, I may establish a position of emotional resilience within which my patient may deepen self-experience while I function largely as a subjective object. On the other hand, that process requires that I tolerate a particularly difficult level of strain, self-doubt, and conflict about maintaining an idealized illusion of parental attunement. My patient also pays a price. Although she has the opportunity to contact split-off aspects of her internal process, she also experiences a level of vulnerability and real dependence on me that renders her highly reactive to my actual failures. Further, she is deprived of the experience of mutual interchange.

At moments like these, a more explicitly relational perspective would be an enormous relief. It would allow me to say, in essence, "Hey, there are two of us here, remember?" Yet such a stance may effectively cut off a critical process for a patient in need of a holding experience. I therefore sometimes choose to remain (quite imperfectly, despite my patient's illusion) within the parental metaphor.

Holding—Choice or Enactment?

A related question of concern to social-constructivist theorists is when, and how, one knows that what is needed is a holding experience. Does the holding function arise spontaneously on the analyst's part in response to the patient's need? To what extent does holding involve the analyst's more or less objective (positivist) assessment of the patient's emotional state? Does holding emerge out of the inherently subjective, negotiated interaction between patient and analyst? That is, in what way does the analyst who holds *choose* to do so, and how is her choice influenced by her unconscious identification with the parental metaphor?

Hoffman (1991, 1992), especially, underlines the centrality of the analyst's *uncertainty* and of her inability to "know," in any absolute sense, what the patient needs. Hoffman believes that the psychoanalytic dyad struggles together toward a deeper understanding even while both participants are continuously aware of the power of their individual subjective experiences. His position argues against the analyst's ability to engage in anything like an objective assessment of the patient's need for a holding process.

My own view is that the movement toward a holding stance involves an inherently paradoxical interweaving of the apparently objective and subjective elements in the holding situation. Simultaneous with my feeling that I choose to enter a holding process is the sense that I have, in fact, no choice except to work within a holding frame![2] The relative weight of these two elements fluctuates as a function of variations in the analytic interaction.

If my patient's responses indicate to me that she consistently reacts violently to evidence of my separate personhood, or to my even slightly discrepant emotional experience, I will begin to question the nature of our interaction. Several possibilities may emerge here. It may be that the source of my patient's difficulty involves what or the *way* that I have interpreted. Alternatively, it may be the patient's *conflicts* around recognizing some aspect of our mutual interaction that interfere, and that further exploration of these issues will open up the process. It is clearly impossible ever to be absolutely sure that holding is the only appropriate therapeutic choice. Nevertheless, when my patient's toxic reactions to evidence of my separateness and her vulnerability to emotional "misses" have a consistently adverse effect both on our work and on her outside life, I am likely to move toward a holding position.

Yet it is also clear that my decision to hold is always made under the impact of subjective factors. My sense of the patient's relative vulnerability, of the force of her need, of her anger, and of her reactivity to impingement, will always be informed by my emotional experience of her. Do I feel like mothering her? Do I feel "shut out" of the analytic interaction? Am I aware of the desire to insulate myself from my patient's anger? The more powerful my subjective response to the patient (whatever its particular color), the more likely I am to feel

---

[2] Mayes and Spence (1994) misunderstand my position when they suggest that I believe that the decision to hold is quite conscious and deliberate. It is my belief that the analyst's holding stance emerges out of a partially or quite fully *unconscious* response to the patient's communications.

forced to choose to hold. These dilemmas are cogently discussed by Mitchell (1991a, 1993), Ghent (1992), and Shabad (1993).

When a patient is able to move beyond an overt demandingness that serves to camouflage underlying vulnerability, a radical shift often takes place in the analyst's subjective experience. A patient who moves beyond neediness and expresses need (Ghent, 1992) is likely to leave the analyst in a reciprocal emotional state. From this parental position, holding feels right. Offering a response within a holding metaphor does not seem to require much thought. Of course it is possible to articulate the patient's need to experience a previously split-off or hidden vulnerability, her reactivity to analytic responses, and the positive therapeutic effect of a holding stance in allowing her a fuller experience of herself. Nevertheless, to the extent that the analyst sees herself as choosing to hold, she may be partially unaware of the powerful, mutual emotional pulls within the dyad. Her holding response has emerged spontaneously out of a complex of communications on the patient's part, some of which were not even fully registered.

The decision to work within a holding frame always requires that the analyst study what she knows about the patient. How is the patient responding to their interaction? What does she seem (both consciously and implicitly) to need? Unless I am temporarily in the throes of an intense reaction to a patient, I believe that I can hear and identify the central thrust of her communications. Although I may feel pulled emotionally in one direction or another, I struggle to find some space within which to bracket that reaction, and then to think about the patient's communications and my possible responses. In this sense, the movement toward a holding stance in part represents a conscious, deliberate choice on the analyst's part. This choice entails the analyst's assessment of the patient's emotional state and of her issues (conflicts) as well as of her needs.

The holding theme may be relevant in a variety of treatment situations where pivotal issues surround not only dependence, but also self-involvement or hate. Here again, the holding function provides a protective setting within which feeling states can be experienced without requiring that the patient respond to the analyst as a discrete other. It is quite clear that to tolerate a patient's hateful attacks or narcissistic obliteration will not leave the analyst in a position to seamlessly respond in a containing way, that is, to enact the nurturing parental metaphor. In fact, in these situations, it is most tempting to break into the holding frame with interpretations that actually function as disguised attacks (Epstein, 1979, 1987). The purpose of such attacks is to rid the analyst of the intense rage and/or helplessness that tend to be evoked when one is subjected to a continually tense analytic situation. It is similarly close to impossible to retain a position of conviction about the therapeutic efficacy of a holding process in these treatment situations. Instead, holding here involves the analyst's containment of self-doubt about her own competence and about the treatment process itself (see Chapters 4 and 5). In this sense, the maintenance of a holding stance requires considerable active struggle and internal work on the analyst's part. Inevitably, the analyst's struggle will at moments be reflected by her attempts (conscious and unconscious) to inject something of her subjectivity into the process.

I have been working for some time with John, a patient who has recently begun to articulate both his longing for and his dread of needing me. Both of these states tend to result in a sense of rage at my failures. At the end of one session that felt rather close and easy (and thus perhaps uncomfortably near to a regression to dependence), I (as usual) sat forward in my chair to signal that I was about to end the session. John reacted by looking at his watch and loudly stated that our time was not up. Slightly puzzled, I checked my clock and watch again, silently noting that according to my timepieces, the session was over.

Here, then, we were once again on the edge of the holding process; John's challenge regarding the treatment boundary placed at the center of our dialogue a multitude of issues regarding my willingness to adapt to him and the potentially disruptive effects of a break in the holding experience. The dilemma was rather dramatically clear-cut—whose clock would I go by, who got the disputed minutes?

On one hand, I wanted to prove myself to John, to reassure him of my holding potential. On the other hand, it was impossible for me to ignore the stretch of myself that this required; the tension between my perceptions and needs and John's was absolute.

It was not unusual that this quandary occurred at the end of the session, when there was literally no time. As I tried to find space within which to work, I was aware of a combination of thoughts. I was somewhat pressed for time, having a heavy schedule and a patient already waiting for me. The obvious, and in some way, easy response would be to articulate John's desire for more of me and his anger and hurt at my "stealing" from him, or more implicitly rejecting him. I was acutely aware, however, that to interpret John's protest or wish would feel horribly humiliating to him.

I felt in a bit of a bind. Should I insist that I was right and disregard his implicit request for more time in order to protect my own needs? Should I continue the session for a few minutes, and set aside my subjectivity? What of my awareness that we had both started and ended on time according to my own clocks? What would he make of my giving up my subjectivity in the face of his protest? What would I make of it? I struggled briefly with my wish to meet both his needs and my own. Finally I said, "According to my clock, which may or may not be accurate, we started and ended on time, so I feel it's time to end. I understand that it may not be time from your point of view." John sat up, looked ironically at me, said firmly, "It's not time," and left.

For many reasons, in this situation I moved out of a holding stance and intervened with John from a more separate, intersubjective position. That is, I neither fully bracketed nor deleted my subjective experience and need. Why? To what degree was my move responsive to what John could tolerate? The fact that John presented his need in a challenging rather than vulnerable manner made it easier for me to hold my own, because he implicitly showed me something of his own resilience. Additionally, however, John challenged me around an area that I use to express my own subjectivity, and he thus came up against my separateness (I do tend to keep to firm time limits). In addition, John's challenge involved a relatively objective aspect of external reality—time. My movement away from a holding position was thus probably influenced simultaneously by my awareness of real time, the press of my subjectivity, and my sense of what John could manage emotionally.

It is inevitable that even in work with extremely vulnerable patients who appear to need a holding process, the analyst only in part chooses when and how to hold, because fluctuations in the patient's experience, the shifting presence of the analyst's subjectivity, and, at times, the analyst's objective assessment of the clinical situation will all limit her capacity to maintain a holding stance. The holding position therefore cannot and probably must not dominate the analyst's work in a uniform way, but instead remains a choice or alternative. The analyst's movement in and out of a holding stance is inevitably affected by a mixture of factors that include the patient's need, the analyst's perceptions of that need, and the analyst's own subjective experience.

The inclusion within the holding theme of the analyst's subjectivity, albeit a bracketed subjectivity, places holding squarely within a relational perspective. I see holding processes to be an essential addition to the relational position. In their absence, a danger exists that we may attribute to our patients a tolerance for interpretation and for collaborative work that sometimes represent highly elusive goals.

Freudian Perspectives on Holding

It is rarely simple to take an aspect of one theory out of context and then compare it to another (Goldberg, 1988) without in some way doing an injustice to the complexities of the alternative position. Despite what I believe to be some areas of clear divergence, many contemporary psychoanalytic theories have moved in the direction of including many of the relational issues addressed in this book (Kernberg, 1993). To some extent a comparison of positions requires that differences be highlighted in a way that may partially stereotype both perspectives. With that caveat, I would like to address some of the areas of overlap and difference between my perspective and that of first some Freudian positions, and then contemporary self psychologists.

Whereas social constructivists have challenged the positivist elements in the holding stance, a positivist, quasi-authoritarian, "tilted" perspective is actually consistent with a Freudian tradition. Both left- and right-wing Freudian analysts (Druck, 1989) often do know what the patient needs. Further, although some Freudians emphasize the unique mutative effect of interpretation, many others (including Pine, 1984; Bach, 1985; Modell, 1988; and Jacobs, 1994) underline the importance of noninterpretive (holding) work—at least with certain patient groups.

The Freudian group's relatively greater comfort with a position of certainty vis-à-vis the patient's needs differs markedly from my own. The Freudian analyst's certainty tends to exclude doubt about the "correctness" of the analyst's holding stance, and to leave the analyst more or less outside the intersubjective dialogue. The Freudian holding analyst chooses to hold because she knows that this is what the patient needs. In doing so, she works to neutralize whatever countertransference responses were involved. In contrast to my belief that holding always includes at least an element of enactment, the Freudian view of holding does not see the analyst as under the sway of an enactment but rather as making a clinical decision from a position of relative analytic neutrality. Movement into a holding position derives from the analyst's diagnostic skill. Countertransference factors here represent an avoidable interference with the analyst's process rather than an inevitable contributor to the analyst's partial choice of a holding stance.

As I see it, a danger lies in this perspective on holding because it tends to protect the analyst from doubt. The analyst may be less likely to question the correctness of the holding stance, or the nature of the dynamics behind the patient's toxic response to the analyst's interpretive interventions. The analyst may also be more fully protected from experiencing her own contribution to the patient's process because of her relatively greater degree of removal from the analytic dialogue.

For the Freudian, the analyst's subjective response to the patient—whether it involves a wish to hold from a nurturing position or an effort to hold onto the analyst's anger at the patient—is problematic. Preferably it will be analyzed privately in order for the analyst to return to a more fully neutral holding position. In contrast, it is my view that analytic neutrality is actually impossible. From a relational perspective, neutrality implies defensive disengagement, because the analyst is seen to be more completely embedded in the analytic dialogue. I believe that holding processes always include the analyst's subjectivity, that the holding analyst must make use of her self-experience by simultaneously tolerating and bracketing sometimes intensely subjective affective states.

The classical emphasis on the maintenance of analytic neutrality is also, to some extent at least, incompatible with the level of (implicit or explicit) self-expression inherent in the use of affectively toned interventions that I have described, especially in work with hateful patients. From a classical perspective, such interventions would represent a countertransference acting out rather than a potentially therapeutic move. The classical analyst is far less likely to feel comfortable making direct use of her affective responses in moving toward a holding position, and instead ordinarily will try to sift out the patient's need from her response more completely than I believe to be possible.

Classical Freudian theorists do not view countertransference and transference experiences always or even usually to be intersubjectively derived. Instead, these reactions are thought to be located more or less within the subjective unconscious experience of analyst or patient. In this sense, Freudians tend not to study the interplay between patient's and analyst's process so much as to examine how the analyst reacts to the patient's transference, that is, to isolate the separate subjectivities of the individuals based on their own personal historical issues. From my perspective, a focus on two separate subjectivities may limit the analyst's capacity to address the analytic dyad as a basic unit, within which the patient's transference can never be absolutely isolated from the analyst's actual impact.

On a more theoretical level, a further area of difference concerns the therapeutic aims of psychoanalytic work. In general, classical Freudian positions (and many British school theorists as well; Symington, 1996) view the ultimate goal of psychoanalytic work to be deepened insight on the patient's part. The intersubjective aspects of analytic interchange are considered secondary to the aim of deepened insight. For traditional theorists, issues of knowing are primary within the treatment context, and the relational positions are believed to reify experience at the expense of deepened internal understanding.

Is this so? Do we pay a price—in terms of deepened understanding of individual dynamics—for our focus on the intersubjective aspects of personal experience? I certainly have struggled with this issue at times, and have wondered about the relative benefits to be accrued from a more pointed focus on internal dynamics versus intersubjective process.

In the end, however, I come to a different conclusion from that of traditional theorists. Ultimately I am not convinced that the patient or analyst can know about his or her subjective process unless they begin within the intersubjective field. In this sense, whether I am working around issues related to holding, or during what I would call ordinary analytic moments, I find myself repeatedly rediscovering how embedded the patient's dynamic process is within her experience of the dyad.

Although some traditional analysts (Symington, 1996) believe that the patient's negative reactions to interpretations reflect the presence of deep or psychotic anxieties that can be managed via interpretation and/or more frequent sessions, I disagree. Although psychotic issues may underlie the patient's reactions to evidence of the analyst's separateness, it has not been my experience that this is always the case. The patient's intense reactivity to the analyst's separate input may indicate that the patient has not fully integrated a capacity for collaborative psychoanalytic work, or for object usage in Winnicott's sense. The failure to integrate a capacity for collaboration reflects, in my view, not the presence of psychotic process, but an undeveloped or unintegrated dimension of self-experience. The patient's tolerance, albeit with intense anxiety, of the analyst's separate perspective, implies some ability to work with and integrate alien ideas about the self without excessive threat to the viability of self-experience. In the relative absence of that ability (even if there is no evidence of psychotic process), all interpretations, even about the patient's difficulty tolerating the analyst's separate understanding, tend to be highly disturbing and do not necessarily move the work forward. I have found that more frequent sessions actually may intensify rather than resolve the patient's acute reactivity if the analyst uses the additional sessions to work interpretively with the patient's anxiety. I believe that a commitment to interpretation assumes the patient to have sufficiently resolved issues around object usage. This certainly often is the case. It is only when collaboration itself results in disorganization—for whatever dynamic reason—that I turn away from issues of deepened insight and toward work around holding the patient's self-experience.

At those times, although I do not abandon a search for meaning, I silently speculate as to why the patient experiences me as he or she does. I find that I cannot actively use that understanding in the work without disrupting the patient in a way that does not result in therapeutic movement. For me, this is pivotal; if the patient can make use of interpretive understanding, there is no need for the analyst to bracket her subjectivity in such a careful way. Further, I believe that work around the holding arena, even in the absence of interpretation and externally derived insight, sometimes produces profound emotional shifts in the patient's experience. Ultimately the work may move toward a fuller elaboration of dynamic process in a way that is closer to a traditional perspective.

I would say that Freudian analysts locate the goals of the work more fully *in the patient* than in the relational arena, and herein lies the core difference in our perspectives. Freudians emphasize insight as the aim of the work. Although they may view deepened intersubjective experience to be a consequence rather than a goal of the process (Symington, 1996), I would say that insight is more of a consequence, and deepened capacity to experience self and other more of a goal. For my purposes, insight and a developed inner mental life cannot be of much value to the patient in the absence of a tolerance for intersubjective exchange. It is therefore the latter that represents my emphasis. This does not mean that I am uninterested in the patient's inner life or in meaning; it does perhaps mean, however, that I am more comfortable living "in the dark" for a bit, while addressing the nature of our interchange. I assume that eventually the patient and I will come to know about her experience and its origins because insight will evolve naturally out of the greater safety and freedom associated with a fuller capacity for intersubjective work.

Given a commitment to deepening the patient's capacity for self-experience, an emphasis on the analyst's willingness to bracket or hold her subjectivity is a paradoxical one. It represents a response to compelling evidence of the patient's intolerance for the analyst's separate input, which itself is reflective of a complex of unconscious anxieties that, for the moment, cannot be addressed usefully.

My perspective on holding reflects a relational position vis-à-vis psychoanalytic process wherein the analyst's knowledge, and insight itself, are given somewhat less weight. Of course, I may know quite a bit about the sources of my patient's difficulty with analytic interventions, for example, about underlying issues of rage, destructive envy, fear of annihilation, and so on. The question is what to do with that knowledge. It is my assumption, and frequently my experience, that work around issues of holding is followed or even accompanied (at other moments) by an investigation into the dynamics behind the patient's particular holding need. I am therefore not particularly worried by my focus on technique because I believe it to be bound up with a view of the nature of relatedness and of psychoanalytic work.

Self Psychology and Holding

My perspective on holding emphasizes the importance of the analyst's capacity to bracket aspects of her dysjunctive responses in order to remain a subjective object to the patient. In some ways, this places me close to the self psychologists' position on the treatment process. However, although our positions converge, my own work has focused on a somewhat different arena of psychoanalytic experience. That arena centers around the analyst's capacity to contain her own process, the nature of the *analyst's* subjective experience in difficult periods of work, and the centrality of paradox and illusion within the holding frame.

In part, the self-psychological perspective on the role of empathy *as a mode of observation* is closely related to my own understanding of one aspect of the analyst's task during moments of holding. Kohut (1984), Stolorow (1993), and Lachmann and Beebe (1993) all underline the importance of the analyst's use of empathy not as a technical intervention, but instead as a method of data gathering that helps the analyst understand the nature of the patient's subjective process.

Certainly, the movement toward a holding stance is predicated on the analyst's ability to experience the patient's reactivity to externally derived input. To the degree that this ability is intrinsically related to the use of empathy *as observation*, I am close to the self psychological perspective on empathy. Like Kohut, I am emphasizing the use of empathy not for the expression of affective resonance, but for information that the analyst can use to deepen her understanding of the patient's vulnerabilities.

In his more recent work, Stolorow (1994) has delineated a perspective that diverges somewhat from mainstream self psychology. He emphasizes the intersubjective nature of the psychoanalytic situation, suggesting that all experience is generated at the intersection of two different subjectivities. This is a relational stance with which I am largely in agreement. My focus is on a particular aspect of intersubjective process—its impact on the analyst's subjectivity and on her capacity to make effective clinical use of it. I understand the analyst to bracket her subjectivity during difficult periods of work in order to deepen the patient's self-experience. In that sense, my view is that when holding processes predominate, the analyst's and the patient's subjectivity do not fully intersect within the clinical interaction (although on a more theoretical level they very well may); I believe that a fuller and more mutual analytic experience requires that the patient tolerate the presence of two separate subjectivities in a way that is relatively absent during these moments.

Winnicott (1947) also recognized both the curative effect of analytic holding and the potential therapeutic impact of the analyst's empathic failures. Winnicott noted that a pivotal therapeutic element occurred when what was traumatically experienced in childhood was reexperienced within the analytic situation, this time within the patient's omnipotence. Kohut (1984) similarly viewed the selfobject experience to be intrinsically curative, but emphasized the potential mutative effect that the analysis of selfobject failures may have in the treatment process. It is clear, of course, that the therapeutic impact of work around enactments requires of the patient a level of resilience and a tolerance for the analyst's failure, at least to some small degree. Although it is inevitable that the analyst will fail the patient even during moments of holding, there are times when such failures are anything but potentially helpful. Especially during times when the patient is acutely in need of a holding experience, the analyst's failures are simply noxious in effect (Winnicott, 1963b; Fosshage, 1992).

Other self psychologists (Kohut, 1984; Ornstein, 1995) emphasize the analyst's effort to enter *the patient's* subjective world. Their emphasis on the analyst's sustained movement into the patient's process does not necessarily imply that the analyst must abandon her own. It is clear that many self psychologists view that effort to be far from easy, and regard it instead as an ongoing struggle.

However, to the degree that any theoretical perspective does not explicitly address the differences between patient's and analyst's separate subjectivities, the analyst may be quite vulnerable to a movement away from her own process. In this sense, self psychologists' relative failure to investigate the analyst's subjectivity may limit, if not exclude, the analyst's ongoing study of her process, and possibly her capacity to *hold her own experience* when it is not congruent with the patient's experience.

A focus on the use of empathy may leave the analyst in something of an emotional dilemma to the extent that the analyst is, in fact, not in tune with the patient's affective experience; here, the self psychologist tries to see things as the patient does. As Kohut (1984) explains it:

> The task that the analyst faces at such moments . . . is largely one of self scrutiny. To hammer away at the analysand's transference distortions brings no results . . . only the analyst's continuing sincere acceptance of the patient's reproaches as (psychologically) realistic followed by a prolonged . . . attempt to look into himself and remove the inner barriers that stand in the way of his empathic grasp of the patient, ultimately have a chance to turn the tide [p. 182].

In a way, of course, this is precisely what I view the analyst's task to involve—ongoing work to understand the patient's affective process. However, I am perhaps less optimistic than Kohut about the analyst's capacity to decenter, especially with difficult patients. Because I believe that it sometimes may be impossible for the analyst to decenter, I prefer to emphasize the analyst's need to study the nature of her subjective process *without* necessarily trying to shift it.

In contrast to the self psychological perspective, I believe that there may be moments, or even protracted periods, when the analyst will not find a way into the patient's process easily, and instead, must find a way to work from the outside that is not felt to be impinging by the patient. In that context, I emphasize the analyst's capacity to *hold herself* as she attempts to maintain a holding position with the patient.

A further area of difference between my position and that of self psychology lies, I believe in the core role that I view *illusion* to play. During holding processes, patient and analyst implicitly make use of illusion in order to render the holding process real and affectively powerful. The notion of illusion here implies that both analyst and patient know, at least at moments, that the holding metaphor is in fact illusory. I do not understand the self-psychological emphasis on empathy to include the notion that such understanding is at least in part based on metaphor.

Another relevant issue concerns the ubiquitous presence of a therapeutic potential within the patient. Ornstein (1995) underscores the therapeutic impact on the patient of the analyst's capacity to understand the nature of the patient's curative fantasy. Ornstein suggests that if the analyst can communicate her appreciation for the hope embedded in the patient's otherwise destructive or self-destructive actions, a healing process is set in motion.

I believe that the self psychologists tend to minimize the pathogenic power of the patient's unconscious attachments, while I am somewhat more cautious with regard to my confidence in the patient's intrinsic push toward healing. Where Ornstein appears to view reenactments to always contain a positive potential for growth, I have found that reenactments sometimes do and at other times do not reflect such potential. My position is that in fact reenactments are sometimes quite toxic in effect. Additionally, it has not been my experience that a healing potential can be contacted in all patients; instead, for some patients, a powerful unconscious attachment to self-destruction (what Joseph, 1989, called "addiction to near death") represents a formidable challenge to the analyst who wishes to help. In treatment situations with certain extremely difficult patients, I have been impressed not with the forward thrust embedded in the pull to reenact painful scenarios, but instead with the intractability of such repetitions (see Chapter 7).

Perhaps a more central difference in perspective lies in my relatively stronger emphasis on the therapeutic impact of the patient's experience of the object rather than of self-experience per se. I especially emphasize the importance of the patient's experience of the object's survival as pivotal to the emergence of a capacity for collaboration and more mutual relatedness. That process goes beyond the patient's fuller sense of being understood. Whereas I emphasize the impact of holding processes on the nature of the patient's object relationships (real and internal), self psychologists tend to focus on the impact of the analyst on the patient's self-experience. Although, inevitably, holding processes alter the self in crucial ways, I have focused on describing the evolution of the patient's relations with those internal and external objects. In this sense, I place the pivotal therapeutic leverage somewhat more squarely between patient and analyst than does the self-psychological emphasis on shifts in the patient's experience of self as understood by the analyst.

Because my perspective is deeply embedded in the analyst's subjective process, a comparison might also be made between my position and that of Schwaber (1981, 1983a, b). Schwaber argues that the focus of analytic inquiry involves a position in which the patient's subjective process is pivotal. The analyst's task involves an ongoing attempt to avoid the intrusion of her own subjectivity.

Mitchell (1993) has summarized the relational critique to this phenomenological approach, which implies the possibility that a single subjective truth exists, and would be "findable" if only the analyst could avoid interfering with the patient's process. I would merely note the difference between an analytic stance in which the analyst struggles with what she knows because *at the moment* the patient cannot tolerate her input, and Schwaber's assumption that in fact it is only the patient who ultimately knows. In this sense, I believe that the analyst's position is always informed by a combination of her own affective and cognitive responses to the patient's material, and also by the patient's subjective experience. This perspective is, I believe, a long way from a purely phenomenological approach.

Chapter 10

The Evolution of
Psychoanalytic Collaboration

Holding as Noncollaborative Psychoanalytic Interchange

Despite the crucial importance of the holding theme within psychoanalysis, a treatment model based on holding processes alone
inevitably would be inadequate. People come for treatment suffering
from a painfully limited capacity to experience the self and from a
related narrowing of experience with internal and external objects. It is
primarily the former area that is addressed by holding processes.

During moments of holding, the analyst allows the patient to treat
her as a subjective rather than an objective object (Winnicott, 1969).
She usually does not introduce her separate understanding of the
patient's process, and she brackets her own dysjunctive reactions to
the patient. The analyst thus places herself in a position that permits
the patient to experience her as if she were in an emotionally reciprocal, that is, conjunctive position vis-à-vis the patient's subjective process. Although a holding experience potentially can deepen the
patient's contact with her internal world, the analyst inevitably
remains somewhat unknown during moments of holding because of
the necessity that she bracket rather than make use of her subjectivity.
She largely remains within the illusion of parental attunement, and to
a great degree does not break into the patient's process. The assumption behind the holding stance is that even small shifts in the analyst's
affective presence will disrupt the patient's self-experience by breaking into the patient's self-elaborative process and into her perception
of the analyst.

In his discussion of the "unclassical patient," Bach (1985) notes, "For
every interpretation, no matter how empathic, always proclaims the
analyst to be someone else, over there, and serves at least the double
function of communicating content and commenting on separation"
(p. 234).

In order to facilitate the holding process, then, the analyst ordinarily
does not intrude on the patient's experience with interpretations or
emotional communications that relate to the analyst's own (subjective)

159

understanding of the patient. I, however, do not believe that the analyst always must avoid interpreting; instead, the analyst must be more careful than usual only to use interpretive interventions that fall within the patient's subjective frame. In this way, the analyst largely protects the patient from the impact of the analytic object's separately generated subjectivity. This stance allows the patient to experience projections and identifications as real rather than as subjectively perceived.

A price is paid, however, for the protection provided during periods of holding, for the patient suffers from a high degree of emotional reactivity. That reactivity leaves the patient somewhat at the mercy of the analyst's affective evenness, without much resilience vis-à-vis her inevitable variability. Ultimately, it would be far preferable for the patient's emotional state to be less hooked into the analyst's (inevitably uneven) presence at any particular moment; that is, for the patient to be able to respond to and integrate the object's variability. For this capacity to evolve within the treatment context, it will be critical that the analytic process addresses the patient's experience of the object in conjunction with an elaboration of the self. Not until the patient can tolerate the analyst's separate, alive presence can mutual relatedness be usefully integrated by the patient.

For this reason, the therapeutic effectiveness of holding processes is limited in significant ways. The holding process tends to deprive the patient of the experience of fully taking in, responding to, and ultimately integrating the reality of the analyst's externality as an object. This will require a shift out of a holding process toward *collaborative interchange*. By collaboration I mean the patient's ability to work with the analyst around the multitude of possible meanings reflected in the patient's process. Collaboration requires some ability to tolerate an ongoing awareness of the existence of a set of distinctively separate subjectivities.

I do not mean to imply that the patient who can engage in collaborative interchange necessarily sees the analyst clearly, or welcomes her interpretations or other interventions. However, a capacity for collaboration is reflected in the patient's relative tolerance for the analyst's separate and distinct, if sometimes unwelcome, understanding of the patient's process and of their interchange. Here, the patient's ability to elaborate on her experience and the transference is facilitated rather than truncated by the analyst's active yet separate engagement. Only when the analyst's separateness can be experienced by the patient to be potentially enriching rather than simply threatening, can the analyst move toward a collaborative stance from which she no longer continually brackets aspects of her own process.

Winnicott's (1969) notions of object relating and object usage refer to a closely related concept. The meanings of these terms have remained somewhat elusive, probably because Winnicott's idiosyncratic use of them is not consistent with their everyday meaning. He rather paradoxically referred to object relating as a developmental achievement that precedes object use. Object relating describes an early period during which the maternal object is subjectively rather than objectively perceived, and the infant is allowed an experience of omnipotence vis-à-vis that maternal object.

In my view, it is the experience of analytic holding that allows the patient to acquire a capacity for object relating (Slochower, 1994). The holding situation facilitates object relating precisely because the analyst assumes a posture which does not require that the patient sift out the projective from the real aspects of the analytic object; in that sense, the object remains subjectively perceived.

The concept of analytic collaboration is predicated on Winnicott's (1969) notion of object usage. He used object usage to describe the acquisition of a secure awareness of the object's autonomous existence, of the patient's capacity for loving and hating without threatening the object's survival. Object usage describes the emotional tolerance for the object's externality that is essential if collaborative work is to take place. Winnicott (1969) wrote:

> In the sequence one can say that first there is object-relating, then in the end there is object-use; in between, however, is the most difficult thing, perhaps, in human development; or the most irksome of all the early failures that come for mending. This thing that there is in between relating and use is the subject's placing of the object outside the area of the subject's omnipotent control; that is, the subject's perception of the object as an external phenomenon, not as a projection . . . after "subject relates to object" comes "subject destroys object" (as it becomes external); and then may come "object survives destruction by the subject" . . . From now on the subject says: "Hullo object!" "I destroyed you." "I love you." "You have value for me because of your survival of my destruction of you." [pp. 89–90].

I use the concept of collaboration in a way that assumes a capacity for object use but explicitly includes its relational implications. It is only when the patient can use the object that collaboration with the analyst becomes possible. The capacity to enjoy fuller and deeper object relationships is dependent on the ability to experience the object's separateness in a nontoxic way.

Winnicott did not explicitly address how he viewed the connections between holding, object relating, and object usage. He seemed, however, to imply that a capacity for object usage spontaneously evolves out of a good experience of object relating. In contrast, I regard the shift from a position in which the object is subjectively perceived to one where its reality can be tolerated to be a most difficult and complex treatment process. It involves an interplay between moments of holding and failures in holding, and ultimately represents a critical juncture in the evolution of a capacity for collaboration.

Holding and the Evolution of Collaborative Interchange

To the degree that collaborative analytic process is a treatment goal, the holding experience ultimately is not. Despite its ubiquity within psychoanalytic work, holding limits the patient's capacity to tolerate and make use of the analyst's subjective presence. It is my belief that holding processes provide a bridge toward collaboration by facilitating an increased tolerance for subjective process. That tolerance will not be fully evidenced, however, until the patient can work with evidence of the analyst's external existence to further her own affective elaboration; when the analyst's separate contribution to that elaboration represents a potential enrichment rather than a derailment to the patient.

Although I understand the development of a capacity for collaborative analytic work to represent a treatment goal, I do not view this evolution to be unidirectional. The need for holding experiences pervades the lifetime, and the analytic process as well. Nevertheless, I view the treatment process to aim for a decreased need on the patient's part for the analyst to bracket her subjectivity. Ideally, moments of holding will evolve into a more peripheral aspect of the work, as a capacity for collaborative investigation is deepened.

I would like to address the nature of the evolution of analytic process from holding toward collaboration. It is my assumption that the holding environment itself is pivotal in facilitating a movement toward collaboration. Although that process is most clear and complete in work with schizoid patients, it also is evident in treatments dominated by other core issues. I therefore first will describe how collaborative process evolved in an analysis dominated by a holding process around dependence, and then will address the emergence of a capacity for collaboration in work with patients whose core issues involve self-involvement or ruthlessness and hate.

Holding Dependence and the Evolution
of Collaborative Interchange

David[1] was an intelligent and sensitive man who entered analysis complaining of intense anxiety despite relatively good external func-

---

[1] This case is also described in Slochower (1994).

tioning. During the first few years of treatment, he engaged in an apparently open way, presenting both current difficulties and earlier experiences with clarity and directness. However, David was oddly unaffected emotionally by the analytic process. He described his internal experience only from the outside, resulting in a subtle but ongoing sense of "as if" that pervaded our interchanges. When I brought this up, David indicated with difficulty that he was not prepared to be vulnerable with me. We were able to analyze how this experience recapitulated his relationship with his emotionally fragile mother, and with his literally absent father. Such work seemed important, yet at the same time made no impact on my (or his) experience of this somewhat detached, "as if" treatment. Even transference work reflected both David's inability to relinquish false self defenses, and his very sensitive awareness of what he "should" be doing in treatment.

While the first three years of analysis resulted in some gains in the evenness of David's external functioning, these gains were small and did not seem to reflect the depth of the analytic work. It was not until the fourth year of analysis that a noticeable shift occurred in the emotional tone of the sessions. Shortly before my vacation, David experienced a serious rejection at work that greatly undermined his somewhat defensively independent stance and his complacent sense of security at his firm (this rejection appeared to result from a shift in management goals rather than from David's performance). For the first time, David reacted with anxiety to my impending departure. David had never before permitted himself to feel, let alone acknowledge, a sense of dependence on another person. The riskiness of this position was evident in the shaky, sometimes terrified tone with which David presented himself, and from his overwhelming relief when he felt fully understood.

As David moved with such intensity into a dependent position, I found myself moving toward a holding one. With David, my holding stance very much included interpretive work. We addressed the nature of his early experience with a brutal father and a depressed mother; his precociously developed sense of autonomy and the vulnerability that it masked; and his terror of relatedness with its inherent risks. David continued to bring in dreams, memories, and associations and to make good use of our work around all of these.

How, then, did our work involve a holding process? First, the tone of our sessions had extraordinary emotional power. During this period of time, David made use of me almost exclusively as a protective parental presence. He expressed his dependence on me and his sensitivity to my reactions quite directly. As long as my emotional presence felt "right" to him, we worked easily and deeply; however, my failures to understand felt devastating to David. David's emotional reactivity was intense. I could fail by being moments late for a session, by mis-understanding the feeling state he was describing, or by sounding even slightly emotionally "off" in any way. I was aware of David's (and my) fantasy that he was my child, and of my extreme care in finding the right words and emotional tone to use with him.

During this period, David experienced much of his (very compe-tent) external functioning as "fake" (i.e., reflecting false self-adapta-tion) because so little of his internal experience was integrated therein. David frequently articulated how much he needed me to temporarily retain aspects of real life functioning for him.

> I need you to do the things my parents couldn't do—to be calm and reassuring and like an emotionally present mother, only here for me. But I also need you to hold onto the outside for me—to remember and to remind me that I do function well in the world. Also to keep track of what we're doing, of what the limits should be and to take care of everything in here. I need you to have confidence that I do manage things on the outside, because I sometimes forget. Then I think I really will fall apart.

David's involvement in a holding process around dependence was such that he bracketed much of his awareness of my limitations as well as of his strengths. He seemed relatively oblivious to my subjec-tive experience of him in this dependent state. My own experience with David was similar to that described with Sarah (Chapter 3). I felt enormously involved in the work and attempted as much as possible to provide a protected space for David. I also felt some strain, although considerably less than I had felt with Sarah. My greater sense of freedom with David was probably due to the fact that David worked so intensely and moved so quickly that I did not find myself in a holding situation that felt stagnant and without end.

Over the course of that year, David's tolerance for emotional contact deepened progressively, and with it, his personal relationships shifted so that he experienced intimacy for the first time and a new pleasure in sexuality. In this sense, at first one might view the holding experience to have largely effected its therapeutic goal. However, on closer examination, it becomes abundantly clear that this is a considerable overstatement. David continued to suffer from an extreme sensitivity to other's failures to respond "just right." He was, from his point of view, far too reactive to the emotional variability of people in his life (including me). This should not be particularly surprising. During this period of dependence, David's need for a highly adapted level of affec-tive responsiveness predominated. As a result, he remained at the mercy of my ability to stay sufficiently attuned so that this tenuous balance was not disturbed.

This phase of treatment had permitted David sufficiently to relinquish false self functioning so that the exposure of more deeply felt experience became possible for the first time. It was through a presentation of these aspects of his internal life that David made himself directly vulnerable to me. During this period, however, it felt essential to David that I not fail him, for he was not able to be angry with me as an external object. When I was "off" even a bit, David tended to retreat into a defensively hopeless position.

In this sense, the analytic holding setting did not move the therapeutic work in the direction of a capacity for collaboration. To the degree that it precludes the possibility of knowing both self and object simultaneously, it describes what ultimately is a highly limited level of contact. When the patient cannot allow the analyst to work from a position of partial separateness, the patient cannot experience a deeper sense of self in the context of truly intersubjective interchange.

For these reasons, the analytic holding environment, like the infant's experience during the early holding period, is by necessity a temporary state of affairs. Just as the mother cannot tolerate remaining at the literal mercy of her infant's needs for long, so analyst (and patient) within a holding situation are under considerable strain. The analyst's need to reassert her subjectivity creates a pressure that may result in a gradual process of deadaptation to the patient's need for near perfect holding. At times, the patient also may tend unconsciously to push the analyst in this direction because of the intolerable sensitivity that is an intrinsic part of the holding experience. The transition toward more mutual collaborative work will represent a solution to this dilemma.

The Evolution of Collaborative Process

Thus, despite the therapeutic potential of the holding environment, its gradual dissolution is, paradoxically, as essential as was its establishment. In order to move toward a collaborative process, the patient and analyst must gradually abandon the protection and the limits of the holding situation. In fact, when the patient and analyst begin to move out of a holding process, what becomes central is the analyst's willingness to tolerate alternately being experienced as a real, external object and as a subjective one. Winnicott (1969) noted that as an external object, the analyst is potentially vulnerable and is also capable of retaliation. The shift toward collaboration will thus involve testing by the patient—testing of the safety and reliability of the analyst's separateness, the potentially destructive effects of the patient's love and hate, and the analyst's ability to survive.

Much of the psychoanalytic literature has addressed Winnicott's concept of object usage by emphasizing the analyst's survival of the patient's destructive attacks (Pizer, 1992). When the analyst survives such attacks, the patient is reassured (on a powerful unconscious level) both about her own destructive potential and about the analytic object's resiliency. Only when the patient is sufficiently confident that neither member of the analytic dyad is vulnerable to destruction can collaborative process take place.

The possibility that two separate subjectivities can coexist in ways that are mutually enriching can, I believe, also evolve in more subtle, less overtly aggressive processes. At times, that discovery may be the consequence of the patient's exposure of her ruthless love for the analyst (Winnicott, 1963c). Ruthless love describes the all-out quality of the infant's love for the mother, which frequently lacks an awareness of the mother's own vulnerability. Such expressions of love for the object can have destructive potential although they are not intentionally destructive (e.g., the eagerly nursing infant can squeeze the mother's breast too hard). In a similar way, the intensity of the patient's affective connection to the analyst can be hard for the analyst to take at times, because the analyst must contain, unexpressed, a sense of being overwhelmed and even exploited by the patient's ruthlessness. Yet it is critical that the analyst accept and survive the patient's expressions of such love.

I suggest, though, that at other moments a new openness to collaborative interchange may be reflected in the patient's very quiet discovery of the analyst-as-external-object. That discovery may be based on nothing more than an apparently small indication of the analyst's otherness that is noticed for the first time. This otherness may be used by the patient to facilitate a transition from the holding position within which the analyst remains a subjective object. Overt aggressive attack is not involved here in that the patient does not attack the analyst for her otherness. However, in order to situate the analyst as an object in the world, the patient may temporarily need to destroy the analyst *as she was subjectively known*. The transition from holding to collaboration requires that the patient make the analyst over in a way that more fully includes the analyst's externality. Part of that process may include the patient's rejection of aspects of the analyst as she had been. The analyst's survival of destruction here implies her willingness to be remembered incorrectly or misunderstood (Winnicott, 1963b) without correcting the patient's perceptions. This process will be therapeutic for the patient only if it is accompanied by the analyst's genuine recognition of the real (i.e., not "merely" subjective) elements in the patient's attack.

It seems likely that the evolution of collaborative process involves mutual movement by patient and analyst. That is, the analyst unconsciously may exert pressure on the patient to recognize the reality of her separateness in response to subtle cues on the patient's part that some tolerance for difference is now possible. Alternatively, the patient may make the first move toward collaboration; however, unless the analyst responsively shifts toward a more separate position, a mutual collaborative process is unlikely to develop.

As David developed a partial capacity for collaboration, he became increasingly able to react to my real presence; I, perhaps responsively, moved out of a holding position, and introduced aspects of my subjectivity into our exchange. This occurred, for example, when a change in my schedule needs led me to request that David temporarily change one of his session hours. During the acute period of dependence, I had avoided changes whenever possible; when they did occur, David reacted with distress and even disorientation. His upset reflected the anxiety that I could not, after all, be counted on. This time, the reality of my teaching schedule made my need to change our time urgent. However, I was also aware of feeling somewhat more freedom and relatively less anxiety about introducing the disruption. Certainly, the absoluteness of my need bolstered my comfort with making the request. However, I also sensed a shift in David to which I responded with a new freedom of my own.

David responded to my request for a time change with anger. He accused me with passion of putting my selfish needs ahead of his own, and of only pretending to be concerned about the effect of this change on him. When I agreed that in fact I was putting myself first, David responded with quiet fury. He seemed to be attempting to destroy me as an object of dependence. David called me a faker, declaring that he could no longer trust me and that all our good work had been a sham, that is, that I could not be counted on.

This was a difficult period for me; although I felt a measure of relief in David's anger and in his movement out of a dependent position, I found his massive frontal attack (or destruction) of the entire treatment hard to take. However, although I was tempted to remind him of the far more shaded nature of his experience and of the positive changes that had already taken place, ultimately I contained myself. Instead I confirmed to David that I was behaving selfishly (i.e., that I did exist as an object in the world), but that I had confidence in our ongoing work (in myself as both bad in the present and potentially good). I tried to communicate a comfort with his hatred of me that simultaneously underlined my awareness of our ongoing connection.

The next few months of treatment were focused largely on David's efforts to assess my capacity to survive his anger, ruthlessness, and scrutiny. Increasingly, David became openly confrontative of my failures to hold, and demanded that I change. At the same time, he made use of aspects of my character and life that he had noticed for the first time. He was now especially intent on defining what he viewed as our differences. For example, he discovered by chance that I have children, while he did not. This had meaning to him far beyond the potential threat posed by these symbolic siblings. David accused me of being caught up in "bourgeois" family life and therefore not capable of understanding him. He repeatedly challenged my capacity to bridge the gap between us, and accused me of having seduced him into believing that I could help him. I tried explicitly and undefensively to accept his doubts and views of me and to maintain a matter-of-fact stance that did not involve explanation, interpretation, or attempts to rectify a failure. Interpretations tended to push David back into an intellectualized position vis-à-vis his experience. Explanation, reassurance, or overt repair on my part left him feeling either that his anger had not been justified, or that I could not tolerate his scrutiny.

David's responses to these disruptions were intense, and seemed to put into question the viability of our relationship. At times he felt convinced that we were so different that I could not possibly help him. However, we repeatedly survived these episodes, returning periodically to his feelings of dependence. David subsequently struggled with the worry that I had been injured by his anger. His feelings of guilt regarding his actual attacks on me (rather than his fantasies) and his concern for my feelings surfaced for the first time. Gradually, David began to respond to me as if he were not quite as fragile as before. He reported with amazement that an extraordinary shift had taken place in his life. Within a few weeks' time, David felt able to sever several emotionally untenable relationships to which he had felt bound; he sought and found a very desirable new job with a firm that clearly appreciated his talents; and he began, for the first time in his life, to attend to his appearance by purchasing a new wardrobe. His understanding of these changes was characterized by joy.

> It's incredible to me. I am all here. It's as if I got free of my family and of you for the first time. I finally said no to them, drew a line and found myself. I know it's because of our work. It was your being there for me, but even more your being able to be—to take my being mad or unreasonable or wanting all of you without collapsing. You weren't afraid and you didn't lose confidence either. That meant everything.

David's new capacity to tolerate my separateness was powerfully demonstrated at the beginning of one session. Throughout our work,

David had rarely made direct eye contact with me at the beginning or end of sessions, and when he did, it was to scan me with some anxiety, because David felt that our connection hung in the balance and would be determined by what he saw. That day, however, David looked at me directly as he entered, smiling slightly, and maintaining eye contact until he lay down. David spoke haltingly and with much feeling about the fact that this was the first time he had allowed himself to actually see me—to see me as myself, as different from him in ways that were no longer so threatening. There was room for both of us in the analytic dialogue, and David recognized this.

This moment was for me both enormously moving and a relief. For the first time, I felt seen, and the strain that had accompanied my struggle to contain aspects of myself dissolved for that moment. Although our sessions did not progress in a linear way, I increasingly felt free in our work and aware of the strength within David as we struggled together to deepen his experience.

David continued to develop his own sense of strength and inner emotional integrity at an impressive and steady rate. Now, what had felt to him like false self functioning was again real, and he was able to bring his competent self-experience into the treatment setting. He was increasingly free with me—free to express his poignantly felt gratitude and loving feelings as well as his rather accurate and critical perception of my limitations and failures.

During the next year of analysis our work continued to alternate between moments of holding and failures in holding, to which David responded with distress or anger, but with increasing confidence in his ability to ride out the disruption. Over the subsequent years holding receded markedly as a treatment theme. As we increasingly engage in collaborative analytic work, David persists in his struggle fully to integrate the reality of my separate subjectivity; periodically, he attempts to identify and sometimes to powerfully challenge me around an aspect of my work or of my person that has been revealed to him. However, as his own capacity for self-definition evolves, David is at times able to see me for myself and to deal directly with me without great anxiety.

Collaboration and the Analyst's "Failures"

Paradoxically, then, it is the establishment of a reliable holding situation that allows the patient to stage a failure, or even a trauma, within the analytic setting and then to integrate that experience. The latter is the pivotal element in "cure" as Winnicott (1963b) saw it:

But even so, the corrective provision is never enough. What is it that may be enough for some of our patients to get well? In the end the patient uses the analyst's failures, often quite small ones, perhaps manoeuvred by the patient, or the patient produces delusional transference elements . . . and we have to put up with being in a limited context misunderstood. The operative factor is that the patient now hates the analyst for the failure that originally came as an environmental factor, outside the infant's area of omnipotent control, but that is *now* staged in the transference.

So in the end we succeed by failing—failing the patient's way. This is a long distance from the simple theory of cure by corrective experience. In this way, regression can be in the service of the ego if it is met by the analyst, and turned into a new dependence in which the patient brings the bad external factor into the area of his or her omnipotent control, and the area managed by projection and introjection mechanisms [p. 258].

The patient's capacity to tolerate and address trauma develops in conjunction with her deeper access to internal process within the protective holding setting. The protective space created by the holding position permits the patient fully to experience and respond to the analyst's failure in ways that were not previously possible. Winnicott focused on the patient's integration of trauma, now within the arena of control. I would add that the relational matrix is also enormously expanded in this process. Only as the patient becomes able to integrate the analyst's failures without a loss of self-experience does intersubjective collaboration become possible within the analytic dyad.

The provision of a reliable analytic holding environment permitted David to develop his capacity to tolerate a deep level of personal experience. However, the move toward a more fully collaborative process required that he be able both to react to, and ultimately integrate, disruptions in the holding experience without losing either himself or me.[2] The almost perfectly attuned holding environment must become imperfect, through either spontaneous analytic failures or the patient's ability to make use of aspects of the analysis for this purpose. It is through the discovery of the analyst's subjectivity, and of her willingness to tolerate being loved and hated as an external object, that collaboration begins. It is often, though not always, true that apparent analytic failures actually represent unconscious attempts on the analyst's part to renegotiate the boundaries of the treatment interaction.

---

[2] As I discussed in Chapter 3, Kohut (1971, 1984) also addressed the integrative effects of "optimal" empathic failures in treatment. His focus, however, was on the effect of these failures and the analyst's empathic response to the patient's selfobject relationships. My emphasis is on the patient's experience of the object, and especially on the patient's capacity to view the external object objectively, and not just subjectively. It is thus the object's capacity to survive the patient's anger that is critical. Here, the therapeutic centrality of analytic failures is believed to be temporary, and part of a developmental progression rather than an ongoing curative factor in treatment.

At other times, it seems as if the patient creates a failure in order to push the (excessively?) attuned analyst into a more fully external position.

The Analyst's Subjectivity and the Evolution of Collaboration

The analyst's difficulty establishing and maintaining a holding environment is paralleled by the complex strains involved in the period of transition toward collaborative interchange. The analyst may derive considerable gratification from the holding stance, especially with a dependent patient (see Chapter 3). This gratification is related to her emotional centrality in the patent's life, to her feeling that the patient is being saved by the work of holding. The analyst's position as a good object is preserved in the patient's mind and in her own eyes and this may offset the strain inherent in the work. Consequently, considerable resistance to a disruption in holding may arise on the analyst's part. Whether unconsciously motivated by efforts at moving toward collaboration or not, the patient's experience of the analyst's failures is likely to result in the patient's disillusionment with the analyst, and may tend to disrupt the analyst's own "good analyst feeling" (Epstein, 1984, 1987). In response, the analyst may attempt to maintain a holding position beyond the patient's need for it, and to respond to the patient's anger by placating the patient rather than by meeting the anger directly.

At the same time, a strain exists that may tend to push the analyst toward prematurely abandoning the holding stance. During moments of holding, the analyst must fully contain her own subjectivity in order to provide the patient with the protection required. Over time, maintaining a holding stance may feel increasingly wearing, particularly when the analyst is unable to use this subjectivity creatively by interpreting. The analyst may wish, at times, to make herself known by breaking into the holding position. Additionally, the strain of maintaining this level of evenness may leave the analyst wishing to be done with it already and for the patient to grow up and free the analyst to be her inevitably variable self. At moments, the analyst may therefore tend to create premature breaks in empathic holding.

In David's analysis, I was well aware of the gratification I derived from my importance to him, and especially from his powerful positive therapeutic reaction to our work. His anger disrupted this, and it was with considerable difficulty that I contained my anxiety in the face of his angry reaction and resisted my impulse to fix my first major "error"—to withdraw the time change request. Allowing myself to fail David also meant tolerating being perceived from the outside, as real, selfish, very human, and thus not as a subjective object. Both relief and loss were involved here. I was simultaneously aware that my desire to reschedule David's hour derived from a growing sense of impatience with the pressure I was under to be absolutely consistent with him. I felt, at times, a need to be known, to break into the purity of his experience in order to be acknowledged as a separate and real object in the world, free to have a variety of feelings with him and about him. I was not at all certain until afterward that my desire had emerged at least partly in response to David's growing readiness to tolerate my very imperfect subjective presence.

Interestingly, David made use of real breaks in holding and at other times created "failures" in order to continue this work. That is, David sometimes reexperienced and reworked an aspect of my response in a way that permitted him to become angry with me retrospectively. These disruptions usually occurred following a smoother period of holding, and again seemed to permit a transition toward collaborative work. For example, several months following David's rejection at work, he became quite angry with me for having failed to forewarn and thus protect him. I struggled with a sense of being unappreciated, and with an angry desire to defend myself. After all, how could I have known this would happen? Yet what was therapeutic at those moments was my avoidance of explanations or declarations of my innocence reflecting a desire to restore my good intentions in his eyes. By communicating my willingness to be seen as bad, I confirmed for David both my capacity to survive intact and his ability to view me as an objective and not subjective object.

Object Probing and the Analyst's Subjectivity

In his important discussion of the notion of object usage, Ghent (1992) proposed that the term object probing might better describe the dynamics of the process by which a patient moves from object relating toward object usage and that object usage would better reflect the final achievement of that phase.

> As I see it, there is an evolving reciprocity between the process and the goal of object usage such that I tend to use the term "use of the object" both for the process, which involves destruction of the subjective object, and for the goal, namely, the capacity to use the object. A spiraling evolution in the capacity for object usage is probably never fully complete. If I were to seek a term that distinguishes between the process and the goal, I think I would employ the term *object probing* for the process and *object usage* for the capacity, the goal. Probing implies a degree of "penetration" and effort to reach and recognize that "use" does not. It carries also the connotation that there is a possibility that what is being probed, or proved, could break and be destroyed by the process, hence fail the implied test [p. 150].

Ghent here underlines the real risks involved in the transition toward object usage, and thus the possibility of failure.

I find that the term probing is also far more evocative of the analyst's subjective experience during this period. How *does* the analyst experience this process? Being "probed" can leave me feeling simultaneously quite exposed, alive, and "poked at," alternately clearly seen (or felt) and quite unseen. Both David's accusations and his observations of me were sometimes painfully accurate and sometimes uncomfortably skewed. However, in addition to my intermittent discomfort at being seen so clearly (or in so distorted a manner), David's intense probing of me and my aliveness and the powerful contacts that followed were also oddly satisfying. This transition toward object usage had resulted in my own freedom to feel more fully with David. It seems to me that an emphasis on the analyst's survival of the patient's destructive attacks tends to obscure the possibility that the analyst also may derive real pleasure from the patient's probing. The mother's response to the baby's not always gentle examination of her face and body may contain an element of "ouch," but often is simultaneously highly pleasurable. The analyst's reaction to her patient's all-out use of her may also confirm her own aliveness and her internal richness in a highly gratifying way.

The Evolution of Collaboration With Self-Involved Patients

David's analysis describes the evolution of a capacity for collaborative work in the treatment of an extremely vulnerable, rather schizoid patient. In such analyses, a holding theme may unfold relatively spontaneously as the patient's resistances to dependence are resolved. Yet holding, object probing, and collaboration are also relevant in treatment situations with more difficult, self-involved patients.

In work with patients who struggle with severe narcissistic issues, a holding stance is unlikely to emerge organically because these patients persist in defending against dependence even while needing a holding experience (see Chapter 4). In this sense, the analyst may find herself frequently working within a holding frame even before the patient can allow herself to need or to collaborate with the analyst. With self-involved patients, holding keeps the analyst a nonperson, and permits the illusion of self-sufficiency (Modell, 1975) to be maintained. The analyst is not present as either an objective or a subjective object but rather as a container. It is the *resolution* of the holding phase that allows the patient a direct experience of the analyst. Only then can the patient begin the process of object relating in a way that includes the patient's real dependence on the analyst. The evolution of a capacity to tolerate any level of need for the analyst is often quite gradual, and, in many cases, treatment may be terminated before a solid level of collaborative interchange has been reached. Collaboration may remain partially elusive because these individuals have such difficulty contacting intense experiences of dependence, love, and object-related hate.

Alice, an artist in her mid-30s, entered treatment complaining of a pervasive though low-level depression and difficulty making connections with men. She appeared to be considerably younger than her chronological age, and had a rather sulky, schoolgirl appearance. Somehow, nothing was ever right for her, and she frequently complained about how dissatisfied she was with her parents' gifts, their overtures of help, her friends' availability, and so on. Although Alice received my input regarding what was "off" about, for example, her parents' responses to her, she was absolutely intolerant of any attempt on my part to investigate her own impact on those interactions. At times I attempted to shift the work slightly by focusing on Alice's chronic sense of dissatisfaction and its effect on others. I tried to engage her in an active way around the possibility that people were put off by her irritable discontent, and that this ultimately contributed to her hurt feelings. However, my efforts to work with her anger and injury were not especially fruitful; Alice remained sulky and unresponsive as I tried to address how I had upset her in a way that included her own participation. Only when I remained altogether within her frame and indicated simply how misunderstood she felt by me did she become slightly more accessible and less withdrawn. This pattern persisted over months despite my efforts to enter the process from a variety of angles. It became clear that Alice could not yet tolerate an active investigation of her process *from the outside.*

As I moved toward a holding position with Alice, she gradually elaborated on her own experience, especially vis-à-vis her parents, with whom she was actively involved. Over a three-year period, Alice became progressively more conscious of her process and more able to articulate her experience directly, rather than silently accusing others with angry or hurt silences. Alice's relationships with her parents improved, and she gradually developed a less intensely reactive stance toward people in her life. Although she always had a fairly active social life, she did not yet feel deeply connected to a man.

I view this period of our work to have largely focused on the process of self-elaboration, with a fairly minimal investigation of Alice's impact on the object. Alice did not appear to have especially strong feelings toward me outside of her reactions when she felt me to be critical of her. Instead, she treated me like a consultant, and almost always behaved "appropriately," denying or avoiding transferential aspects of her responses. In this sense, the holding process had not yet permitted Alice fully to expose all aspects of her affective experience. Alice also did not take me in *as a subject* in my own right, and in that sense she reacted to my input largely in terms of its relative good fit with her own understandings. She expressed neither anger nor need vis-à-vis me or the treatment, and maintained a somewhat distant though friendly stance.

By the end of the third year of our work, Alice had become a bit more able to tolerate my input. She emerged partially from a self-involved stance that excluded the possibility of a second subjectivity. In this sense, Alice acquired a slightly greater capacity for collaboration; she began to express need for others in her life, and her dreams now contained a quality of affective vulnerability that was not always covered over by narcissistic rage. At times Alice seemed to need a second holding process that involved dependence rather than self-involvement. It is notable that her dependent feelings were contained within moments or sessions. I view this shift to reflect a crucial movement in the direction of a deepened potential for collaborative work.

Now (several years later), Alice continues to relate to me more or less as an object without my own subjectivity. However, a shift is evident in her intimate relationships outside the treatment; she increasingly is able to make room for the experience of others even as she struggles with her own responses. What remains to be seen is whether Alice will be able to tolerate the intensity of feeling involved in a fuller movement toward collaboration. I still feel that she partially mutes her own responses. In this way, she protects both herself and the object from the intensity of her affective state.

It has been my experience that severely narcissistic individuals do not usually remain in treatment for as long as Alice. It is not often that these patients can altogether work through the vulnerability that is an intrinsic part of the holding experience and the shift toward collaboration. Alice has remained in the work for an extended time period. She has used it first to elaborate and integrate aspects of her own process, and later, her impact on others. She has not, however, been able to tolerate the full and intensely risky affective states that inevitably accompany loving, and in this sense, the movement toward collaboration remains incomplete.

Hateful Patients and the Evolution of Collaboration

In other treatment situations where the patient struggles with issues of hate and of self-hate, holding may allow the patient to assess the analyst's ability to tolerate her complex and intensely negative feelings (see Chapter 5). Emotional communications are often based on unconscious feelings of rage and envy and take little notice of the analyst as an external object. Here again, holding will precede the experience of dependence and of collaboration. The analyst must first establish the viability of the treatment setting before the patient will feel it safe to react to her actual (not projected or "staged") failures. For these patients, both holding and collaboration involve the exposure and analysis of the patient's hate. The final and most difficult analytic work requires that the patient test the analyst's capacity to receive and tolerate dependence. The patient then may need a second holding experience (in which dependence is held) before moving toward collaboration.

Robert had been working with me for a fairly short time when I first experienced the rather subtle but unremitting quality of denigration that would later pervade the work. Robert was a highly intelligent businessman with a background in psychology and a sophisticated understanding of psychoanalytic theory. He spent much of the treatment engaged in an apparently cooperative investigation of his relationships and his considerable difficulties dealing with both men and women. I caught onto the fairly embedded way in which he put me down when he noted with some condescension that I was repeating something I had previously said. When I addressed his tone directly, he acknowledged irritation but insisted that he was simply annoyed at me for wasting his time; there was no dynamic meaning to his reaction —it was entirely understandable, justified, and deserved.

Over time Robert became increasingly consistent in his way of responding to me; he would appear to be engaged in an analytic process, and then would react to my statement, question, or silence with a tone that communicated contempt even where his words did not. Robert sometimes acknowledged how critical he was of me. For example, I wasn't a real analyst because I had a Ph.D. and not an M.D.; I was not a classical Freudian (he deduced this because I practiced in my living room). Robert concluded that I was therefore theoretically unsophisticated. He insisted that such observations were simple realities, and did not deserve to be further investigated. On a few occasions I was extremely active in confronting Robert with how denigrating he was. The impact of my confrontation was considerable; Robert became intensely depressed and moved into a self-attacking position that he was unable to work with.

Over the course of several years, Robert periodically demeaned me quietly for my error of the moment. I struggled with a mixture of fury and defensiveness. Because Robert had such difficulty tolerating or working with his self-hate and rage, I eventually moved toward a

holding position. I tried to maintain a stance of active, alive engagement with Robert that did not reflect either retaliation or collapse on
my part (see Chapter 4 and the case of Karen for a fuller discussion of
these clinical issues). That position allowed me to hold Robert while
holding onto my periodic feelings of anger at him.

Robert very slowly became capable of tolerating some exploration
of his process in a more affectively real way. I continued, however, to
function as a subjective object for Robert. In moments of distress, he
experienced me as a container for his own split-off self-loathing. At
quieter, more reflective times, Robert engaged in a deeper level of self-
exploration, using me as a holding object.

In some ways, this shift seemed remarkable to me; Robert no longer
denigrated me continually in order to deflect his own self-hatred. He
began to elaborate on his feelings about himself and to examine the
nature and sources of his excruciating self-image, and he was able to
tolerate the painful affects that were thereby generated. Yet, Robert
remained affectively *outside* the transference, unable to address the
nature or meaning of his denigrating object relationships. Robert still
did not see me as an external object. For example, despite the fact that
a diploma indicating where and when I trained was in full view, he
persisted in implying that I had not received formal psychoanalytic
training. In an attempt to prod Robert to address the reality of my
objective existence (and also to vindicate myself), I asked him whether
he had noticed the diploma on the wall. Robert, with surprise, said no.
Of course, that data did not impact on his essential mistrust of me, and
instead he began questioning the quality of the training that I had
received.

Paradoxically, then, Robert made use of the psychoanalytic situation largely by allowing me to hold its imperfections for him. He
thereby protected himself from toxic feeling states until they became
tolerable. In order for Robert and me to move toward collaborative
work, he would have to integrate the reality of the analytic object as a
real source of help and also as a real source of failure. That would
require his willingness to tolerate some degree of dependence on the
analytic process.

At times, Robert seems to be moving in the direction of a capacity
for collaborative interchange. That capacity has seemed potentially
present when, for example, he criticized me for an error in understanding rather than for a mistake that he himself set up (e.g., my
"failure" to receive psychoanalytic training). At other moments,
Robert has appeared to be moving toward moments of dependence on
my holding function; he has occasionally voiced both need and appreciation for my willingness to be there with him and for having "put
up" with his subtle nastiness. Yet, whenever I begin to feel especially

hopeful that we have finally rounded a corner together, Robert returns to a denigrating position, perhaps worried that I will in some way take credit for his progress. I remain uncertain as to whether Robert ever will be able fully to integrate a capacity to love and hate the object for its real attributes and thereby to fully move to a position of relatively open collaboration.

Collaboration in Everyday Psychoanalytic Process

Although the acquisition of a capacity for collaboration is especially troublesome for patients who suffer from massive resistances to tolerating their real dependence on good-enough analysis, issues related to the analytic object's separate existence will emerge even in the most ordinary treatment. In the best of analyses, patient and analyst move relatively fluidly among varied aspects of internal and real experience in ways that may take for granted both the analyst's otherness and her relatedness. Yet even here, an implicit dimension of analytic interchange involves the patient's struggle to integrate the analyst as objective and subjective object.

Sharon, toward the end of her analysis with me, had developed a much fuller capacity to feel and to express her internal life both with me and with others. We worked well together in the transference and around other issues. As Sharon elaborated on her process, she made good use of the treatment boundaries and of me as a subjective and objective object. I felt *myself* with her and quite free to work and react in a variety of ways.

During our last year together, my father died, and I called all my patients to cancel our sessions for that week, indicating that there had been a death in the family. Sharon returned for treatment having noted an obituary about my father in the newspaper. Many of my patients had expressed their condolences, and their hope that I was all right, that is, able to be fully with them again. Sharon's concern, however, was a bit different. She asked me whether I would feel comfortable telling her something about my father, about who he was for me. She would, she said, like to know me, to have some sense of me in my own life, not as an analyst. She said that she did not want me to say anything that I felt uncomfortable saying, but would be grateful if I would share something of myself with her (Sharon had lost both parents and this death had special meaning to her). I felt quite moved by the sincerity of Sharon's wish and by the openness of her approach, which left room for both her subjectivity and for my own.

After some discussion about the meaning that such disclosure would have for Sharon, I ultimately shared something about my father with her. I found Sharon's response to be both appreciative and empathic. My self-revelation neither moved nor derailed the treatment; instead, I think it was a marker on the way toward termination for Sharon, in that it symbolized the establishment of a more fully mutual and adult relationship between us. In this sense, Sharon had already developed a reliable capacity for collaboration, and had reached a point in her treatment where she could both tolerate and value evidence of my externality.

Conclusion

The purpose of this book has been to elaborate on the nature and impact of the analyst's capacity to hold both her patient and herself within a psychoanalytic frame. I hope it is evident how much the affective tone of a holding situation will vary as a function of the particular emotional picture presented by the patient. Although holding still may be associated with the nurturing parent–infant relationship, a more thorough examination of the process of parenting makes quite clear that holding remains a theme throughout the life span, with ever-widening emotional implications. In the same way, I hope that a broader view of the notion of "holding" within psychoanalysis may offer a useful framework within which to understand the nature of the analyst's subjective experience and its implications, especially in work with difficult patients.

I end this book with a wish to underscore my belief that holding processes never adequately describe the therapeutic impact of psychoanalytic work. Instead, I am pointing to a perspective that includes moments of holding along with interpretive work and, ultimately, some level of mutual interchange around the intersubjective nature of patient's and analyst's experiences. I hope that by explicitly addressing the implications of the holding theme for relational psychoanalysis, I have succeeded in demonstrating that the two are not in fact incompatible. If the nature and centrality of illusion within the psychoanalytic relationship is pivotal, then there may be moments when we all need a holding experience. It is my hope that this book clarifies the therapeutic impact of holding in psychoanalytic work, either as a dominant or as a latent force.

It is, of course, intrinsically risky for the patient fully to acknowledge the external reality of the analyst while simultaneously living with the very powerful loving and destructive feelings that are inevitably evoked in this work. In this sense, the achievement of a capacity for collaborative interchange implies that we, as analysts, have allowed our patients to know us (both objectively and subjectively) as people capable of doing and receiving real and projected harm as well as good. Our patients, of course, struggle with the dangers inherent in such an awareness. Nevertheless, the achievement of a simultaneously and paradoxically subjective and objective relationship is, I believe, intrinsic to any psychoanalytic treatment.

Paradoxically, it will be the loss of the illusion of attunement implicit in the holding experience that ultimately will allow for a more mutual and alive relationship between patient and analyst. As the patient's capacity for collaboration evolves, I find that both my patient and myself are increasingly free—to move, breathe, and *be* within the psychoanalytic context. The transitional space, which was quite narrow and constraining during the holding period, widens in a way that permits both of us more emotional leeway, and ultimately a fuller integration of the mutual yet asymmetrical aspects of our relationship.

References

Abraham, K. (1924), A short study of the development of the libido: Viewed in the light of mental disorders. In: *Selected Papers on Psychoanalysis*. London: Hogarth Press, pp. 418–501, 1950.

Adler, G. (1989), Transitional phenomena, projective identification, and the essential ambiguity of the psychoanalytic situation. *Psychoanal. Quart.*, 58:81–104.

Aron, L. (1991), The patient's experience of the analyst's subjectivity. *Psychoanal. Dial.*, 1:29–51.

——— (1992), Interpretation as expression of the analyst's subjectivity. *Psychoanal. Dial.*, 2:475–508.

——— (1995), The internalized primal scene. *Psychoanal. Dial.*, 5:195–237.

Bach, S. (1985), *Narcissistic States and the Therapeutic Process*. New York: Aronson.

Balint, M. (1968), *The Basic Fault*. London: Tavistock.

Bass, A. (1996), Holding, holding back, and holding on: Reflections on "Holding and the Fate of the Analyst's Subjectivity" (by J. Slochower, this issue). *Psychoanal. Dial.*, 6:361–378.

Bassin, D., Honey, M. & Kaplan, M. M. (eds.). (1994), *Representations of Motherhood*. New Haven, CT: Yale University Press.

Beebe, B. & Lachmann, F. (1988), The contribution of mother–infant mutual influence to the origins of self and object representations. *Psychoanal. Psychol.*, 5:305–337.

Benjamin, J. (1988), *The Bonds of Love*. New York: Pantheon.

——— (1994), The omnipotent mother: A psychoanalytic study of fantasy and reality. In: D. Bassin, M. Honey & M. M. Kaplan (eds.), *Representations of Motherhood*. New Haven, CT: Yale University Press, pp. 129–146.

Bibring, E. (1953), The mechanism of depression. In: P. Greenacre (ed.), *Affective Disorders*. New York: International Universities Press, pp. 14–48.

Bion, W. (1959), *Experiences in Groups*. London: Tavistock.

——— (1962), *Learning From Experience*. London: Heinemann.

——— (1963), *Elements of Psychoanalysis*. London: Heinemann.

Bollas, C. (1978), The transformational object. *Internat. J. Psycho-Anal.*, 60:97–107.

——— (1987), *The Shadow of the Object*. New York: Columbia University Press.

Bowlby, J. (1960), Grief and mourning in infancy and early childhood. *The Psychoanalytic Study of the Child*, 15:9–52. New York: International Universities Press.

——— (1969), *Attachment*. New York: Basic Books.

——— (1980), *Loss: Sadness and Depression*. New York: Basic Books.

Bromberg, P. M. (1991), On knowing one's patient inside out: The aesthetics of unconscious communication. *Psychoanal. Dial.*, 1:399–422.

——— (1993), Shadow and substance: A relational perspective on clinical process. *Psychoanal. Psychol.*, 10:147–168.

——— (1995), Resistance, object-usage, and human relatedness. *Contemp. Psychoanal.*, 31:173–191.

Burke, W. F. (1992), Countertransference disclosure and the asymmetry/mutuality dilemma. *Psychoanal. Dial.*, 2:241–271.

Butler, J. (1990), *Gender Trouble*. New York: Routledge.

Carpy, D. V. (1989), Tolerating the countertransference: A mutative process. *Internat. J. Psycho-Anal.*, 70:287–294.

Casement, P. (1991), *Learning From the Patient*. New York: Guilford.

Chodorow, N. (1978), *The Reproduction of Mothering*. Berkeley: University of California Press.

Davies, J. M. & Frawley, M. G. (1994), *Treating the Adult Survivor of Childhood Sexual Abuse*. New York: Basic Books.

Dimen, M. (1991), Deconstructing difference: Gender, splitting and transitional space. *Psychoanal. Dial.*, 1:335–352.

Druck, A. (1989), *Four Therapeutic Approaches to the Borderline Patient*. Northvale, NJ: Aronson.

Epstein, L. (1977), The therapeutic function of hate in the countertransference. *Contemp. Psychoanal.*, 13:442–461. Also in: L. Epstein & A. Feiner (eds.) (1979), *Countertransference—The Therapist's Contribution to the Therapeutic Situation*. New York: Aronson, pp. 213–234.

——— (1979), The therapeutic use of countertransference data with borderline patients. *Contemp. Psychoanal.*, 15:248–275.

——— (1984), An interpersonal-object relations perspective on working with destructive aggression. *Contemp. Psychoanal.*, 20:651–662.

——— (1987), The problem of the bad-analyst-feeling. *Modern Psychoanal.*, 12:35–45.

Fairbairn, W. R. D. (1952), *An Object Relations Theory of the Personality*. New York: Basic Books.

First, E. (1994), Mothering, hate and Winnicott. In: D. Bassin, M. Honey & M. M. Kaplan (eds.), *Representations of Motherhood*. New Haven, CT: Yale University Press, pp. 147–161.

Fosshage, J. L. (1992), Self psychology: The self and its vicissitudes within a relational matrix. In: N. J. Skolnick & S. C. Warshaw (eds.), *Relational Perspectives in Psychoanalysis*. Hillsdale, NJ: The Analytic Press, pp. 21–42.

Freud, S. (1917), Mourning and melancholia. *Standard Edition*, 14:243–248. London: Hogarth Press, 1957.

———— (1920), Beyond the pleasure principle. *Standard Edition*, 18:7–64. London: Hogarth Press, 1955.

Fromm, E. (1964), *The Heart of Man*. New York: Harper & Row.

Gabbard, G. O. (1989), Patients who hate. *Psychiat.*, 52:96–106.

Gedo, J. (1979), *Beyond Interpretation*. Hillsdale, NJ: The Analytic Press, 1993.

Ghent, E. (1992), Paradox and process. *Psychoanal. Dial.*, 2:135–159.

Gill, M. (1983), The interpersonal paradigm and the degree of the therapist's involvement. *Contemp. Psychoanal.*, 19:200–237.

Goldberg, A. (1988), *A Fresh Look at Psychoanalysis*. Hillsdale, NJ: The Analytic Press.

Grunes, M. (1984), The therapeutic object relationship. *Psychoanal. Rev.*, 71:123–143.

Hamilton, N. G. (1990), The containing function and the analyst's projective identification. *Internat. J. Psycho-Anal.*, 71:445–453.

Harris, A. (1991), Gender as contradiction. *Psychoanal. Dial.*, 1:197–224.

Heimann, P. (1950), On counter-transference. *Internat. J. Psycho-Anal.*, 31:81–84.

Hirsch, I. (1987), Varying modes of analytic participation. *J. Amer. Acad. Psychoanal.*, 15:205–222.

Hoffman, I. Z. (1991), Discussion: Toward a social-constructivist view of the psychoanalytic situation. *Psychoanal. Dial.*, 1:74–105.

———— (1992), Some practical implications of a social-constructivist view of the psychoanalytic situation. *Psychoanal. Dial.*, 2:287–304.

Horowitz, L. (1985), Divergent views on the treatment of borderline patients. *Bull. Menn. Clinic*, 49:525–545.

Jacobs, T. (1994), Nonverbal communications: Some reflections on their role in the psychoanalytic process and psychoanalytic education. *J. Amer. Psychoanal. Assn.*, 42:741–762.

Jacobson, E. (1957), Denial and repression. *J. Amer. Psychoanal. Assn.*, 5:61–92.

Joseph, B. (1982), Addiction to near death. In: M. Feldman & E. B. Bott Spillius (eds.), *Psychic Equilibrium and Psychic Change*. London: Routledge, pp. 127–138.

Kernberg, O. F. (1975), *Borderline Conditions and Pathological Narcissism*. New York: Aronson.

———— (1993), Convergences and divergences in contemporary psychoanalytic technique. *Internat. J. Psycho-Anal.*, 74:659–673.

Khan, M. (1963), *The Privacy of the Self*. New York: International Universities Press.

Klein, M. (1955), *Envy and Gratitude and Other Works*. New York: Delacorte.

——— (1975), *Love, Guilt and Reparation*. New York: Delta.

Kohut, H. (1959), Introspection, empathy and psychoanalysis. In: P. Ornstein (ed.), *The Search for the Self*. New York: International Universities Press, pp. 459–483.

——— (1971), *The Analysis of the Self*. New York: International Universities Press.

——— (1984), *How Does Analysis Cure?* A. Goldberg & P. Stepansky (eds.). Chicago: University of Chicago Press.

Kraemer, S. (in press), "Betwixt the dark and the daylight" of maternal subjectivity: Meditations on the threshold. *Psychoanal. Dial.*

Lachmann, F. M. & Beebe, B. (1993), Interpretation in a developmental perspective. In: A. Goldberg (ed.), *Progress in Self Psychology, Vol. 9: The Widening Scope of Self Psychology*. Hillsdale, NJ: The Analytic Press, 9:45–52.

Lamm, M. (1988), *The Jewish Way in Death and Mourning*. New York: Jonathan David.

Levenson, E. (1972), *The Fallacy of Understanding*. New York: Basic Books.

Little, M. (1951), Countertransference and the patient's response to it. *Internat. J. Psycho-Anal.*, 32:32–40.

——— (1959), *Toward a Basic Unity*. New York: Aronson.

——— (1990), *Psychotic Anxieties and Containment*. Northvale, NJ: Aronson.

Loewald, H. (1960), On the therapeutic action of psychoanalysis. In: *Papers on Psychoanalysis*. New Haven, CT: Yale University Press, 1980, pp. 221–256.

Mahler, M. (1972), Rapprochement subphase of the separation-individuation process. *Psychoanal. Quart.*, 41:487–506.

Mandelbaum, D. G. (1959), Social uses of funeral rites. In: H. Feifel (ed.), *The Meaning of Death*. New York: McGraw-Hill.

Mayes, C. & Spence, D. P. (1994), Understanding therapeutic action in the analytic situation: A second look at the maternal metaphor. *J. Amer. Psychoanal. Assn.*, 42:789–817.

Mitchell, S. (1988), *Relational Concepts in Psychoanalysis*. Cambridge, MA: Harvard University Press.

——— (1991a), Wishes, needs and interpersonal negotiations. *Psychoanal. Inq.*, 11:147–170.

——— (1991b), Contemporary perspectives on self: Toward an integration. *Psychoanal. Dial.*, 1:121–148.

———— (1993), *Hope and Dread in Psychoanalysis*. New York: Basic Books.

Modell, A. (1975), A narcissistic defense against affects and the illusion of self sufficiency. *Internat. J. Psycho-Anal.*, 56:275–282.

———— (1976), The holding environment and the therapeutic action of psychoanalysis. *J. Amer. Psychoanal. Assn.*. 24:285–307.

———— (1988), On the protection and safety of the therapeutic setting. In: A. Rothstein (ed.), *The Therapeutic Action of Psychoanalytic Psychotherapy*. Madison, CT: International Universities Press.

Ogden, T. H. (1979), On projective identification. *Internat. J. Psycho-Anal.*, 60:357–373.

———— (1986), *The Matrix of the Mind*. Northvale, NJ: Aronson.

———— (1994), *Subjects of Analysis*. Northvale, NJ: Aronson.

———— (1991), The therapeutic relationship as paradox. *Psychoanal. Dial.*, 1:13–28.

Ornstein, A. (1995), The fate of the curative fantasy in the psychoanalytic treatment process. *Contemp. Psychoanal.*, 31:113–123.

Phillips, A. (1993), *On Kissing Tickling and Being Bored*. Cambridge, MA: Harvard University Press.

Pick, I. B. (1985), Working through in the countertransference. *Internat. J. Psycho-Anal.*, 66:157–166.

Pine, F. (1984), The interpretive moment: Variations on classical themes. *Bull. Menn. Clinic*, 48:54–71.

Pizer, S. A. (1992), The negotiation of paradox in the analytic process. *Psychoanal. Dial.*, 2:215–240.

Poggi, R. G. & Ganzarain, R. (1983), Countertransference hate. *Bull. Menn. Clinic*, 47:15–35.

Robbins, M. (1988), The adaptive significance of destructiveness in primitive personalities. *J. Amer. Psychoanal. Assn.*, 36:627–652.

Sandbank, T. (1993), Psychoanalysis and maternal work—Some parallels. *Internat. J. Psycho-Anal.* 74:715–727.

Sandler, J. (1960), The background of safety. *Internat. J. Psycho-Anal.*, 41:352–356.

Schwaber, E. (1981), Empathy: A mode of analytic listening. *Psychoanal. Inq.*, 1:357–392.

———— (1983a), Psychoanalytic listening and psychic reality. *Internat. Rev. Psychoanal.*, 10:379–392.

———— (1983b), Construction, reconstruction and the mode of clinical attunement. In: A. Goldberg (ed.), *The Future of Psychoanalysis*. New York: International Universities Press, pp. 273–291.

Seinfeld, J. (1993), *Interpreting and Holding*. Northvale, NJ: Aronson.

Shabad, P. (1993), Resentment, indignation, entitlement: The transformation of unconscious wish to need. *Psychoanal. Dial.*, 3:481–494.

Siggins, L. D. (1966), Mourning: A critical survey of the literature. *Internat. J. Psycho-Anal.*, 47:14–25.

Slochower, J. (1991), Variations in the analytic holding environment. *Internat. J. Psycho-Anal.*, 72:709–718.

—— (1992), A hateful borderline patient and the holding environment. *Contemp. Psychoanal.*, 28:72–88.

—— (1993), Mourning and the holding function of shiva. *Contemp. Psychoanal.*, 29:352–367.

—— (1994), The evolution of object usage and the holding environment. *Contemp. Psychoanal.*, 30:135–151.

—— (1996), The holding environment and the fate of the analyst's subjectivity. *Psychoanal. Dial.*, 6:323–353.

Stern, D. (1992), Commentary on Constructivism in Clinical Psycho-Analysis. *Psychoanal. Dial.*, 2:331–364.

—— (1994), Needed relationships and repeated relationships: An integrated relational perspective. *Psychoanal. Dial.*, 4:317–346.

Stolorow, R. D. (1993), Thoughts on the nature and therapeutic action of psychoanalytic interpretation. In: A. Goldberg (ed.), *Progress in Self Psychology, Vol. 9: The Widening Scope of Self Psychology*. Hillsdale, NJ: The Analytic Press, pp. 31–52.

—— (1994), *The Intersubjective Perspective*. Northvale, NJ: Aronson.

Symington, N. (1983), The analyst's act of freedom as an agent of therapeutic change. *International Review of Psychoanalysis*, 10:283–291.

—— (1990), The possibility of human freedom and its transmission (with particular reference to the thoughts of Bion). *Internat. J. Psycho-Anal.*, 71:95–106.

—— (1996), Commentary on Slochower's paper, "The Analytic Holding Environment," *Psychoanal. Dial.*, 6:323–353.

Tansey, M. J. (1992), Psychoanalytic expertise. *Psychoanal. Dial.*, 2:305–316.

Winnicott, D. W. (1945), Primitive emotional development. In: *Through Paediatrics to Psycho-Analysis*. New York: Basic Books, 1975, pp. 145–203.

—— (1947), Hate in the countertransference. In: *Through Paediatrics to Psycho-Analysis*. New York: Basic Books, 1975, pp. 194–203.

—— (1951), Transitional objects and transitional phenomenon. In: *Through Paediatrics to Psycho-Analysis*. New York: Basic Books, pp. 229–242.

—— (1954), Withdrawal and regression. In: *Through Pediatrics to Psychoanalysis*. London: Hogarth Press.

—— (1958), The capacity to be alone. In: *The Maturational Processes and the Facilitating Environment*. New York: International Universities Press, 1965, pp. 29–36.

—————— (1960a), The theory of the parent–infant relationship. In: *The Maturational Processes and the Facilitating Environment*. New York: International Universities Press, 1965, pp. 37–55.

—————— (1960b), Ego distortion in terms of true and false self. In: *The Maturational Processes and the Facilitating Environment*. New York: International Universities Press, 1965, pp. 140–152.

—————— (1963a), Psychiatric disorder in terms of infantile maturational processes. In: *The Maturational Processes and the Facilitating Environment*. New York: International Universities Press, 1965, pp. 230–241.

—————— (1963b), Dependence in infant-care, in child-care, and in the psycho-analytic setting. In: *The Maturational Processes and the Facilitating Environment*. New York: International Universities Press, 1965, pp. 249–259.

—————— (1963c), The mentally ill in your caseload. In: *The Maturational Processes and the Facilitating Environment*. New York: International Universities Press, 1965, pp. 217–229.

—————— (1963d), The development of the capacity for concern. In: *The Maturational Processes and the Facilitating Environment*. New York: International Universities Press, 1965, pp. 73–82.

—————— (1963e), Communicating and not communicating leading to a study of certain opposites. In: *The Maturational Processes and the Facilitating Environment*. New York: International Universities Press, 1965, pp. 179–192.

—————— (1964a), *The Child, the Family, and the Outside World*. New York: Penguin.

—————— (1964b), The importance of the setting in meeting regression in psycho-analysis. In: *Psychoanalytic Explorations*. Cambridge, MA: Harvard University Press, 1989, pp. 96–102.

—————— (1965), *The Maturational Processes and the Facilitating Environment*. New York: International Universities Press.

—————— (1966), The split-off male and female elements to be found in men and women. In: *Psychoanalytic Explorations*. Cambridge, MA: Harvard University Press, 1989, pp. 168–193.

—————— (1969), The use of an object and relating through identifications. In: *Playing and Reality*. New York: Basic Books, 1971, pp. 86–94.

—————— (1971), *Playing and Reality*. New York: Basic Books.

—————— (1972), *Holding and Interpretation*. London: Hogarth Press.

—————— (1989), *Psychoanalytic Explorations*. Cambridge, MA: Harvard University Press.

Index